War and Conflict Quotations

ALSO BY MICHAEL C. THOMSETT
AND JEAN FREESTONE THOMSETT
(AND PUBLISHED BY McFARLAND)

*Political Quotations: A Worldwide Dictionary of
Thoughts and Pronouncements from Politicians, Literary Figures,
Humorists and Others*
(1994)

*Sex and Love Quotations: A Worldwide Dictionary of
Pronouncements About Gender and Sexuality Throughout the Ages*
(1995)

ALSO BY MICHAEL C. THOMSETT
(AND PUBLISHED BY McFARLAND)

Insurance Dictionary Illustrated
(1989)

Investment and Securities Dictionary
(1986)

*Musical Terms, Symbols and Theory:
An Illustrated Dictionary*
(1989)

Real Estate Dictionary
(1988)

A Treasury of Business Quotations
(1990)

War and Conflict Quotations

A Worldwide Dictionary of
Pronouncements from Military Leaders,
Politicians, Philosophers, Writers and Others

by
MICHAEL C. THOMSETT
JEAN FREESTONE THOMSETT

McFarland & Company, Inc., Publishers
Jefferson, North Carolina, and London

British Library Cataloguing-in-Publication data are available

Library of Congress Cataloguing-in-Publication Data

Thomsett, Michael C.
　　War and conflict quotations : a worldwide dictionary of
pronouncements from military leaders, politicians, philosophers,
writers and others / by Michael C. Thomsett, Jean Freestone
Thomsett.
　　　　p.　cm.
　　Includes indexes.
　　ISBN 0-7864-0314-4 (library binding : 50# alkaline paper) ♾
　　1. War — Quotations, maxims, etc.　I. Thomsett, Jean F., 1947–　　.
II. Title.
PN6084.W35T48　1997
303.6'6 — dc21　　　　　　　　　　　　　　　　　　　96-47324
　　　　　　　　　　　　　　　　　　　　　　　　　　　　　CIP

Manufactured in the United States of America

McFarland & Company, Inc., Publishers
　Box 611, Jefferson, North Carolina 28640

CONTENTS

vi   *Contents*

INTRODUCTION

War and conflict have been major topics of discussion in literature as well as in philosophy and in history. It may be said that history is primarily a chronicle of the conflicts of the human race, and politicians and philosophers have had much to say on these topics.

A compiler of quotations has to deal constantly with questions of judgment. What belongs in the compilation? To what extent should the details of the topic be expanded? Whose observations have merit? We have attempted in this work to fairly represent as broad a range as possible of opinions concerning war and conflict, and have included not only political and military persons, but philosophers, poets, writers, social commentators, entertainers — anyone whose words, in our opinion, provided insight and value to the researcher, writer, speaker, librarian, student or other reader of this work.

A quotation may be located in several ways in this book.

First, one may search under the categories in the body of the book. They are arranged alphabetically and ample cross-referencing is included at the beginning of each section. Thus, a reader who needs more than the quotations supplied within a specific area can easily refer to related sections.

Second, a reader may search the Index of Persons to find quotations of a specific author. References in the indexes are to the serially numbered entries (the quotations) throughout the book.

Third, the reader may refer to the Index of Key Words in Context. Words and phrases are arranged alphabetically and references are again to the entry numbers.

The book has been arranged to be of practical use. Within each category, the sequence of quotations might appear to be arbitrary at first glance. The arrangement was, however, determined with great care and effort. Many quotations books use a chronological order, or are alphabetical by author. In our opinion, these arrangements are not very useful. We have arranged the quotations within each classification so that complementary or similar statements are together, and so that contradictory statements are in close proximity. This provides readers with insight and enjoyment, perhaps adding elements of enrichment or controversy to the expressions that catch their interest.

Some very popular statements have traditionally been credited to more than one individual. In such cases, we have attributed it to the earliest source found. Some similar quotations are included and placed next to their companions.

Modern interests call for sensitivity to the fact that both men and women are welcome to express their opinions on any topic, including that of war and conflict. This has not always been the prevalent rule. As a consequence, this book represents a predominantly male point of view. Furthermore, people in the past have preferred masculine references currently out of favor, such as "man" and "mankind." As compilers and researchers, we are fully aware of this problem. However, it would be inappropriate for us to alter a quotation, and we have respected the original expression in every case. Still, we have attempted to compile as comprehensive a reference as possible, for and by both men and women.

M.C.T. and J.F.T.
Fall, 1996

THE QUOTATIONS

Action

See also Battles; Courage; Heroes; Leadership

1. The test of any man lies in action.
— Pindar, *Odes,* 5th c. B.C.

2. Action springs not from thought, but from a readiness for responsibility.
— Dietrich Bonhoeffer, *Letters and Papers from Prison,* 1953

3. The great end of life is not knowledge but action.
— T. H. Huxley, "Technical Education," 1877

4. Nothing is ever done in this world until men are prepared to kill one another if it is not done.
— George Bernard Shaw, *Major Barbara,* 1905

5. There is a time for all things, a time to preach and a time to pray, but those times have passed away. There is a time to fight, and that time has now come.
— Peter Muhlenberg, sermon, January, 1776

6. Every great action is extreme when it is undertaken. Only after it has been accomplished does it seem possible to those creatures of more common stuff.
— Stendhal, *The Red and the Black,* 1830

7. The profit on a good action is to have done it.
— Seneca, *Letters to Lucilius,* 1st c.

8. Effective action is always unjust.
— Jean Anouilh, *Catch As Catch Can,* 1960

9. Some men succeed by what they know; some by what they do; and a few by what they are.
— Elbert Hubbard, *The Note Book,* 1927

10. A man's most open actions have a secret side to them.
— Joseph Conrad, *Under Western Eyes,* 1911

Aggression

See also Conflict; Expansion; Force; Strength

11. Isn't the best defense always a good attack?
— Ovid, *The Art of Love,* ca. 8

12. He who would be free must strike the first blow.
— Frederick Douglass, *My Bondage and My Freedom,* 1855

13. Our capacity to retaliate must be, and is, massive in order to deter all forms of aggression.
—John Foster Dulles, speech, December 8, 1955

14. Aggressiveness is the principal guarantor of survival.
—Robert Ardrey, *The Social Contract,* 1970

15. History is not a web woven with innocent hands.
—John E. E. Dalberg, *The Home and Foreign Review,* 1862

16. Aggressive conduct, if allowed to go unchecked and unchallenged, ultimately leads to war.
—John F. Kennedy, speech, October 22, 1962

17. We kill everybody, my dear. Some with bullets, some with words, and everybody with our deeds. We drive people into their graves, and neither see it nor feel it.
—Maxim Gorki, *Enemies,* 1906

18. Man, biologically considered, is the most formidable of all beasts of prey, and, indeed, the only one that preys systematically on his own species.
—William James, *Memories and Studies,* 1911

19. Today there's more fellowship among snakes than among mankind. / Wild beasts spare those with similar markings.
—Juvenal, *Satires,* ca. 100

20. At worst, is not this an unjust world, full of nothing but beasts of prey, four-footed or two-footed?
—Thomas Carlyle, "Count Cagliostro," 1833

Alliances

See also the Cold War; Diplomacy; Foreign Policy; International Relations; Treaties

21. Union gives strength.
—Aesop, *Fables,* "The Bundle of Sticks," ca. 550 B.C.

22. By uniting we stand, by dividing we fall.
—John Dickinson, "The Liberty Song," 1768

23. When bad men combine, the good must associate; otherwise they will fall, one by one, an unpitied sacrifice in a contemptible struggle.
—Edmund Burke, *Thoughts on the Cause of the Present Discontents,* 1770

24. Woes unite foes.
—Proverb

25. The enemy of my enemy is my friend.
—Proverb

26. Coalitions though successful have always found this, that their triumph has been brief.
—Benjamin Disraeli, speech, December 16, 1852

27. Gratitude, like love, is never a dependable international emotion.
—Joseph Alsop, in *The Observer,* November 30, 1952

28. It's hard to imagine anything that would give our allies more cause to consider us unreliable than that we say one thing in public and secretly do another.
—George Mitchell, at Iran-Contra hearings, July 13, 1987

29. An alliance is like a chain. It is not made stronger by adding weak links to it.
—Walter Lippmann, in *New York Herald Tribune,* August 5, 1952

30. To make war upon those who trade with us is like setting a bulldog upon a customer at the shop door.
— Thomas Paine,
The Age of Reason, 1794

31. We cannot always assure the future of our friends; we have a better chance of assuring our future if we remember who our friends are.
— Henry Kissinger,
White House Years, 1979

32. Men may be linked in friendship. Nations are linked only by interests.
— Rolf Hochhuth,
The Soldiers, 1967

33. Living next to you is in some ways like sleeping with an elephant. No matter how friendly and even-tempered is the beast, if I can call it that, one is affected by every twitch and grunt.
— Pierre Trudeau, on Canadian relations with the United States, in *New York Times,* March 26, 1969

34. Be my brother, or I will kill you.
— Sébastien-Roch Nicholas de Chamfort, in T. Carlyle, *History of the French Revolution,* 1837

35. Any alliance whose purpose is not the intention to wage war is senseless and useless.
— Adolf Hitler,
Mein Kampf, 1924

36. If Hitler invaded hell I would make at least a favorable reference to the devil in the House of Commons.
— Winston S. Churchill,
The Grand Alliance, 1950

37. It is our true policy to steer clear of permanent alliance with any portion of the foreign world.
— George Washington, farewell address, September 17, 1796

38. Peace, commerce, and honest friendship with all nations — entangling alliances with none.
— Thomas Jefferson, inaugural address, March 4, 1801

39. An alliance should be hard diplomatic currency, valuable and hard to get, and not inflationary paper from the mimeograph machine in the State Department.
— Walter Lippmann, in *New York Herald Tribune,* August 5, 1952

Anti-War *see* Pacifism

Appeasement
See also Causes of War; Conflict; Defeat; Foreign Policy; International Relations

40. Submit to the present evil, lest a greater one befall you.
— Phaedrus, *Fables,* 1st c.

41. You may either win your peace or buy it: win it, by resistance to evil; buy it, by compromise with evil.
— John Ruskin,
The Two Paths, 1859

42. Peace at any price.
— Alphonse de Lamartine,
Méditations poétiques, 1820

43. So enamored on peace that he would have been glad the king should have bought it at any price.
— Henry Hyde,
History of the Rebellion, 1703

44. There is a price which is too great to pay for peace, and that price can be put in one word. One cannot pay the price of self-respect.
— Woodrow Wilson, speech, February 1, 1916

45. The most disadvantageous peace is better than the most just war.
— Desiderius Erasmus,
Adagia, 1500

46. The name of peace is sweet and the thing itself good, but between peace and slavery there is the greatest difference.
— Cicero, *Philippics*, 44–43 B.C.

47. Better beans and bacon in peace than cakes and ale in fear.
— Aesop, *Fables*,
"The Town Mouse and the Country Mouse," ca. 550 B.C.

48. Certain peace is better and safer than anticipated victory.
— Livy, *Ab Urbe Condita*,
ca. 29 B.C.

49. No man can sit down and withhold his hands from the warfare against wrong and get peace from his acquiescence.
— Woodrow Wilson, speech,
May 7, 1911

50. Nothing's as good as holding on to safety.
— Euripedes, *The Phoenician Women*, ca. 410 B.C.

51. They that can give up essential liberty to obtain a little temporary safety deserve neither liberty nor safety.
— Benjamin Franklin, *Historical Review of Pennsylvania*, 1759

52. We should do all in our power to hasten the day when there shall be peace among the nations — a peace based upon justice and not upon cowardly submission to wrong.
— Theodore Roosevelt,
message to Congress,
December 4, 1906

53. Lord Salisbury and myself have brought you back peace — but a peace I hope with honor.
— Benjamin Disraeli, speech,
July 16, 1878

54. I believe it is peace for our time.
— Neville Chamberlain,
announcement following conclusion of the Pact of Munich with Adolf Hitler, September 30, 1938

55. The Pact of Munich was a greater blow to humanity than the atomic bomb at Hiroshima.
— Dwight D. Eisenhower, speech,
March 23, 1950

56. England has been offered a choice between war and shame. She has chosen shame and will get war.
— Winston S. Churchill, speech,
September, 1938

57. The concessions of the weak are the concessions of fear.
— Edmund Burke,
On Conciliation with America,
1775

58. We should seek by all means in our power to avoid war, by analyzing possible causes, by trying to remove them, by discussion in a spirit of collaboration and good will.
— Neville Chamberlain, speech,
October 6, 1938

59. Before you go to war, you should pursue every reasonable alternative. That is not called surrender. That is intelligence and civility in progress.
— Mario M. Cuomo,
in *U.S. News and World Report*,
March 25, 1991

60. You start out giving your hat, then you give your coat, then your shirt, then your skin and finally your soul.
— Charles DeGaulle, statement on relations with the Soviet Union, in *New York Herald Tribune*, September 22, 1961

61. A just war is in the long run far better for a nation's soul than the most prosperous peace obtained by acquiescence in wrong or injustice.
— Theodore Roosevelt, message to Congress, December 4, 1906

62. There is no avoiding war; it can only be postponed to the advantage of others.
— Niccolò Machiavelli,
The Prince, 1513

63. Appeasement but begets new and bloodier wars.
— Douglas MacArthur, speech,
April 19, 1951

Arms *see* Weapons

the Atomic Age

See also the Cold War; International Relations

64. Gods are born and die, but the atom endures.
— Alexander Chase, *Perspectives*,
1966

65. There is no evil in the atom; only in men's souls.
— Adlai Stevenson, speech,
September 18, 1952

66. We have grasped the mystery of the atom and rejected the Sermon on the Mount.
— Omar Bradley, speech, 1948

67. The more horrible a depersonalized scientific mass war becomes, the more necessary it is to find universal ideal motives to justify it.
— John Dewey, *Human Nature
and Conduct*, 1922

68. Only technology has permitted us to put a city to the sword without quite realizing what we are doing.
— Joseph W. Krutch, in
The American Scholar,
Summer, 1967

69. We turned back to look at Hiroshima. The city was hidden by that awful cloud ... boiling up, mushrooming, terrible and incredibly tall.
— Paul W. Tibbets, pilot of the
Enola Gay, in *Saturday Evening
Post*, June 8, 1946

70. As the bomb fell over Hiroshima and exploded, we saw an entire city disappear. I wrote in my log the words: "My God, what have we done?"
— Robert Lewis, co-pilot of the
Enola Gay, on *NBC TV*,
May 19, 1955

71. The force from which the sun draws its powers has been loosed against those who brought war to the Far East.
— Harry S Truman, speech,
August 6, 1945

72. If I had known that the Germans would not succeed in constructing the atomic bomb, I would never have lifted a finger.
— Albert Einstein, in R. Jungk,
Brighter than A Thousand Suns,
1958

73. Statesmen must learn to live with scientists as the Medici once lived with artists.
— Oswald Mosley, in
R. Skidelsky, *Oswald Mosley*, 1975

74. This idea of weapons of mass extermination is utterly horrible and is something which no one with one spark of humanity can tolerate. I will not pretend to obey a government which is organizing a mass massacre of mankind.
— Bertrand Russell, speech,
April 15, 1961

75. Law not served by power is an illusion; but power not ruled by law is a

menace which our nuclear age cannot afford.
— Arthur J. Goldberg, in *Time*,
June 17, 1966

76. The way to win an atomic war is to make certain it never starts.
— Omar Bradley, speech,
November 10, 1948

77. War in our time has become an anachronism. Whatever the case in the past, war in the future can serve no useful purpose. A war which became general, as any limited action might, would only result in the virtual destruction of mankind.
— Dwight D. Eisenhower, in
M. Wallace, *Fund for the
Republic*, 1959

78. Global war has become a Frankenstein's monster, threatening to destroy both sides.
— Douglas MacArthur, speech,
July 5, 1961

79. For the first time in the history of mankind, one generation literally has the power to destroy the past, the present and the future, the power to bring time to an end.
— Hubert H. Humphrey, speech,
October 29, 1964

80. The unleashed power of the atom has changed everything save our modes of thinking and we thus drift toward unparalleled catastrophe.
— Albert Einstein, in
New York Times,
May 25, 1946

81. We have genuflected before the god of science only to find that it has given us the atomic bomb, producing fears and anxieties that science can never mitigate.
— Martin Luther King, Jr.,
Strength to Love, 1963

82. It is impossible, except for theologians, to conceive of a worldwide scandal or a universe-wide scandal; the proof of this is the way people have set-tled down to living with nuclear fission, radiation poisoning, hydrogen bombs, satellites, and space rockets.
— Mary McCarthy,
On the Contrary, 1961

83. The terror of the atom age is not the violence of the new power but the speed of man's adjustment to it — the speed of his acceptance.
— E. B. White,
The Second Tree from the Corner,
1954

84. The world has achieved brilliance without wisdom, power without conscience. Ours is a world of nuclear giants and ethical infants.
— Omar Bradley, speech, 1948

85. The new and terrible dangers which man has created can only be controlled by man.
— John F. Kennedy, speech,
November 2, 1959

86. It may be that we shall by a process of sublime irony have reached a stage in this story where safety will be the sturdy child of terror and survival the twin brother of annihilation.
— Winston S. Churchill,
statement on the hydrogen bomb,
March 3, 1955

87. A world without nuclear weapons would be less stable and more dangerous for all of us.
— Margaret Thatcher, in *Time*,
April 27, 1987

88. The atom bomb was no "great decision" ... It was merely another powerful weapon in the arsenal of righteousness.
— Harry S Truman, speech,
April 28, 1959

89. No country without an atom bomb could properly consider itself independent.
— Charles DeGaulle, in
New York Times Magazine,
May 12, 1968

Battle Cries

See also Courage; Patriotism; Slogans and Mottoes

90. Attack — Repeat — Attack.
— William F. Halsey, Jr., dispatch
at the battle of Santa Cruz
Islands, October 26, 1942

91. By push of bayonets, no firing till
you see the whites of their eyes.
— Frederick the Great,
order at Prague, May 6, 1757

92. Don't one of you fire until you see
the whites of their eyes.
— William Prescott, order at
Bunker Hill (also attributed to
Israel Putman), June 17, 1775

93. Come on, you sons of bitches! Do
you want to live forever?
— Daniel Daly, at Belleau Wood,
June 4, 1918

94. Let the storm rage ever stronger!
— Maxim Gorki,
Song of a Stormy Petrel, 1903 (a
rallying cry for revolutionaries)

95. Damn the torpedoes — full speed
ahead!
— David Glasgow Farragut, order
at the battle of Mobile Bay,
August 5, 1864

96. Hit hard, hit fast, hit often.
— William F. Halsey, Jr., remark

97. Carthage must be destroyed.
— Cato the Elder, in Pliny the
Elder, *Naturalis Historia*, 1st c.

98. *Ils ne passeront pas.* (They shall
not pass.)
— slogan, French army at
Verdun, 1916

99. The enemy say that Americans are
good at a long shot, but cannot stand the
cold iron. I call upon you instantly to give
a lie to the slander. Charge!
— Winfield Scott, to the 11th
Infantry Regiment at Chippewa,
Canada, June 5, 1814

100. Give them the cold steel, boys!
— Lewis Addison Armistead,
attributed during Civil War, 1863

101. Praise the Lord and pass the
ammunition.
— Howell Fogey, during the attack
on Pearl Harbor, December 7, 1941

102. Remember the Alamo!
— Sidney Sherman, battle cry at
San Jacinto, April 21, 1836

103. Stout hearts, my laddies! If the row
comes, Remember the Maine and show the
world how American sailors can fight.
— Clifford K. Berryman, cartoon
caption that became the battle
cry of the Spanish American War,
in *Washington Post*, April 3, 1898

104. Send them our latitude and lon-
gitude.
— William F. Halsey, Jr., remark
in response to the enemy's
question, "Where is the
American fleet?" October, 1944

105. Stand your ground. Don't fire
unless fired upon, but if they mean to have
a war let it begin here!
— John Parker, order to the
Minutemen at Lexington,
April 19, 1775

106. Tell him to go to hell.
— Zachary Taylor, response to
Santa Anna's demand for
surrender at Buena Vista,
February 23, 1847

107. I looked out and saw a Jerry standing with a not-very white hanky tied to a
rifle. He shouted "Surrender!" ... [I told
him] Get the hell out of here. We're taking
on prisoners.
— Eric Mackay, at the battle of
Arnhem Bridge, September 1944,
in C. Ryan, *A Bridge Too Far*,
1974

108. Tell the men to fire faster and not to give up the ship; fight her till she sinks.
— James Lawrence, on board the U.S. frigate Chesapeake, June 1, 1813

109. Tora, Tora, Tora!
— Attack command, Japanese fleet, December 7, 1941

110. You may fire when you are ready, Gridley.

— George Dewey, to the flagship captain at the battle of Manila Bay, May 1, 1898

111. *Vae victis.* (Woe to the defeated.)
— Brennus, battle cry upon the capture of Rome, 390 B.C.

112. War and the knife.
— José de Palafox, response to demand for surrender at the siege of Saragossa, August 4, 1808

Battle Dispatches and Reports

See also Courage, Patriotism; Resolve

113. All quiet on the Western Front.
— Erich M. Remarque, title of book, 1929

114. Peace reigns in Warsaw.
— Horace François Bastien Sébastiani, announcing the fall of Warsaw, 1831

115. The die is cast.
— Julius Caesar, upon crossing the Rubicon, 1st c. B.C.

116. The war has started incredibly badly. Therefore, it must be continued.
— Charles DeGaulle, *Mémoires de guerre: L'Appel*, 1955

117. Ever forward, but slowly.
— Gebhard von Blücher, order to Russian troops at Leipzig, October 19, 1813

118. The first twenty-four hours of the invasion will be decisive ... for the Allies, as well as Germany, it will be the longest day.
— Erwin Rommel, remark concerning the anticipated Allied invasion of France, April 22, 1944

119. Greetings, we win!
— Philippides, last words, after running from Marathon to

Athens with news of victory over the Persian army, 490 B.C.

120. *Ave, Caesar, moritori te salutant.* Hail, Caesar, we who are about to die salute you.
— Suetonius, *Life of Claudius*, 2nd c.

121. Hold the fort, for I am coming.
— William T. Sherman, message, October, 1864

122. I came through and I shall return.
— Douglas MacArthur, statement after breaking through the Japanese lines, March 20, 1942

123. We fight, get beat, rise, and fight again.
— Nathanael Greene, letter after the battle of Hobkirk's Hill, April, 1781

124. I have nothing to offer but blood, toil, tears and sweat.
— Winston S. Churchill, speech, May 13, 1940

125. I offer neither pay, nor quarters, nor provisions; I offer hunger, thirst, forced marches, battles, and death. Let him who loves his country in his heart

and not with his lips only, follow me.
> — Giuseppe Garibaldi, in G. M.
> Trevelyan, *Garibaldi's Defense of
> the Roman Republic*, 1907–11

126. I think we might be going a bridge too far.
> — Frederick Browning, comment
> regarding the invasion of
> Holland, September 10, 1944, in
> R. E. Urguhart, *Arnhem*, 1958

127. It is the beginning of the end.
> — Charles-Maurice de Tallyrand,
> remark on the battle of Borodino,
> 1812, in E. Fournier, *L'Esprit dans
> l'Historie*, 1857

128. There must be a beginning of any great matter, but the continuing unto the end until it be thoroughly finished yields the true glory.
> — Francis Drake, dispatch,
> May 17, 1587

129. It is magnificent, but it is not war.
> — Pierre Bosquet, remark on the
> charge of the Light Brigade,
> October 25, 1854

130. A landing was made this morning on the coast of France, by troops of the Allied Expeditionary Force. This landing is part of the concerted United Nations plan for the liberation of Europe.
> — Dwight D. Eisenhower, radio
> broadcast on D-Day, June 6, 1944

131. My center is giving way, my right is in retreat; situation excellent. I shall attack!
> — Ferdinand Foch, in G. Aston,
> *Marshal Foch*, 1929

132. They've got us surrounded again, the poor bastards.
> — Creighton W. Abrams, describ-
> ing the Battle of the Bulge in the
> Second World War, in *Time*,
> February 16, 1968

133. We are so outnumbered there's only one thing to do. We must attack.
> — Andrew Browne Cunningham,

remark before attacking the Italian fleet, November, 1940

134. One if by land and two if by sea; / And I on the opposite shore will be, / Ready to ride and spread the alarm / Through every Middlesex village and farm.
> — Henry Wadsworth Longfellow,
> *Tales of a Wayside Inn*,
> "Paul Revere's Ride," 1863–74

135. From the east to the west blow the trumpet to arms! / Through the land let the sound of it flee; / Let the far and the near all unite with a cheer, / In defense of our Liberty Tree.
> — Thomas Paine,
> *The Liberty Tree*, 1775

136. The mother of battles.
> — Saddam Hussein, speech,
> January 6, 1991

137. Nuts!
> — Anthony McAuliffe, response
> to demand for surrender at
> Bastogne, December 22, 1944

138. Sighted sub, sank same.
> — Donald F. Mason, radio
> message, January 28, 1942

139. Taxation without representation is tyranny.
> — James Otis, coined phrase of
> the American Revolution,
> ca. 1761

140. There is Jackson, standing like a stone wall!
> — Bernard Elliott Bee, said of
> General T. E. Jackson at the battle
> of Bull Run (at which Bee died),
> July 21, 1861

141. *Veni, vidi, vici.* (I came, I saw, I conquered.)
> — Julius Caesar, announcement
> of victory at Zela, 1st c. B.C.

142. We are waiting for the long-promised invasion. So are the fishes.
> — Winston S. Churchill,
> radio broadcast concerning the
> threatened invasion of Britain by
> Germany, October 21, 1940

143. We beat them today or Molly Stark's a widow.
— John Stark, said before the battle of Bennington, August 16, 1777

144. Before this time tomorrow, I shall have gained a peerage, or Westminster Abbey.
— Horatio Nelson, before the battle of the Nile, in R. Southey, *Life of Nelson*, 1813

145. What a glorious morning for America!
— Samuel Adams, statement in response to the sound of gunfire at Lexington, April 19, 1775

146. It would be superfluous in me to point out to your Lordship that this is war.
— Charles Francis Adams, dispatch to Earl Russell, September 5, 1863

147. Yesterday, December 7, 1941 — a date which will live in infamy — the United States of America was suddenly and deliberately attacked by naval and air forces of the Empire of Japan.
— Franklin D. Roosevelt, message to Congress, December 8, 1941

Battles

See also Action; Conflict; Soldiers; Strategy and Tactics; Strength

148. The first blow is half the battle.
— Oliver Goldsmith, *She Stoops to Conquer*, 1773

149. There can be no reconciliation where there is no open warfare. There must be a battle, a brave boisterous battle, with pennants waving and cannon roaring, before there can be peaceful treaties and enthusiastic shaking of hands.
— Mary E. Braddon, *Lady Audley's Secret*, 1862

150. A bold heart is half the battle.
— Proverb

151. Half-heartedness never won a battle.
— William McKinley, speech, January 27, 1898

152. He that is afraid of wounds, must not come nigh a battle.
— Proverb

153. In a battle all you need to make you fight is a little hot blood and the knowledge that it's more dangerous to lose than to win.
— George Bernard Shaw, *Man and Superman*, 1903

154. No battle is worth fighting except the last one.
— Enoch Powell, in *Observer*, January 2, 1983

155. Waterloo is a battle of the first rank won by a captain of the second.
— Victor Hugo, *Les Misérables*, 1862

156. The battle of Waterloo was won on the playing fields of Eton.
— Arthur Wellesley, Duke of Wellington, in W. Fraser, *Words on Wellington*, 1889

157. The terrible grumble, and rumble, and roar, / Telling the battle was on once more, / And Sheridan twenty miles away.
— Thomas Buchanan Read, *Sheridan's Ride*, 1865

158. There's no such thing as a crowded battlefield. Battlefields are lonely places.
— Alfred M. Gray, in *Newsweek*, July 9, 1984

159. Our business in the field of fight / Is not to question, but to prove our might.
— Homer, *The Iliad*, ca. 700 B.C.

160. How are the mighty fallen in the midst of the battle!
— Bible, *II Samuel*, 1:24

161. Two armies fighting each other are one great army in the act of suicide.
— Henri Barbusse, *Under Fire: The Story of a Squad*, 1917

162. You cannot choose your battlefield, / The gods do that for you, / But you can plant a standard / Where a standard never flew.
— Nathalia Crane, *The Colors*, ca. 1925

Bravery *see* Courage

Causes of War

See also Diplomacy; Enemies; Expansion;
Foreign Policy; Good and Evil; International Relations;
Predictions of War; Tyranny

163. Life is warfare.
— Seneca, *Epistolae Morales*, 1st c.

164. This life of ours is a very enjoyable fight, but a very miserable truce.
— Gilbert K. Chesterton, *Charles Dickens*, 1906

165. The savage in man is never quite eradicated.
— Henry David Thoreau, *Journal*, September 26, 1859

166. It is unfair to blame man too fiercely for being pugnacious; he learned the habit from Nature.
— Christopher Morley, *Inward Ho!* 1923

167. Is war a biological necessity?
— Bronislaw Malinowski, speech, September 17, 1936

168. War is a biological necessity of the first importance, a regulative element in the life of mankind which cannot be dispensed with.
— Friedrich von Bernhardi, *Germany and the Next War*, 1912

169. He who knows history knows also that to banish war from the world would be to mutilate human nature.
— Heinrich von Treitschke, *Politics*, 1897–98

170. The condition of man ... is a condition of war of everyone against everyone.
— Thomas Hobbes, *Leviathan*, 1651

171. The foes from whom we pray to be delivered are our own passions, appetites and follies; and against these there is always need that we should war.
— Theodore Roosevelt, statement, November 2, 1905

172. War will never cease until babies begin to come into the world with larger cerebrums and smaller adrenal glands.
— H. L. Mencken, *Minority Report*, 1956

173. War will always find a way.
— Bertolt Brecht, *Mother Courage*, 1939

174. To say that war is madness is like saying that sex is madness: true enough, from the standpoint of a stateless eunuch, but merely a provocative epigram for those who must make their arrangements in the world as given.
— John Updike, *Self-Consciousness: Memoirs*, 1989

175. We used to wonder where war lived, what it was that made it so vile.

And now we realize that we know where it lives, that it was inside ourselves.
— Albert Camus, *Notebooks 1935–1942*, 1962

176. Wars are not caused by nations having armies. Wars are caused by political conflicts that create crises that spin out of control.
— Christopher Layne, in *Atlantic Monthly*, June, 1989

177. The word *state* is identical with the word *war*.
— Peter Kropotkin, *Paroles d'un révolté*, 1884

178. In violence we forget who we are.
— Mary McCarthy, *On the Contrary*, 1961

179. Once blood is shed in a national quarrel reason and right are swept aside by the rage of angry men.
— David Lloyd George, *War Memoirs*, 1942

180. People don't start wars, governments do.
— Ronald Reagan, in *Time*, March 18, 1985

181. It is human nature that rules the world, not governments and regimes.
— Svetlana Alliluyeva, in *New York Times*, November 3, 1984

182. The cause of some going to war, and of others avoiding it, is the same desire in both, attended with different views.
— Blaise Pascal, *Pensées*, 1670

183. All may begin a war, few can end it.
— Proverb

184. What mighty contests rise from trivial things!
— Alexander Pope, *The Rape of the Lock*, 1712

185. Fury provides arms.
— Virgil, *Aeneid*, 19 B.C.

186. Hate is still the main enemy of the human race, the fuel that heats the furnaces of genocide.
— I. F. Stone, in *I. F. Stone's Weekly*, September 9, 1968

187. Wars are caused by undefended wealth.
— Douglas MacArthur, in *New York Daily News*, November 18, 1945

188. Is there any man ... who does not know that the seed of war in the modern world is industrial and commercial rivalry?
— Woodrow Wilson, speech, September 5, 1919

189. Conflicting economic interest is relatively unimportant as a cause of war.
— Frank H. Knight, *Freedom and Reform*, 1947

190. What causes war is not patriotism, not that human beings are willing to die in defense of their dearest ones. It is the false doctrine, fostered by the few, that war spells gain.
— Henry Ford, in *Forum*, October, 1928

191. Gold and riches, the chief causes of war.
— Cornelius Tacitus, *Histories*, ca. 100

192. From the first day to this, sheer greed was the driving force of civilization.
— Friedrich Engels, *The Origin of the Family*, 1894

193. Every new stroke of civilization has cost the lives of countless brave men, who have fallen defeated by the "dragon," in their efforts to win the apples of the Hesperides, or the fleece of gold. Fallen in their efforts to overcome the old, half sordid savagery of the lower stages of creation, and win the next stage.
— D. H. Lawrence, *St. Mawr*, 1925

194. What we believe is more important than our material existence, therefore warfare is a legitimate extension of values.

— Edward Johnson, in
Independent, April 26, 1988

195. Opinions cannot survive if one has no chance to fight for them.

— Thomas Mann,
The Magic Mountain, 1924

196. If you want war, nourish a doctrine. Doctrines are the most frightful tyrants to which men are subject, because doctrines get inside a man's reason and betray him against himself. Civilized men have done their fiercest fighting for doctrines.

— William Graham Sumner, *War*,
1903

197. The right is more precious than peace.

— Woodrow Wilson, speech,
April 2, 1917

198. We fight not to enslave, but to set a country free, and to make room upon the earth for honest men to live in.

— Thomas Paine, in
The American Crisis, 1776–83

199. War is an evil thing; but to submit to the dictation of other states is worse.

— Thucydides,
History of the Peloponnesian War,
431–413 B.C.

200. Without war no state could exist. All those we know of arose through war … War, therefore, will endure to the end of history, as long as there is a multiplicity of states.

— Heinrich von Treitschke,
Politics, 1897–98

201. The blood of a nation ought never to be shed except for its own preservation in the utmost extremity.

— François Fenalon, *Télémaque*,
1699

202. The blood of man should have never been shed but to redeem the blood of man. It is well shed for our family, for our friends, for our God, for our coun-

try, for our kind. The rest is vanity; the rest is crime.

— Edmund Burke,
Letters on a Regicide Peace,
1797

203. We have always said that in our war with the Arabs we had a secret weapon — no alternative.

— Golda Meir, in *Life*,
October 3, 1969

204. Necessity never made a good bargain.

— Benjamin Franklin,
Poor Richard's Almanack,
April, 1735

205. Urgent necessity prompts many to do things, at the very thoughts of which they perhaps would start at other times.

— Miguel de Cervantes,
Don Quixote, 1605–15

206. Necessity is the plea for every infringement of human freedom. It is the argument of tyrants; it is the creed of slaves.

— William Pitt, speech,
November 18, 1783

207. It is not merely cruelty that leads men to love war, it is excitement.

— Henry Ward Beecher,
Proverbs from Plymouth Pulpit,
1887

208. America is addicted to wars of distraction.

— Barbara Ehrenreich, in *Times*,
April 22, 1991

209. My biggest concern is that anytime things get complicated in this country, we like to start a war.

— Ross Perot, in *Washington Post*,
May 8, 1993

210. The only war I ever approved of was the Trojan War; it was fought over a woman and the men knew what they were fighting for.

— William L. Phelps, sermon,
June 25, 1933

Civil War

See also Freedom; Rebellion; Revolution; Slavery

211. A foreign war is a lot milder than a civil war.
— Michel de Montaigne,
Essays, 1580

212. In a civil war the firing line is invisible, it passes through the hearts of men.
— Antoine de Saint-Exupéry,
Wind, Sand, and Stars, 1939

213. The wars of the people will be more terrible than those of the kings.
— Winston S. Churchill, speech,
May 12, 1901

214. If we do not make common cause to save the good old ship of the Union on this voyage, nobody will have a chance to pilot her on another voyage.
— Abraham Lincoln, speech,
February 15, 1861

215. If a house be divided against itself, that house cannot stand.
— Bible, *Mark* 3:25

216. The war of a community — of whole nations, and particularly of civilized nations — always starts from a political condition, and is called forth by a political motive. It is, therefore, a political act.
— Karl von Clausewitz,
On War, 1833

217. Every man's sword was against his fellow.
— Bible, *I Samuel* 14:20

218. Every man's sword shall be against his brother.
— Bible, *Ezekiel* 38:21

219. The war is over — the rebels are our countrymen again.
— Ulysses S. Grant, after Lee's
surrender at Appomattox,
April 9, 1865

220. All quiet along the Potomac.
— George B. McClennan,
attributed

221. Now we are engaged in a great civil war, testing whether that nation or any nation so conceived and so dedicated can long endure.
— Abraham Lincoln,
Gettysburg Address,
November 19, 1863

222. Still a Union that can only be maintained by swords and bayonets, and in which strife and civil war are to take the place of brotherly love and kindness, has no charm for me.
— Robert E. Lee, letter,
January 23, 1861

223. From hence, let fierce contending nations know / What dire effects from civil discord flow.
— Joseph Addison, *Cato*, 1713

Civilians

See also Horrors of War; Morale; Neutrality;
Propaganda; Public Opinion

224. Make war on the men — the ladies have too-long memories.
— Stephen Vincent Benét,
John Brown's Body, 1928

225. The butter to be sacrificed because of the war always turns out to be the margarine of the poor.
— James Tobin, speech,
December 27, 1967

226. In moral terms, wars follow a perverse pattern: the more highfalutin the motive, the more pain inflicted on civilians.
— Harrison Rainie, in
U.S. News and World Report,
February 18, 1891

227. I will not wage war against women and children. I have instructed my air force to limit their attacks to military objectives. However, if the enemy should conclude from this that he might get away with waging war in a different manner he will receive such an answer that he'll be knocked out of his wits!
— Adolf Hitler, in G. Stein,
Hitler, 1968

228. What difference does it make to the dead, the orphans and the homeless, whether the mad destruction is wrought under the name of totalitarianism or the holy name of liberty or democracy?
— Mohandas K. Gandhi,
Non-Violence in Peace and War,
1948

229. War alone grants to mankind the magnificent spectacle of a general submission to a general aim.
— Jakob Christoph Burckhardt,
Reflections on History, 1943

230. War means an ugly mob-madness, crucifying the truthtellers, choking the artists, sidetracking reforms, revolutions, and the working of social forces.
— John Reed, in *The Masses*,
April, 1917

231. To lead an uninstructed people to war is to throw them away.
— Confucius, *Analects*,
ca. 480 B.C.

232. A free people ought not only to be armed, but disciplined; to which end a uniform and well-digested plan is requisite.
— George Washington, message
to Congress, January 8, 1790

233. Those men and women are fortunate who are born at a time when a great struggle for human freedom is in progress.
— Emmeline Pankhurst,
My Own Story, 1914

234. I find war detestable but those who praise it without participating in it even more so.
— Romain Rolland, in *Journal de Genève*, October 30, 1914

235. Can anything be more ridiculous than that a man should have the right to kill me because he lives on the other side of the water, and because his ruler has a quarrel with mine, though I have none with him?
— Blaise Pascal, *Pensées*, 1670

236. The most shocking fact about war is that its victims and its instruments are individual human beings, and that these individual beings are condemned by the monstrous conventions of politics to murder or be murdered in quarrels not their own.
— Aldous Huxley, *The Olive Tree*,
1937

237. Older men declare war. But it is youth who must fight and die.
— Herbert Hoover, speech,
June 27, 1944

238. I maintain that Congress has the right and the duty to declare the object of the war, and the people have the right and the obligation to discuss it.
— Robert M. LaFollette, Sr.,
speech, October 6, 1917

239. Civilization is not by any means an easy thing to attain to. There are only two ways by which man can reach it. One is by being cultured, the other by being corrupt.
— Oscar Wilde, *The Picture of Dorian Gray*, 1891

240. The civilized are those who get more out of life than the uncivilized, and for this we are not likely to be forgiven.
— Cyril Connolly,
The Unquiet Grave, 1944

241. Civilization is the lamb's skin in which barbarism masquerades.
— Thomas B. Aldrich, *Pankapog Papers*, 1903

242. Our sympathy is cold to the relation of distant misery.
— Edward Gibbon, *The Decline and Fall of the Roman Empire*, 1776–88

243. In wartime, the degree of patriotism is directly proportional to distance from the front.
— Philip Caputo, in *New York Times Magazine*, February 24, 1991

244. Frankly, I'd like to see the government get out of war altogether and leave the whole field to private industry.
— Joseph Heller, *Catch-22*, 1955

the Cold War

See also the Atomic Age; Foreign Policy;
International Relations

245. Let us not be deceived — we are today in the midst of a cold war.
— Bernard Baruch, speech, April 16, 1947

246. The Cold War began with the division of Europe. It can only end when Europe is whole.
— George Bush, in *Daily Telegraph*, June 1, 1989

247. A strange, a perverted creed that has a queer attraction both for the most primitive and for the most sophisticated societies.
— Harold Macmillan, regarding Communism, in *New York Herald Tribune*, October 15, 1961

248. Communism has never come to power in a country that was not disrupted by war or corruption, or both.
— John F. Kennedy, speech, July 3, 1963

249. Whether you like it or not, history is on our side. We will bury you.
— Nikita Khrushchev, speech, September 15, 1959

250. An evil empire.
— Ronald Reagan, speech, describing the Soviet Union, March 8, 1983

251. An iron curtain has descended across the continent.
— Winston S. Churchill, speech, March 5, 1946

252. The Iron Curtain still stretches from Stettin to Trieste. But it's a rusting curtain.
— George Bush, speech, October 18, 1988

253. It is better to discuss things, to argue and engage in polemics than make perfidious plans of mutual destruction.
— Mikhail Gorbachev, in *New York Times*, April 19, 1987

254. We may be likened to two scorpions in a bottle, each capable of killing the other, but only at the risk of his own life.
— J. Robert Oppenheimer, in *Foreign Affairs*, July 1953

255. The superpowers often behave like two heavily armed blind men feeling their way around a room, each believing himself in mortal peril from the other, whom he assumes to have perfect vision.
— Henry Kissinger, in *The Observer*, September 30, 1979

256. The Cold War has ended, or in ending, not because there are victors and

vanquished, but because there is neither one nor the other.
— Mikhail Gorbachev, speech, November 29, 1989

257. [President Bill Clinton] has devel-

oped something new under the sun: the idea of bloodless war. The only problem is that it doesn't exist.
— Robert W. Tucker, in *Los Angeles Times*, August 1, 1994

Conflict

See also Aggression; Battles; Expansion; Force; Strength, War and Peace

258. An association of men who will not quarrel with one another is a thing which has never yet existed, from the greatest confederacy of nations down to a town meeting or a vestry.
— Thomas Jefferson, letter, June 1, 1798

259. We are quick to flare up, we races of men on the earth.
— Homer, *The Odyssey*, ca. 700 B.C.

260. For I have been a man, and that means to have been a fighter.
— Johann Wolfgang von Goethe, *West-östlicher Diwan*, 1819

261. My life is a warfare.
— Voltaire, *Mahomet*, 1741

262. I respect only those who resist me, but I cannot tolerate them.
— Charles DeGaulle, in *New York Times*, May 12, 1968

263. The Lord is a man of war.
— Bible, *Exodus*, 15:3

264. If you fear making anyone mad, then you ultimately probe for the lowest common denominator of human achievement.
— Jimmy Carter, speech, November 9, 1978

265. The struggle between liberty and authority is the most conspicuous feature in the portions of history with which we are earliest familiar, particularly in that of

Greece, Rome and England.
— John Stuart Mill, *On Liberty*, 1859

266. The urge to destroy is a creative urge.
— Mikhail Bakunin, *Reaction in Germany*, 1842

267. No mortal man has ever served at the same time his passions and his best interests.
— Sallust, *The War with Catiline*, ca. 40 B.C.

268. The most effective way of utilizing human energy is through an organized rivalry, which by specialization and social control is, at the same time, organized cooperation.
— Charles Horton Cooley, *Human Nature and the Social Order*, 1902

269. It is not by the principles of humanity that man lives or is able to preserve himself above the animal world but solely by means of the most brutal struggle.
— Adolf Hitler, speech, February, 1928

270. Perhaps catastrophe is the natural human environment, and even though we spend a good deal of energy trying to get away from it, we are programmed for survival amid catastrophe.
— Germaine Greer, *Sex and Destiny*, 1984

Conquest

See also Battles; Expansion; Strength; Victory

271. No one conquers who doesn't fight.
— Gabriel Biel, *Exposito Canonis Missae*, 15th c.

272. Every State must conquer or be conquered.
— Mikhail Bakunin, *Federalism, Socialism and Anti-Theologism*, 1868

273. We are a conquering race. We must obey our blood and occupy new markets and if necessary new lands.
— Albert J. Beveridge, speech, April 27, 1898

274. Conquest is the missionary of valor, and the hard impact of military virtues beats meanness out of the world.
— Walter Bagehot, *Physics and Politics*, 1872

275. Conquering kings their titles take.
— John Chandler, title of hymn, 1837

276. See, the conquering hero comes! / Sound the trumpets, beat the drums!
— Thomas Morell, *Judas Maccabeus*, 1747

277. Whoever can surprise well must conquer.
— John Paul Jones, letter, February 10, 1778

278. Our cruel and unrelenting enemy leaves us only the choice of brave resistance, or the most abject submission. We have, therefore, to resolve to conquer or die.
— George Washington, to the Continental Army before the battle of Long Island, August 27, 1776

279. You cannot conquer America.
— William Pitt, speech, November 18, 1777

280. If there is one principle more deeply rooted than any other in the mind of every American, it is that we should have nothing to do with conquest.
— Thomas Jefferson, letter, July 28, 1791

281. Rats and conquerors must expect no mercy in misfortune.
— Charles Caleb Colton, *Lacon*, 1820–22

282. The desire to conquer is itself a sort of subjection.
— George Eliot, *Daniel Deronda*, 1876

283. A peace is of the nature of a conquest; / For then both parties nobly are subdued, / And neither party loser.
— William Shakespeare, *Henry IV, Part II*, 1597

284. The rare case where the conquered is very satisfied with the conqueror.
— Konrad Adenauer, said of Allied occupation of West Berlin, in *New York Times*, March 21, 1960

285. We seem, as it were, to have conquered and peopled half the world in a fit of absence of mind.
— John Seeley, *The Expansion of England*, 1883

Cost of War

See also the Cold War; Death; Futility of War;
Horrors of War; Pacifism; Strategy and Tactics; Weapons

286. Endless money forms the sinews of war.
— Cicero, *Philippics*, 44–43 B.C.

287. War begun without good provision of money beforehand for going through with it is but a breathing of strength and blast that will quickly pass away. Coin is the sinews of war.
— François Rabelais, *Gargantun and Pantagruel*, 1532

288. The first and most imperative necessity in war is money, for money means everything else — men, guns, ammunition.
— Ida Tarbell, *The Tariff in Our Times*, 1906

289. War seldom enters but where wealth allures.
— John Dryden, *The Hind and the Panther*, 1687

290. Sooner or later every war of trade becomes a war of blood.
— Eugene V. Debs, speech, June 16, 1918

291. Capitalism carries within itself war, as clouds carry rain.
— Jean Jaurés, *Studies in Socialism*, 1902

292. Give capital thirty days to think it over and you will learn by that time that there will be no war. That will stop the racket — that and nothing else.
— Smedley D. Butler, in *The Forum and Century*, September, 1934

293. Take the profit out of war.
— Bernard Baruch, in *Atlantic Monthly*, January, 1926

294. Make wars unprofitable and you make them impossible.
— A. Philip Randolph, *The Messenger*, 1919

295. Wars are made to make debt.
— Ezra Pound, in *Writers at Work*, 1963

296. Each generation should be made to bear the burden of its own wars, instead of carrying them on, at the expense of other generations.
— James Madison, in *National Gazette*, February 2, 1792

297. Probably no nation is rich enough to pay for both war and education.
— Abraham Flexner, *Universities*, 1930

298. There is no instance of a country having benefited from prolonged warfare.
— Sun Tzu, *The Art of War*, ca. 500 B.C.

Courage

See also Courage Is … ; Courageous People;
Cowards; Duty; Greatness; Heroes; Morale; Resolve

299. Bravery never goes out of fashion.
— William M. Thackeray, *The Four Georges*, 1860

300. The weapon of the brave is in his heart.
— Proverb

301. None but the brave deserves the fair.
— John Dryden,
Alexander's Feast, 1697

302. The red badge of courage.
— Stephen Crane, title of book,
1895

303. It is courage, courage, courage, that raises the blood of life to crimson splendor.
— George Bernard Shaw,
Back to Methusalah, 1921

304. Quit yourselves like men, and fight.
— Bible, *I Samuel* 4:9

305. Blessings on your young courage, boy; that's the way to the stars.
— Virgil, *Aeneid*, 19 B.C.

306. Courage leads to the stars, fear toward death.
— Seneca, *Hercules Furens*, ca. 50

307. They are surely to be esteemed the bravest spirits who, having the clearest sense of both the pains and pleasures of life, do not on that account shrink from danger.
— Thucydides, *History of the Peloponnesian War*, 431–413 B.C.

308. If we take the generally accepted definition of bravery as a quality which knows no fear, I have never seen a brave man. All men are frightened. The more intelligent they are, the more they are frightened.
— George S. Patton,
War as I Knew It, 1947

309. God of battles! Steal my soldiers' hearts; / Possess them not with fear; take from them now / The sense of reckoning, if the opposèd numbers / Pluck their hearts from them.
— William Shakespeare,
Henry V, 1599

310. Life without the courage for death is slavery.
— Seneca, *Letters to Lucilius*, 1st c.

311. The courage we desire and prize is not the courage to die decently, but to live manfully.
— Thomas Carlyle,
On Boswell's Life of Johnson, 1832

312. For without belittling the courage with which men have died, we should not forget those acts of courage with which men ... have *lived*.
— John F. Kennedy,
Profiles in Courage, 1956

313. Life shrinks or expands in proportion to one's courage.
— Anaïs Nin,
The Diary of Anaïs Nin, 1966

314. Life is mostly froth and bubble, / Two things stand like stone, / Kindness in another's trouble, / Courage in your own.
— Adam Lindsay Gordon,
Ye Wearie Wayfarer, 1866

315. Of courage ... oh yes! If only one had that ... Then life might be livable, in spite of everything.
— Henrik Ibsen,
Hedda Gabler, 1890

316. The paradox of courage is that a man must be a little careless of his life in order to keep it.
— Gilbert K. Chesterton,
All Things Considered, 1908

317. It is a brave act of valor to condemn death; but where life is more terrible than death, it is then the truest valor to dare to live.
— Thomas Browne,
Religio Medici, 1642

318. Sometimes even to live is an act of courage.
— Seneca, *Letters to Lucilius*, 1st c.

319. 'Tisn't life that matters! 'Tis the courage you bring to it.
— Hugh Walpole, *Fortitude*, 1913

320. This will remain the land of the free only as long as it is the home of the brave.
— Elmer Davis, *But We Were Born Free*, 1954

321. My valor is certainly going, it is sneaking off! I feel it oozing out as it were, at the palms of my hands!
— Richard B. Sheridan,
The Rivals, 1775

322. There is plenty of courage among us for the abstract but not for the concrete.
— Helen Keller,
Let Us Have Faith, 1940

323. Valor delights in the test.
— Proverb

324. "I'm very brave generally," he went on in a low voice, "only today I happen to have a headache."
— Lewis Carroll, *Through the Looking-Glass*, 1872

325. It is easy to be brave from a safe distance.
— Aesop, *Fables*,
"The Wolf and the Lamb,"
ca. 550 B.C.

326. No one can answer for his courage when he has never been in danger.
— François La Rochefoucauld,
Maxims, 1665

327. To act coolly, intelligently and prudently in perilous circumstances is the test of a man — and also of a nation.
— Adlai Stevenson, in
New York Times, April 11, 1955

328. Valor lies just half way between rashness and cowheartedness.
— Miguel de Cervantes,
Don Quixote, 1605–15

329. Courage mounteth with occasion.
— William Shakespeare,
King John, 1596–97

330. A great part of courage is the courage of having done the thing before.
— Ralph Waldo Emerson,
The Conduct of Life, 1860

331. Familiarity with danger makes a brave man braver, but less daring.
— Herman Melville,
White Jacket, 1850

332. Without justice, courage is weak.
— Benjamin Franklin,
Poor Richard's Almanack,
January, 1734

333. All bravery stands upon comparisons.
— Francis Bacon, *Essays*, 1625

334. Some of your countrymen were unable to distinguish between their native dislike for war and the stainless patriotism of those who suffered its scars. But there has been a rethinking ... now we can say to you, and say as a nation, thank you for your courage.
— Ronald Reagan, speech concerning the Vietnam War,
November 11, 1984

335. Courage does not always march to airs blown by a bugle: is not always wrought out of the fabric ostentation wears.
— Frances Rodman, in
New York Times, May 13, 1961

336. Noble deeds are most estimable when hidden.
— Blaise Pascal, *Pensées*, 1670

337. Despair gives courage to a coward.
— Proverb

338. Between cowardice and despair, valor is gendered.
— John Donne, *Paradoxes: Problems and Essays*, 1633

339. Everyone becomes brave when he observes one who despairs.
— Friedrich Wilhelm Nietzsche,
Thus Spake Zarathustra, 1883–92

340. In a false quarrel there is no true valor.
— William Shakespeare,
Much Ado About Nothing,
1598–99

341. Valor is of no service, chance rules all, and the bravest often fall by the hands of cowards.
— Cornelius Tacitus,
Histories, ca. 100

342. War alone brings up to their highest tension all human energies and imposes the stamp of nobility upon the peoples who have the courage to make it.
— Benito Mussolini,
"The Political and Social Doctrine of Fascism," 1932

343. Fighting is like champagne. It goes to the heads of cowards as quickly as of heroes. Any fool can be brave on a battlefield when it's be brave or else be killed.
— Margaret Mitchell,
Gone with the Wind, 1936

344. The courage of a soldier is found to be the cheapest and most common quality of human nature.
— Edward Gibbon, *The Decline and Fall of the Roman Empire*, 1776–88

345. Physical courage is never in short supply in a fighting army. Moral courage sometimes is.
— Matthew B. Ridgway,
The Korean War, 1967

346. For fools rush in where angels fear to tread.
— Alexander Pope,
An Essay on Criticism, 1711

347. When valor preys on reason, / It eats the sword it fights with.
— William Shakespeare,
Antony and Cleopatra, 1606–07

348. Two o'clock in the morning courage: I mean unprecedented courage.
— Napoleon Bonaparte,
statement, December 5, 1815

349. Uncommon valor was a common virtue.
— Chester W. Nimitz, statement concerning the Marine Corps at Iwo Jima, February to May, 1945

Courage Is ...

See also Courage; Courageous People

350. Courage is a kind of salvation.
— Plato, *The Republic*, ca. 370 B.C.

351. Courage is the thing. All goes if courage goes.
— J. M. Barrie, speech,
May 3, 1922

352. Courage is not simply *one* of the virtues but the form of every virtue at the testing point, which means at the point of highest reality.
— C. S. Lewis, in C. Connolly,
The Unquiet Grave, 1944

353. Courage is a quality so necessary for maintaining virtue, that it is always respected, even when it is associated with vice.
— Samuel Johnson, in J. Boswell,
Life of Samuel Johnson, 1791

354. Courage without conscience is a wild beast.
— Robert G. Ingersoll, speech,
May 29, 1882

355. Courage is like love; it must have hope for nourishment.
— Napoleon Bonaparte,
Maxims, 1804–15

356. Grace under pressure.
— Ernest Hemingway, defining 'guts,' in *New York Times*,
November 24, 1963

357. Bravery is the capacity to perform properly even when scared half to death.
— Omar Bradley, in J. Garagiola,
Baseball Is a Funny Game, 1960

358. Courage is resistance to fear, mastery of fear — not absence of fear.
— Mark Twain, *Pudd'nhead Wilson*, 1894

359. Perfect courage and utter cowardice are two extremes which rarely occur.

— François La Rochefoucauld,
Maxims, 1665

360. Perfect courage is to do without witnesses what one would be capable of doing with the world looking on.

— François La Rochefoucauld,
Maxims, 1665

361. Valor is a gift. Those having it never know for sure whether they have it till the test comes. And those having it in one test never know for sure if they will have it when the next test comes.

— Carl Sandburg, news
summaries, December 14, 1954

362. Valor is the nobleness of the mind.

— Proverb

363. Courage is almost a contradiction in terms. It means a strong desire to live taking the form of a readiness to die.

— Gilbert K. Chesterton,
Orthodoxy, 1908

364. Courage is the price that life exacts for granting peace.

— Amelia Earhart, *Courage*, 1927

Courageous People

See also Greatness; Heroes; Leadership

365. Fortune favors the brave.

— Terence, *Phormio*, 161 B.C.

366. A man of courage never wants weapons.

— Proverb

367. A brave man's wounds are seldom on his back.

— Proverb

368. He wishes that he, too, had a wound, a red badge of courage.

— Stephen Crane,
The Red Badge of Courage, 1895

369. The Lord is with thee, thou mighty man of valor.

— Bible, *Judges*, 6:12

370. Brave men are brave from the very first.

— Pierre Corneille, *Le Cid*, 1636

371. A valiant man's look is more than a coward's sword.

— Proverb

372. Brave men are all vertebrates; they have their softness on the surface and their toughness in the middle.

— Gilbert K. Chesterton,
Tremendous Trifles, 1909

373. Every man has his own courage, and is betrayed because he seeks in himself the courage of other persons.

— Ralph Waldo Emerson,
Journals, 1847

374. The strongest man in the world is he who stands most alone.

— Henrik Ibsen, *An Enemy of the People*, 1882

375. People with courage and character always seem sinister to the rest.

— Hermann Hesse, *Demain*, 1919

376. Until the day of his death, no man can be sure of his courage.

— Jean Anouilh, *Becket*, 1959

377. Perhaps those, who, trembling most, maintain a dignity in their fate, are the bravest: resolution on reflection is real courage.

— Horace Walpole,
Memoirs of the Reign of King George II,
1846

378. Some have been thought brave because they were afraid to run away.

— Thomas Fuller,
Gnomologia, 1732

379. A brave man struggling in the storms of fate, / And greatly falling with a falling state.
— Alexander Pope, in J. Addison, *Cato*, 1713

380. A man can be physically courageous and morally craven.
— Melvin B. Tolson, in *Washington Tribune*, March 25, 1939

Cowards

See also Appeasement;
Courage; Fear; Futility of War; Morale; Pacifism

381. Cowards die often.
— Proverb

382. To have died once is enough.
— Virgil, *Aeneid*, 19 B.C.

383. Cowards die many times before their deaths; / The valiant never taste of death but once.
— William Shakespeare, *Julius Caesar*, 1599

384. He that fears death lives not.
— Proverb

385. The republic was not established by cowards, and cowards will not preserve it.
— Elmer Davis, speech, 1953

386. Of cowards no history is written.
— Proverb

387. He was just a coward and that was the worst luck any man could have.
— Ernest Hemingway, *For Whom the Bell Tolls*, 1940

388. The most mortifying infirmity in human nature, to feel in ourselves, or to contemplate in another, is, perhaps, cowardice.
— Charles Lamb, *Last Essays of Elia*, 1833

389. Man gives every reason for his conduct save one, every excuse for his crimes save one; and that one is his cowardice.
— George Bernard Shaw, *Man and Superman*, 1903

390. Self-defense is Nature's eldest law.
— John Dryden, *Absalom and Achitophel*, 1681

391. A coward turns away, but a brave man's choice is danger.
— Euripedes, *Iphigenin in Taurus*, ca. 412 B.C.

392. The man who runs may fight again.
— Menander, *Monostikoi*, 4th c. B.C.

393. Even the bold will fly when they see Death / drawing in close enough to end their life.
— Sophocles, *Antigone*, 442–441 B.C.

394. The better part of valor is discretion.
— William Shakespeare, *Henry IV, Part I*, 1597

395. Any coward can fight a battle when he's sure of winning; but give me the man who has pluck to fight when he's sure of losing. That's my way, sir; there are many victories worse than a defeat.
— George Eliot, *Janet's Repentance*, 1857

396. That man is not truly brave who is afraid either to seem to be, or to be, when it suits him, a coward.
— Edgar Allan Poe, *Marginalia*, 1844–49

397. The coward calls the brave man rash, the rash man calls him a coward.
— Aristotle, *Nicomachean Ethics*, 325 B.C.

398. The mob gets out of hand, runs wild, worse / than raging fire, while the man who stands apart / is called a coward.
— Euripedes, *Hecuba*, ca. 425 B.C.

399. Conscience and cowardice are really the same thing.
— Oscar Wilde, *The Picture of Dorian Gray*, 1891

400. Conscience is but a word that cowards use, / Devised at first to keep the strong in awe.
— William Shakespeare, *Richard III*, 1591

401. As an old soldier I admit the cowardice; it's as universal as sea sickness, and matters just as little.
— George Bernard Shaw, *Man and Superman*, 1903

402. Cowards in scarlet pass for men of war.
— George Granville, *The She Gallants*, 1696

403. Military service produces moral inbecility, ferocity and cowardice.
— George Bernard Shaw, *John Bull's Other Island*, 1906

404. All wars are wars among thieves who are too cowardly to fight and who therefore induce the young manhood of the whole world to do the fighting for them.
— Emma Goldman, in *Mother Earth*, July, 1917

405. War spares not the brave, but the cowardly.
— Anacreon, *Fragment 101*, 5th c. B.C.

406. Cowards never use their might, / But against such as will not fight.
— Samuel Butler, *Hudibras*, 1663

407. Nothing gives a fearful man more courage than another's fear.
— Umberto Eco, *The Name of the Rose*, 1980

408. If you knew how cowardly your enemy is, you would slap him. Bravery is knowledge of the cowardice in the enemy.
— Edgar Watson Howe, *Country Town Sayings*, 1911

409. Cowardly dogs bark loudest.
— John Webster, *The White Devil*, 1612

410. Every dog is valiant at his own door.
— Proverb

411. Hatred is the coward's revenge for being intimidated.
— George Bernard Shaw, *Major Barbara*, 1905

412. A plague of all cowards, I say.
— William Shakespeare, *Henry IV, Part I*, 1597

413. Ever will a coward show no mercy.
— Thomas Malory, *Le Morte d'Arthur*, ca. 1469

414. Cruelty ever proceeds from a vile mind, and often from a cowardly heart.
— Lodovico Ariosto, *Orlando Furioso*, 1516

415. That cowardice is incorrigible which the love of power cannot overcome.
— Charles Caleb Colton, *Lacon*, 1820–22

416. When cowardice is made respectable, its followers are without number both from among the weak and the strong; it easily becomes a fashion.
— Eric Hoffer, *The Passionate State of Mind*, 1954

417. Optimism and self-pity are the positive and negative poles of modern cowardice.
— Cyril Connolly, *The Unquiet Grave*, 1944

418. Cowardice, as distinguished from panic, is almost always simply a lack of ability to suspend the functioning of the imagination.
— Ernest Hemingway, *Men at War*, 1942

419. I'm a hero with coward's legs.
— Spike Milligan, *Puckoon*, 1963

the Dead

See also Heroes; Horrors of War

420. In peace sons bury their fathers, but in war fathers bury their sons.
— Croesus, attributed

421. Let the dead bury their dead.
— Bible, *Matthew* 8:22

422. Th' dead ar-re always pop-lar. I knowed a society wanst to vote a mony-ment to a man an' refuse to help his fam'ly all in wan night.
— Finley Peter Dunne, *Mr. Dooley in Peace and in War*, 1898

423. Who will remember, passing through this gate, / The unheroic dead who fed the guns? / Who shall absolve the foulness of their fate —/ Those doomed, conscripted, unvictorious ones?
— Siegfried Sassoon, *On Passing the New Menin Gate*, 1918

424. Fame is so sweet that we love anything with which we connect it, even death.
— Blaise Pascal, *Pensées*, 1670

425. With drums and guns, and guns and drums / The enemy nearly slew ye. / My darling dear, you look so queer, / Oh, Johnny, I hardly knew ye.
— Anonymous, Irish folk song

426. Sons of the dark and bloody ground.
— Theodore O'Hara, *The Bivouac of the Dead*, 1847

427. "You're wounded!" "Nay," the soldier's pride / Touched to you quick, he said: / "I'm killed, Sire!" And his chief beside, / Smiling the boy fell dead.
— Robert Browning, "Incident of the French Camp," 1842

428. Red lips are not so red / As the stained stones kissed by the English dead.
— Wilfred Owen, "Greater Love," 1917

429. Here dead lie we because we did not choose / To live and shame the land from which we sprung. / Life, to be sure, is nothing much to lose; / But young men think it is, and we were young.
— A. E. Housman, *More Poems*, 1936

430. It is only the dead who do not return.
— Bertrand Barère de Vieuzac, speech, 1794

431. In Flanders fields the poppies blow / Between the crosses, row on row.
— John McCrae, "In Flanders Fields," 1915

432. It is foolish and wrong to mourn the men who died. Rather we should thank God that such men lived.
— George S. Patton, speech, June 7, 1945

433. All quiet along the Potomac to-night, / No sound save the rush of the river, / While soft falls the dew on the face of the dead —/ The picket's off duty forever.
— Ethel Lynn Beers, "The Picket Guard," 1861

434. For the dead there are no more toils.
— Sophocles, *The Women of Trachis*, ca. 413 B.C.

435. Remember me when I am dead / And simplify me when I'm dead.
— Keith Douglas, "Simplify me when I'm Dead," 1941

436. He has gone over to the majority.
— Petronius, *Satyricon*, 1st c.

437. Man is a noble animal, splendid in ashes, and pompous in the grave.
— Thomas Browne, *Hydriotaphia*, 1658

438. It is not right to glory in the slain.
— Homer, *The Odyssey*,
ca. 700 B.C.

439. Lafayette, we are here.
— Charles E. Stanton, said at
Lafayette's tomb, July 4, 1917

440. On Fame's eternal camping ground / Their silent tents are spread, / And Glory guards, with solemn round, / The bivouac of the dead.
— Theodore O'Hara,
The Bivouac of the Dead, 1847

441. Fame is a food that dead men eat, —/ I have no stomach for such meat.
— Henry Austin Dobson,
"Fame is a Food," 1906

442. Fame is the sun of the dead.
— Honoré de Balzac,
Le Recherche de l'Absolu, 1834

443. He lives in fame that died in virtue's cause.
— William Shakespeare,
Titus Andronicus, 1590

444. And when the war is done and youth stone dead / I'd toddle safely home and die — in bed.
— Siegfried Sassoon,
Base Details, 1918

445. Those most like the dead are those most loath to die.
— Jean de La Fontaine,
Fables, 1668

446. It is better to be a fool than to be dead.
— Robert Louis Stevenson,
Virginibus Puerisque, 1881

447. A living dog is better than a dead lion.
— Bible, *Ecclesiastes* 9:4

448. Dead men have no victory.
— Euripedes,
The Phoenician Women,
ca. 410 B.C.

Death

See also Horrors of War; Patriotism

449. Old soldiers never die, / They simply fade away.
— J. Foley, "Old Soldiers Never
Die," 1920

450. It is not unseemly for a man to die fighting in defense of his country.
— Homer, *The Iliad*, ca. 700 B.C.

451. Even Rome cannot give us dispensation from death.
— Molière, *L'Etourdi*, 1665

452. The angel of death has been abroad throughout the land; you may almost hear the beating of his wings.
— John Bright, reporting on the
Crimean War, in *Hansard*,
February 23, 1855

453. A single death is a tragedy, a million deaths is a statistic.
— Joseph Stalin, attributed

454. Neither the sun nor death can be looked at steadily.
— François La Rochefoucauld,
Maxims, 1665

455. Death is a thing of grandeur ... a rearrangement of the world.
— Antoine de Saint-Exupéry,
Flight to Arras, 1942

456. I too shall lie in the dust when I am dead, but now let me win noble renown.
— Homer, *The Iliad*, ca. 700 B.C.

457. As for death one gets used to it, even if it's only other people's death you get used to.
— Enid Bagnold, *Autobiography*,
1969

458. Death is swallowed up in victory.
— Bible, *I Corinthians* 15:54

459. Killing cleanly and in a way which gives you esthetic pride and pleasure has always been one of the greatest enjoyments of a part of the human race.
— Ernest Hemingway,
Death in the Afternoon, 1932

460. The word "civilization" to my mind is coupled with death. When I use the word, I see civilization as a crippling, thwarting thing, a stultifying thing.
— Henry Miller, in
Writers at Work, 1963

461. It is always a strain when people are being killed. I don't think anybody has held this job who hasn't felt personally responsible for those being killed.
— Lyndon B. Johnson, in *Time*,
April 15, 1985

462. Let us eat and drink; for tomorrow we shall die.
— Bible, *Isaiah* 22:13

463. Death is the supreme festival on the road to freedom.
— Dietrich Bonhoeffer, *Letters
and Papers from Prison*, 1953

464. To die will be an awfully big adventure.
— J. M. Barrie, *Peter Pan*, 1928

465. So many people are in love with death. They want war.
— Erich Fromm, in *Look*,
May 5, 1964

466. Men reject their prophets and slay them, but they love their martyrs and honor those whom they have slain.
— Fyodor Dostoevski,
The Brothers Karamazov,
1879–80

467. In the depth of the anxiety of having to die is the anxiety of being eternally forgotten.
— Paul Tillich,
The Eternal Now, 1963

468. Men are convinced of your arguments, your sincerity, and the seriousness of your efforts only by your death.
— Albert Camus, *The Fall*, 1956

469. Death is the great leveler.
— Proverb

470. Life levels all men: death reveals the eminent.
— George Bernard Shaw,
Man and Superman, 1903

471. 'Tis after death that we measure men.
— James Barron Hope, *A Wreath
of Virginia Bay Leaves*, 1895

472. But ye shall die like men, and fall like one of the princes.
— Bible, *Psalms* 82:7

473. Death is not the greatest of evils; it is worse to want to die, and not be able to.
— Sophocles, *Electra*, ca. 414 B.C.

474. Fear of death increases in exact proportion to increase in wealth.
— Ernest Hemingway, in A. E.
Hotchner, *Papa Hemingway*, 1955

475. Why, do you know, then, that the origin of all human evils, and of baseness, and cowardice, is not death, but rather the fear of death?
— Epictetus, *Discourses*, 2nd c.

476. A belief in hell and the knowledge that every ambition is doomed to frustration at the hands of a skeleton have never prevented the majority of human beings from behaving as though death were no more than an unfounded rumor.
— Aldous Huxley,
Themes and Variations, 1950

477. All men think all men mortal but themselves.
— Edward Young,
Night Thoughts, 1742–45

478. No young man ever thinks he shall die.
— William Hazlitt, *Table Talk*,
1821–22

479. The best of men cannot suspend their fate: / The good die early, and the bad die late.
— Daniel Defoe, *Character of the
Late Dr. S. Annesley*, 1715

480. To my mind, to kill in war is not a whit better than to commit ordinary murder.
— Albert Einstein, in *Kaizo*, Autumn, 1952

481. It is forbidden to kill; therefore all murderers are punished who kill not in large companies, and to the sound of trumpets.
— Voltaire, *Philosophical Dictionary*, 1764

482. Ez fer war, I call it murder.
— James Russell Lowell, *The Biglow Papers, Series I*, 1848

483. Kill a man, and you are an assassin. Kill millions of men, and you are a conqueror. Kill everyone, and you are a god.
— Jean Rostand, *Pensées d'un Biologiste*, 1939

484. One should die proudly when it is no longer possible to live proudly.
— Friedrich Wilhelm Nietzsche, *Twilight of the Idols*, 1888

485. Death is better, a milder fate than tyranny.
— Aeschylus, *Agememnon*, ca. 458 B.C.

486. We know that the road to freedom has always been stalked by death.
— Angela Davis, in *Daily World*, August 25, 1971

487. To our real, naked selves there is not a thing on earth or in heaven worth dying for.
— Eric Hoffer, *The True Believer*, 1951

488. To die with glory, if one has to die at all, / is still, I think, pain for the dier.
— Euripedes, *Rhesus*, ca. 455–441 B.C.

489. Death is never sweet, not even if it is suffered for the highest ideal.
— Erich Fromm, *Escape from Freedom*, 1941

490. To die for an idea; it is unquestionably noble. But how much nobler it would be if men died for ideas that were true!
— H. L. Mencken, *Prejudices, First Series*, 1919

491. To die for an idea is to place a pretty high price upon conjectures.
— Anatole France, *La Révolte des anges*, 1914

Defeat

See also Conquest; Futility of War; Victory

492. The quickest way of ending a war is to lose it.
— George Orwell, *Shooting an Elephant*, 1950

493. I return with feelings of misgiving from my third war — I was the first American commander to put his signature to a paper ending a war when we did not win it.
— Mark W. Clark, on retiring as United Nations commander in Korea, in *New York Herald Tribune*, October 21, 1953

494. There are defeats more triumphant than victories.
— Michel de Montaigne, *Essays*, 1580

495. We have one foot in genesis and the other in apocalypse, and annihilation is always one immediate option.
— Michael Harrington, *Toward a Democratic Left*, 1968

496. Nothing except a battle lost can be half so melancholy as a battle won.
— Arthur Wellesley, Duke of Wellington, dispatch from Waterloo, 1815

497. Every man meets his Waterloo at last.
— Wendell Phillips, speech, November 1, 1859

498. Post-mortems on defeat are never very useful unless they say something about the future.
— James Reston, in *New York Times*, July 15, 1964

499. You show me a good and gracious loser, and I'll show you a failure.
— Knute Rockne, in *Argosy*, November, 1976

500. Defeat is a school in which truth always grows strong.
— Henry Ward Beecher, *Proverbs from Plymouth Pulpit*, 1887

501. The conventional army loses if it does not win. The guerrilla wins if he does not lose.
— Henry Kissinger, in *Foreign Affairs*, January, 1969

502. If you know neither the enemy nor yourself, you will succumb in every battle.
— Sun Tzu, *The Art of War*, ca. 500 B.C.

503. 'Tis better to have fought and lost, / Than never to have fought at all.
— Arthur Hugh Clough, "Peschiera," 1854

504. A man can be destroyed but not defeated.
— Ernest Hemingway, *The Old Man and the Sea*, 1952

505. Nothing should be left to an invaded people except their eyes for weeping.
— Otto von Bismarck, attributed

506. The only safe course for the defeated is to expect no safety.
— Virgil, *Aeneid*, 19 B.C.

Diplomacy

See also Foreign Policy; International Relations; Treaties

507. Diplomacy, *n.* The patriotic art of lying for one's country.
— Ambrose Bierce, *The Devil's Dictionary*, 1906

508. Diplomacy is to do and say the nastiest things in the nicest way.
— Isaac Goldberg, *The Reflex*, 1930

509. Courtesy, moderation, and self-restraint should mark international, no less than private, intercourse.
— Theodore Roosevelt, directive, March 10, 1904

510. Diplomacy ... the art of nearly deceiving all your friends, but not quite deceiving all your enemies.
— Kofi Busia, statement, February 2, 1970

511. Diplomacy is letting someone else have your way.
— Lester B. Pearson, in *Vancouver Sun*, March 18, 1965

512. Diplomacy is the police in grand costume.
— Napoleon Bonaparte, *Maxims*, 1804–15

513. All diplomacy is a continuation of war by other means.
— Chou En-lai, in *Saturday Evening Post*, March 27, 1954

514. Diplomacy is at its very, very best in preventive diplomacy. The best that can happen to you is that no one notices what you do. And since nobody sees anything, why should anyone say thank you? When a problem appears, then you have failed.
— Lakdhar Brahimi, in *Los Angeles Times*, September 29, 1994

515. Competing pressures tempt one to believe that an issue deferred is a problem avoided: more often it is a crisis invited.
— Henry Kissinger, in *Time*, October 15, 1979

516. It is a great victory that comes without blood.
— Proverb

517. Warfare, no matter what weapons it employs, is a means to an end, and if that end can be achieved by negotiated settlements of conditional surrender, there is no need for war.
— Harry S Truman, *Memoirs*, 1955–56

518. All war represents a failure of diplomacy.
— Tony Benn, speech, February 28, 1991

519. Men and nations do behave wisely, once all other alternatives have been exhausted.
— Abba Eban, in *Vogue*, August 1, 1967

520. You don't promote the cause of peace by talking only to people with whom you agree.
— Dwight D. Eisenhower, press conference, January 30, 1957

521. He is wise who tries everything before arms.
— Terence, *Eunuchus*, ca. 165 B.C.

522. If we are to survive on this planet, there must be compromises.
— Storm Jameson, *A Cup of Tea for Mr. Thorgill*, 1957

523. Compromise does not mean cowardice.
— John F. Kennedy, *Profiles in Courage*, 1956

524. Let us never negotiate out of fear, but let us never fear to negotiate.
— John F. Kennedy, inaugural address, January 20, 1961

525. Only free men can negotiate; prisoners cannot enter into contracts.
— Nelson Mandela, in *Time*, February 25, 1985

526. In setting our military goals we need first of all to recognize that most of the world's most basic woes do not lend themselves to purely military solutions.
— Matthew B. Ridgway, *The Korean War*, 1967

527. The reason that diplomacy is so stilted is that its purpose is to head off the most natural social relation between countries in economic or ideological conflict, namely war.
— Judith Martin, *Common Courtesy*, 1985

528. Our policy is directed not against any country or doctrine but against hunger, poverty, desperation and chaos. Its purpose should be the revival of a working economy in the world so as to permit the emergence of political and social conditions in which free institutions can exist.
— George C. Marshall, address (the Marshall Plan), June 5, 1947

529. Force can only overcome other force. When it has done this, it has spent itself and other means of influencing conduct have to be employed.
— Dean Acheson, *A Democrat Looks at His Party*, 1955

530. Diplomacy and defense are not substitutes for one another. Either alone would fail.
— John F. Kennedy, speech, November 16, 1961

531. American diplomacy is easy on the brain but hell on the feet.
— Charles G. Dawes, speech, June 2, 1931

532. Vacillation and inconsistency are as incompatible with successful diplomacy as they are with the national dignity.
— Benjamin Harrison, speech, September 11, 1888

533. To act with doubleness towards a man whose own conduct was double, was so near an approach to virtue that it deserved to be called by no meaner name than diplomacy.
— George Eliot, *Felix Holt, The Radical,* 1866

534. In ninety-nine cases out of a hundred, when there is a quarrel between two states, it is generally occasioned by some blunder of a ministry.
— Benjamin Disraeli, speech, February 19, 1858

535. Sometimes it takes two or three conferences to scare up a war, but generally one will do it.
— Will Rogers, in *New York Times,* July 6, 1933

536. May the pens of the diplomats not ruin again what the people have attained with such exertions.
— Gebhard von Blücher, statement after the battle of Waterloo, 1813

537. The words of his mouth were smoother than butter, but war was in his heart: his words were softer than oil, yet were they drawn swords.
— Bible, *Psalms* 55:21

538. I don't like hypocrisy — even in international relations.
— Kofi Busia, statement, February 2, 1970

539. To jaw-jaw is better than to war-war.
— Winston S. Churchill, speech, June 26, 1954

540. The favorite cliché of those who advocate summit talks regardless of the circumstances is, "Talking is always better than fighting." This, however, is not the only choice. Talking is not better than not talking when you do not know what you are going to talk about.
— Richard M. Nixon, *The Challenges We Face,* 1960

541. There are few ironclad rules of diplomacy but to one there is no exception. When an official reports that talks were useful, it can safely be concluded that nothing was accomplished.
— John Kenneth Galbraith, in *Foreign Service Journal,* June, 1969

542. Diplomacy means all the wicked devices of the Old World, spheres of influence, balances of power, secret treaties, triple alliances, and, during the interwar period, appeasement of Fascism.
— Barbara Tuchman, in *Foreign Affairs,* October, 1972

543. In statesmanship get the formalities right, never mind about the moralities.
— Mark Twain, *Following the Equator,* 1897

544. I'd rather see America save her soul than her face.
— Norman Thomas, statement, November 27, 1965

545. No terms except an unconditional and immediate surrender can be accepted.
— Ulysses S. Grant, message to General S. B. Buckner, February 16, 1862

546. Neither the sanctions of international law nor the justice of a cause can be depended upon for a fair settlement of differences, when they come into conflict with a strong political necessity on the one side opposed to comparative weakness on the other.
— Alfred Thayer Mahan, *The Interest of America in Sea Power,* 1897

547. You don't negotiate with someone who marches into another country, devastates it, killing whoever stands in his way. You get him out, make him pay and see that he is never in a position to do these things again.
— Margaret Thatcher, in *Newsweek,* October 29, 1990

548. The chief reason warfare is still with us is ... the single fact that no substitute for this final arbiter in interna-

tional affairs has yet appeared on the political scene.

— Hannah Arendt, *Crisis of the Republic*, 1972

Diplomats

See also Appeasement; Foreign Policy;
International Relations

549. A diplomat is a person who can tell you to go to hell in such a way that you actually look forward to the trip.
— Caskie Stinnett,
Out of the Red, 1960

550. Consul, *n.* In American politics, a person who, having failed to secure an office from the people is given one by the Administration on condition that he leave the country.
— Ambrose Bierce,
The Devil's Dictionary, 1906

551. An ambassador is not simply an agent; he is also a spectacle.
— Walter Bagehot,
The English Constitution, 1867

552. The difference between being an elder statesman / And posing successfully as an elder statesman / Is practically negligible.
— T. S. Eliot,
The Elder Statesman, 1958

553. At home, you always have to be a politician; when you're abroad, you almost feel yourself a statesman.
— Harold Macmillan, in *Look*,
April 15, 1958

554. You can always get the truth from an American statesman after he has turned seventy, or given up all hope of the Presidency.
— Wendell Phillips, speech,
November 7, 1860

555. An ambassador is an honest man, sent to lie abroad for the good of his country.
— Henry Wotton, in I. Wolton,
Reliquiae Wottonianae, 1651

556. Diplomats write notes, because they wouldn't have the nerve to tell the same thing to each other's face.
— Will Rogers,
The Autobiography of Will Rogers,
1949

557. My advice to any diplomat who wants to have a good press is to have two or three kids and a dog.
— Carl Rowan, in *New Yorker*,
December 7, 1963

558. Why employ intelligent and highly paid ambassadors and then go and do their work for them? You don't buy a canary and sing yourself.
— Alex Douglas-Home, in
New York Times, April 21, 1969

559. Diplomats were invented simply to waste time.
— David Lloyd George, comment
regarding the Versailles Peace
Conference, November, 1918

560. Diplomats are useful only in fair weather. As soon as it rains they drown in every drop.
— Charles DeGaulle, in
Newsweek, October 1, 1962

561. The only real diplomacy ever performed by a diplomat is in deceiving their own people after their dumbness has got them into a war.
— Will Rogers,
The Autobiography of Will Rogers,
1949

562. The ambassadors of peace shall weep bitterly.
— Bible, *Isaiah* 33:7

563. Diplomats are just as essential to starting a war as soldiers are for finishing

it. You take diplomacy out of war and the thing would fall flat in a week.

— Will Rogers,
The Autobiography of Will Rogers,
1949

564. For a diplomat to think that rival and unfriendly powers cannot be brought to a settlement is to forget what diplomacy is all about. There would be little for diplomats to do if the world consisted of partners, enjoying political intimacy, and responding to common appeals.

— Walter Lippmann,
The Cold War, 1947

Duty

See also Military Command; Patriotism; Resolve

565. Obedience is the first duty of a soldier.

— Proverb

566. My duty is to obey orders.

— Thomas J. (Stonewall) Jackson,
aphorism

567. Without duty, life is soft and boneless; it cannot hold itself together.

— Joseph Joubert, *Pensées,* 1842

568. The reward of one duty is the power to fulfill another.

— George Eliot, *Daniel Deronda,*
1876

569. What better fate for a man than to die in the performance of his duty?

— Douglas MacArthur, in W. Manchester, *American Caesar,*
1978

570. Discipline is the soul of an army. It makes small numbers formidable; procures success to the weak, and esteem to all.

— George Washington, letter,
July 29, 1759

571. Nothing can be more hurtful to the service, than the neglect of discipline; for that discipline, more than numbers, gives one army the superiority over another.

— George Washington, orders,
July 6, 1777

572. The brave man inattentive to his duty, is worth little more to his country, than the coward who deserts her in the hour of danger.

— Andrew Jackson, statement to troops who abandoned the lines during the battle of New Orleans,
January 8, 1815

573. Do your duty, and leave the rest to the gods.

— Pierre Corneille, *Horace,* 1639

574. Duty cannot exist without faith.

— Benjamin Disraeli,
Tancred, 1847

575. Reasonable orders are easy enough to obey; it is capricious, bureaucratic or plain idiotic demands that form the habit of discipline.

— Barbara Tuchman, *Stillwell and the American Experience in China: 1911–1945,* 1970

576. Duty largely consists of pretending that the trivial is critical.

— John Fowles, *The Magus,* 1965

577. The worst of doing one's duty was that it apparently unfitted one for doing anything else.

— Edith Wharton,
The Age of Innocence, 1920

578. The paths of glory at least lead to the grave, but the paths of duty may not get you anywhere.

— James Thurber,
Fables for Our Time, 1943

579. The burning conviction that we have a holy duty toward others is often a

way of attaching our drowning selves to a passing raft.
— Eric Hoffer, *The True Believer*, 1951

580. When a stupid man is doing something he is ashamed of, he always declares that it is his duty.
— George Bernard Shaw, *Caesar and Cleopatra*, 1898

581. England expects that every man will do his duty.
— Horatio Nelson, at the battle of Trafalgar, in R. Southey, *Life of Nelson*, 1813

582. Every subject's duty is the king's; but every subject's soul is his own.
— William Shakespeare, *Henry V*, 1599

583. A sense of duty is moral glue, constantly subject to stress.
— William Safire, in *New York Times*, May 23, 1986

584. To an honest man, it is an honor to have remembered his duty.
— Plautus, *The Three-Penny Day*, ca. 194 B.C.

585. I know the disciplines of war.
— William Shakespeare, *Henry V*, 1599

586. The last pleasure in life is the sense of discharging our duty.
— William Hazlitt, *Characteristics*, 1823

587. Thank God, I have done my duty.
— Horatio Nelson, at the battle of Trafalgar, October 21, 1805

Empire *see* Expansion

Enemies

See also Alliances; the Cold War; Conflict; Good and Evil

588. There is no little enemy.
— Proverb

589. His enemies shall lick the dust.
— Bible, *Psalms* 72:9

590. This is no time for making new enemies.
— Voltaire, attributed last words upon being asked to renounce the devil, 1778

591. The last enemy that shall be destroyed is death.
— Bible, *I Corinthians* 15:26

592. One enemy is too much.
— George Herbert, *Jacula Prudentum*, 1651

593. One of the most time-consuming things is to have an enemy.
— E. B. White, in *Essays of E. B. White*, 1977

594. *Hatred* is an affair of the heart; *contempt* that of the head.
— Arthur Schopenhauer, *Parerga and Paralipomena*, 1851

595. Hast thou found me, O mine enemy?
— Bible, *I Kings* 21:20

596. You will only injure yourself if you take notice of despicable enemies.
— Aesop, *Fables*, "The Bald Man and the Fly," ca. 550 B.C.

597. When our hatred is too keen it puts us beneath those whom we hate.
— François La Rochefoucauld, *Maxims*, 1665

598. Trust not a new friend nor an old enemy.
— Proverb

599. Call no man foe, but never love a stranger.
— Stella Benson,
This is the End, 1917

600. Treating your adversary with respect is giving him an advantage to which he is not entitled.
— Samuel Johnson, in J. Boswell,
Tour of the Hebrides,
August 15, 1773

601. Our worst enemies here are not the ignorant and the simple, however cruel; our worst enemies are the intelligent and corrupt.
— Graham Greene,
The Human Factor, 1978

602. The main enemy is at home.
— Karl Liebknecht, speech, 1914

603. The greatest enemy to man is man.
— Robert Burton, *The Anatomy of Melancholy*, 1621

604. We have met the enemy, and they are ours.
— Oliver H. Perry, announcement of victory at the battle of Lake Erie, September 10, 1813

605. We have met the enemy and he is us.
— Walt Kelly, *Pogo* comic strip,
ca. 1950

606. If it has to choose who is to be crucified, the crowd will always save Barabbas.
— Jean Cocteau,
Le Rallep à Ordre, 1926

607. Mountains interposed / Make enemies of nations, who had else / Like kindred drops, been mingled into one.
— William Cowper,
The Task, 1785

608. No people on earth can be held, as a people, to be an enemy, for all humanity shares the common hunger for peace and fellowship and justice.
— Dwight D. Eisenhower, speech,
April 16, 1953

609. If we could read the secret history of our enemies, we should find in each man's life sorrow and suffering enough to disarm all hostility.
— Henry Wadsworth Longfellow,
Driftwood, 1857

610. Calamities are of two kinds: misfortune to ourselves, and good fortune to others.
— Ambrose Bierce,
The Devil's Dictionary, 1906

611. All our foes are mortal.
— Paul Valéry, *Tel Quel*, 1943

612. He that is taken and put into prison or chains is not conquered, though overcome; for he is still an enemy.
— Thomas Hobbes,
Leviathan, 1651

613. Abatement in the hostility of one's enemies must never be thought to signify they have been won over. It only means that one has ceased to constitute a threat.
— Quentin Crisp,
The Naked Civil Servant, 1968

614. If we are bound to forgive an enemy, we are not bound to trust him.
— Thomas Fuller,
Gnomologia, 1732

615. Hate traps us by binding us too tightly to our adversary.
— Milan Kundera,
Immortality, 1991

616. There is no safety in regaining the favor of an enemy.
— Publilius Syrus,
Moral Sayings, 1st c. B.C.

617. Take heed of enemies reconciled, and of meat twice boiled.
— John Ray,
English Proverbs, 1670

618. Do not trust the horse, Trojans. Whatever it is, I fear the Greeks even when they bring gifts.
— Virgil, *Aeneid*, 19 B.C.

619. Enemies' gifts are no gifts and do no good.
— Sophocles, *Ajax*, ca. 447 B.C.

620. Enemies' promises were made to be broken.
— Aesop, *Fables*, "The Nurse and the Wolf," ca. 550 B.C.

621. Believe no tales from an enemy's tongue.
— Proverb

622. A state which has freshly achieved liberty makes enemies and no friends.
— Niccolò Machiavelli, *The Prince*, 1513

623. If there ever was in the history of humanity an enemy who was truly universal, an enemy whose acts and moves trouble the entire world, threaten the entire world, attack the entire world in any way or another, that real and really universal enemy is precisely Yankee imperialism.
— Fidel Castro, speech, January 12, 1968

624. Opposition may become sweet to a man when he has christened it persecution.
— George Eliot, *Janet's Repentance*, 1857

625. Opposition is not necessarily enmity; it is merely misused and made an *occasion* for enmity.
— Sigmund Freud, *Civilization and Its Discontents*, 1930

626. I hate admitting that my enemies have a point.
— Salman Rushdie, *The Satanic Verses*, 1988

627. Never ascribe to an opponent motives meaner than your own.
— J. M. Barrie, speech, May 3, 1922

628. Let us learn to respect sincerity of conviction in our opponents.
— Otto von Bismarck, speech, December 18, 1863

629. The wise learn many things from their enemies.
— Aristophanes, *The Birds*, 414 B.C.

630. We can learn even from our enemies.
— Ovid, *Metamorphoses*, 1st c.

631. Pay attention to your enemies, for they are the first to discover your mistakes.
— Antisthenes, in Diogenes Laertius, *Lives and Opinions of Eminent Philosophers*, 3rd c.

632. The truth is forced upon us, very quickly, by a foe.
— Aristophanes, *The Birds*, 414 B.C.

633. A wise man gets more use from his enemies than a fool from his friends.
— Baltasar Gracián, *The Art of Worldly Wisdom*, 1647

634. You may have enemies whom you hate, but not enemies whom you despise. You must be proud of your enemy: then the success of your enemy shall be your success too.
— Friedrich Wilhelm Nietzsche, *Thus Spake Zarathustra*, 1883–92

635. You shall judge of a man by his foes as well as by his friends.
— Joseph Conrad, *Lord Jim*, 1900

636. A man cannot be too careful in the choice of his enemies.
— Oscar Wilde, *The Picture of Dorian Gray*, 1891

637. Our friends, the enemy.
— Pierre-Jean de Béranger, in *Chansons de De Béranger*, 1832

638. My near'st and dearest enemy.
— William Shakespeare, *Henry IV, Part I*, 1597

639. Life'd not be worth livin' if we didn't keep our inimies.
— Finley Peter Dunne, *Mr. Dooley in Peace and in War*, 1898

640. I do not approve the extermination of the enemy; the policy of exterminating or, as it is barbarously said, liquidating enemies, is one of the most alarming developments of modern war and peace, from the point of view of those who desire the survival of culture. One needs the enemy.

— T. S. Eliot, *Note Towards the Definition of Culture,* 1948

641. I am the enemy you killed, my friend, / I know you in this dark.

— Wilfred Owen, "Strange Meeting," 1918

642. One must, if one can, kill one's opponent, but never rouse him by contempt and the whiplash.

— Clemens von Metternich, letter, September 10, 1842

643. We can come to look upon the deaths of our enemies with as much regret as we feel for those of our friends, namely, when we miss their existence as witnesses to our success.

— Arthur Schopenhauer, *Parerga and Paralipomena,* 1851

644. I have only ever made one prayer to God, a very short one: "O Lord, make my enemies ridiculous." And God granted it.

— Voltaire, letter, May 16, 1767

645. There's nothing like the sight / Of an old enemy down on his luck.

— Euripedes, *Herekleidai,* ca. 429–27 B.C.

646. Instead of loving your enemy, treat your friend a little better.

— Edgar Watson Howe, *Ventures in Common Sense,* 1919

Esprit de Corps *see* Morale

Expansion

See also Aggression; Conflict; Force; Nationalism; Strength

647. Our manifest destiny to overspread the continent allotted by Providence for the free development of our yearly multiplying millions.

— John L. O'Sullivan, in *U.S. Magazine and Diplomatic Review,* July–August, 1845

648. We National Socialists must hold unflinchingly to our aim in foreign policy, namely, to secure for the German people the land and soil to which they are entitled on this earth.

— Adolf Hitler, explaining the need for *Lebensraum* (living space), *Mein Kampf,* 1924

649. The mission of the United States is one of benevolent assimilation.

— William McKinley, letter, December 21, 1898

650. No man has a right to fix the boundary of the march of a nation; no man has a right to say to his country — thus far shalt thou go and no further.

— Charles S. Parnell, speech, January 21, 1885

651. State boundaries are made by man and changed by man.

— Adolf Hitler, *Mein Kampf,* 1924

652. For Fascism the tendency to empire, that is to say, to the expansion of nations, is a manifestation of vitality; its opposite, staying at home, is a sign of decadence: people who rise or re-rise are

imperialist, peoples who die are renunci-
atory.
— Benito Mussolini, in
M. Oakeshott, *The Social and
Political Doctrines of
Contemporary Europe*, 1944

653. Imperialism, sane imperialism,
as distinguished from what I may call
wild-cat imperialism, is nothing but this —
a larger patriotism.
— Archibald P. Primrose, speech,
May 5, 1899

654. We don't want to fight, / But by
jingo, if we do, / We've got the men, we've
got the ships, / We've got the money too.
— song, Russo-Turkish War, 1878

655. We shall not make Britain's mistake. Too wise to try to govern the world,
we shall merely own it.
— Ludwell Denny,
America Conquers Britain, 1930

656. Imperialism is the monopoly
stage of capitalism.
— Lenin, *Imperialism as the Last
Stage of Capitalism*, 1916

657. The day of small nations has long
passed away. The day of Empires has come.
— Joseph Chamberlain, speech,
May 12, 1904

658. Habit has familiarized men's
minds with the idea of natural power
spreading beyond the bounds of the continent.
— Alfred Thayer Mahan,
The Freedom of Asia, 1900

659. Small nations are like indecently
dressed women. They tempt the evil-
minded.
— Julius Nyerere, in *The Reporter*,
April 9, 1964

660. In the eyes of empire builders
men are not men, but instruments.
— Napoleon Bonaparte, *Maxims*,
1804–15

661. Take up the White Man's burden, / Send forth the best ye breed —/ Go,
bind your sons to exile / To serve your

captain's needs.
— Rudyard Kipling, *The White
Man's Burden*, 1899

662. When we contemplate this primitive world, one is convinced that nothing will drag it out of its indolence unless
one compels the people to work. The Slavs
are a mass of born slaves, who feel the
need of a master.
— Adolf Hitler, in N. Cameron
and R. H. Stevens, *Hitler's Secret
Conversations, 1941–1944*, 1953

663. History tells me that when the
Russians come to a country they don't go
back.
— Mohammad Daoud, in
New York Times, March 28, 1985

664. The conquest of the earth, which
mostly means the taking it away from
those who have a different complexion or
slightly flatter noses than ourselves, is not
a pretty thing when you look into it.
— Joseph Conrad,
The Heart of Darkness, 1902

665. The frontier of America is on the
Rhine.
— Franklin D. Roosevelt,
attributed statement,
January 31, 1939

666. Size is not grandeur, and terri-
tory does not make a nation.
— T. H. Huxley,
On University Education, 1876

667. Liberation wars will continue to
exist as long as imperialism exists.
— Nikita Khrushchev, in
New York Times, July 11, 1965

668. In imperialism nothing fails like
success. If the conqueror oppresses his
subjects, they will become fanatical patriots, and sooner or later have their revenge;
if he treats them well, and "governs them
for their good," they will multiply faster
than their rulers, till they claim their
independence.
— William Ralph Inge,
Outspoken Essays, First Series,
1919

669. Nations, like individuals, have to limit their objectives or take the consequences.
— James Reston,
Sketches in the Sand, 1967

670. Of all follies there is none greater than wanting to make the world a better place.
— Molière, *Le Misanthrope*,
1666

Fanatics

See also Causes of War; Nationalism; Rebellion;
Revolutionaries; Tyrants

671. A fanatic is a man that does what he thinks the Lord would do if He knew the facts of the case.
— Finley Peter Dunne,
Mr. Dooley's Opinions, 1890

672. Defined in psychological terms, a fanatic is a man who consciously overcompensates a secret doubt.
— Aldous Huxley,
Proper Studies, 1927

673. The fanatic is incorruptible. If he kills for an idea, he can just as well get himself killed for one; in either case, tyrant or martyr, he is a monster.
— E. M. Cioran,
A Short History of Decay, 1949

674. A fanatic is one who can't change his mind and won't change the subject.
— Winston S. Churchill, in
New York Times, July 5, 1954

675. If there is anything more dangerous to the life of the mind than having no independent commitment to ideas, it is having an excess of commitment to some special and constricting idea.
— Richard Hofstadter,
*Anti-Intellectualism in American
Life*, 1963

676. A resolute minority has usually prevailed over an easygoing or wobbly majority whose prime purpose was to be left alone.
— James Reston,
Sketches in the Sand, 1967

677. Man can be identified as an animal that makes dogmas.
— Gilbert K. Chesterton,
Heretics, 1905

678. A fanatic is a great leader who is just entering the room.
— Heywood Broun, in
New York World, February 6, 1928

679. When people are less sure, they are often most dogmatic.
— John Kenneth Galbraith,
The Great Crash, 1929, 1955

680. Take away hatred from some people, and you have men without faith.
— Eric Hoffer, *The Passionate
State of Mind*, 1954

681. Fervor is the weapon of choice of the impotent.
— Frantz Fanon,
Black Skins, White Masks, 1952

682. We are capable of destroying America and breaking its nose.
— Muammar Qaddafi, speech,
June 15, 1986

683. We know that this mad dog of the Middle East has a goal of world revolution.
— Ronald Reagan, on Muammar
Qaddafi, April 9, 1986

684. In times of disorder and stress, the fanatics play a prominent role; in times of peace, the critics. Both are shot after the revolution.
— Edmund Wilson,
Memoirs of Hecate County, 1949

685. Extreme positions are not succeeded by moderate ones, but by *contrary* extreme positions.
— Friedrich Wilhelm Nietzsche,
The Will to Power, 1888

686. What is objectionable, what is dangerous about extremists is not that they are extreme, but that they are intolerant. The evil is not what they say about their cause, but what they say about their opponents.

— Robert F. Kennedy,
The Pursuit of Justice, 1964

687. If you see one cold and vehement at the same time, set him down for a fanatic.

— Johann Kasper Lavater,
Aphorisms on Man, 1788

688. There are men in the world who derive as stern an exaltation from the proximity of disaster and ruin, as others from success.

— Winston S. Churchill,
The Malakand Field Force, 1898

689. There in only one step from fanaticism to barbarism.

— Denis Diderot, *Essai sur le mérite de la vertu,* 1745

690. Fanaticism consists in redoubling your effort when you have forgotten your aim.

— George Santayana,
The Life of Reason, 1905–06

Fear

See also Cowards; Heroes; Horrors of War; Resolve

691. Fear is the foundation of most governments.

— John Adams,
Thoughts on Government, 1776

692. Fear is stronger than arms.

— Aeschylus, *Agamemnon,* ca. 458 B.C.

693. Excessive force is always powerless.

— Aeschylus, *The Suppliant Maidens,* 463 B.C.

694. All the weapons of war will not arm fear.

— Proverb

695. War is fear cloaked in courage.

— William C. Westmoreland, in *McCalls,* December, 1966

696. Hate is the consequence of fear; we fear something before we hate it; a child who fears noise becomes a man who hates noise.

— Cyril Connolly,
The Unquiet Grave, 1944

697. He that fears you present will hate you absent.

— Thomas Fuller,
Gnomologia, 1732

698. In time we hate that which we often fear.

— William Shakespeare,
Antony and Cleopatra, 1606–07

699. Fear is the main source of superstition, and one of the main sources of cruelty.

— Bertrand Russell,
Unpopular Essays, 1950

700. Fear could never make virtue.

— Voltaire, *Philosophical Dictionary,* 1764

701. God is good, there is no devil but fear.

— Elbert Hubbard,
The Note Book, 1927

702. The thing I fear most is fear.

— Michel de Montaigne,
Essays, 1580

703. Nothing is terrible except fear itself.

— Francis Bacon, *De Augmentis Scientiarum,* 1623

704. Nothing is so much to be feared as fear.

— Henry David Thoreau, *Journal,* September 7, 1851

705. It is the perpetual dread of fear, the *fear of fear*, that shapes the face of a brave man.
— George Bernanos,
The Diary of a Country Priest,
1936

706. The only thing we have to fear is fear itself.
— Franklin D. Roosevelt,
inaugural address, March 4, 1933

707. Death is not the enemy; living in constant fear of it is.
— Norman Cousins,
The Healing Heart, 1983

708. I'd rather give my life than be afraid to give it.
— Lyndon B. Johnson, comment,
November 25, 1963

709. Neither a man nor a crowd nor a nation can be trusted to act humanely or to think sanely under the influence of a great fear.
— Bertrand Russell,
Unpopular Essays, 1950

710. An ugly sight, a man who is afraid.
— Jean Anouilh, *Antigone,* 1942

711. You can discover what your enemy fears most by observing the means he uses to frighten you.
— Eric Hoffer,
The Passionate State of Mind,
1954

712. Avoiding danger is no safer in the long run than outright exposure. The fearful are caught as often as the bold.
— Helen Keller,
Let Us Have Faith, 1940

713. When our actions do not, / Our fears do make us traitors.
— William Shakespeare,
Macbeth, 1606

714. O! / How vain and vile a passion is this fear! / What base uncomely things it makes men do.
— Ben Jonson, *Sejanus,* 1603

715. What we fear comes to pass more speedily than what we hope.
— Publilius Syrus, *Moral Sayings,*
1st c. B.C.

716. Behind everything we feel, there is always a sense of fear.
— Ugo Betti, *Struggle Till Dawn,*
1949

717. Of all base passions, fear is most accursed.
— William Shakespeare,
Henry VI, Part I, 1592

718. Nothing is more despicable than respect based on fear.
— Albert Camus,
Notebooks 1935–1942, 1962

719. Men are eager to tread underfoot what they have once too much feared.
— Lucretius, *De Rerum Natura,*
1st c. B.C.

720. Thought is one of the manifestations of human energy, and among the earlier and simpler phases of thought two stand conspicuous — Fear and Greed. Fear, which by stimulating the imagination, creates a belief in an invisible world, and ultimately develops a priesthood; and Greed, which dissipates energy in war and trade.
— Brooks Adams,
*The Law of Civilization and
Decay,* 1897

721. Warrior, jailer, priest — the eternal trinity which symbolizes our fear of life.
— Henry Miller,
The Colossus of Maroussi, 1941

722. 'Twas only fear first in the world made gods.
— Ben Jonson, *Sejanus,* 1603

723. Fear is a noose that binds until it strangles.
— Jean Toomer,
Definitions and Aphorisms,
1931

724. Fear betrays unworthy souls.
— Virgil, *Aeneid,* 19 B.C.

725. Fear is the prison of the heart.
— Proverb

726. The most destructive element in the human mind is fear. Fear creates aggressiveness; aggressiveness engenders hostility; hostility engenders fear — a disastrous circle.
— Dorothy Thompson,
The Courage To Be Happy, 1957

727. No passion so effectively robs the mind of all its powers of acting and reasoning as fear.
— Edmund Burke, *A Philosophical Inquiry into the Origin of Our Ideas of the Sublime and Beautiful*, 1756

728. Extreme fear can neither fight nor fly.
— William Shakespeare,
The Rape of Lucrece, 1594

729. When men are ruled by fear, they strive to prevent the very changes that will abate it.
— Alan Paton, in
Saturday Review,
September 9, 1967

730. Fear gives wings.
— Proverb

731. Fear is an emotion indispensable for survival.
— Hannah Arendt, in
New Yorker, November 21, 1977

732. Just as courage imperials life, fear protects it.
— Leonardi Da Vinci,
Notebooks, ca. 1500

733. Fear is sharp-sighted and can see things under ground, and much more in the skies.
— Miguel de Cervantes,
Don Quixote, 1605–15

734. If you're scared, just holler and you'll find it ain't so lonesome out there.
— Joe Sugden, in J. Garagiola,
Baseball Is a Funny Game, 1960

735. There is nothing strange about fear: no matter in what guise it presents itself it is something with which we are all so familiar that when a man appears who is without it we are at once enslaved by him.
— Henry Miller,
The Wisdom of the Heart, 1941

736. True nobility is exempt from fear.
— William Shakespeare,
Henry VI, Part II, 1592

737. An utterly fearless man is a far more dangerous comrade than a coward.
— Herman Melville,
Moby Dick, 1851

738. Men as resolute appear / With too much, as too little fear.
— Samuel Butler, *Hudibras*, 1663

739. Man imagines that it is death he fears; but what he fears is the unforeseen, the explosion. What man fears is himself.
— Antoine de Saint-Exupéry,
Flight to Arras, 1942

740. Men! The only animal in the world to fear!
— D. H. Lawrence,
"Mountain Lion," 1923

741. Where fear is, happiness is not.
— Seneca, *Letters to Lucilius*,
1st c.

742. The first duty of man is that of subduing fear. We must get rid of fear; we cannot act at all till then. A man's acts are slavish, not true but specious; his very thoughts are false, he thinks too as a slave and coward, till he has got fear under his feet.
— Thomas Carlyle, lecture,
May, 1840

743. Any device whatever by which one frees himself from the fear of others is a natural good.
— Epicurus,
"Principal Doctrines," 3rd c. B.C.

744. Who lives in fear will never be a free man.
— Horace, *Epistles*, 13 B.C.

745. A good scare is worth more to a man than good advice.
— Edgar Watson Howe,
Country Town Sayings, 1911

746. The man who has ceased to fear has ceased to care.
— F. H. Bradley, *Aphorisms*, 1930

747. He has not learned the lesson of life who does not every day surmount a fear.
— Ralph Waldo Emerson,
Society and Solitude, 1870

748. We are all dangerous till our fears grow thoughtful.
— John Ciardi,
This Strangest Everything, 1966

749. To conquer fear is the beginning of wisdom.
— Bertrand Russell, *An Outline of Intellectual Rubbish*, 1950

Force

See also Aggression; Conflict; Expansion;
Strategy and Tactics; Strength

750. Force and fraud are in war the two cardinal virtues.
— Thomas Hobbes,
Leviathan, 1651

751. Only force and oppression have made the wrecks in the world.
— William Allen White, in
Emporia Gazette, July 27, 1922

752. The one means that wins the easiest victory over reason: terror and force.
— Adolf Hitler,
Mein Kampf, 1924

753. Justice without force is impotent, force without justice is tyranny.
— Blaise Pascal, *Pensées*, 1670

754. There is no real force without justice.
— Napoleon Bonaparte,
Maxims, 1804–15

755. Force works on servile nations, not the free.
— Ben Jonson,
Every Man in His Humor, 1598

756. Force cannot give right.
— Thomas Jefferson,
"Draft of Instructions to the Virginia Delegates in the Continental Congress,"
August, 1774

757. Force without reason falls of its own weight.
— Horace, *Odes*, 23 B.C.

758. Force has no place where there is need of skill.
— Herodotus, *The History*,
ca. 450 B.C.

759. Force is not a remedy.
— John Bright, speech,
November 16, 1880

760. Whatever needs to be maintained through force is doomed.
— Henry Miller,
The Wisdom of the Heart, 1941

761. The use of force alone is but temporary. It may subdue for a moment; but it does not remove the necessity of subduing again; and a nation is not governed which is perpetually to be conquered.
— Edmund Burke, *On Conciliation with America*, 1775

762. When one by force subdues men, they do not submit to him in heart. They submit because their strength is not adequate to resist.
— Mencius, *Works*, 4th c. B.C.

763. Force is the vital principle and immediate parent of despotism.
— Thomas Jefferson, inaugural address, March 4, 1801

764. Our patience will achieve more than our force.
— Edmund Burke,
Reflections on the Revolution in France, 1790

765. Who overcomes by force hath overcome but half his foe.
— John Milton,
Paradise Lost, 1667

766. Civilization is nothing more than the effort to reduce the use of force to the last resort.
— José Ortega y Gasset,
The Revolt of the Masses, 1930

767. I am not aware that any community has a right to force another to be civilized.
— John Stuart Mill,
On Liberty, 1859

768. The spirit of improvement is not always a spirit of liberty, for it may aim at forcing improvements on an unwilling people.
— John Stuart Mill,
On Liberty, 1859

769. Man your ships, and may the force by with you.
— George Lucas, *Star Wars*, 1977

Foreign Policy

See also the Cold War; Diplomacy;
International Relations; Treaties

770. Foreign policy, like a river, cannot rise above its source.
— Adlai Stevenson, speech,
December 4, 1954

771. In foreign relations, as in all other relations, a policy has been formed only when commitments and power have been brought into balance.
— Walter Lippmann,
U.S. Foreign Policy, 1943

772. Foreign relations are like human relations. They are endless. The solution of one problem usually leads to another.
— James Reston,
Sketches in the Sand, 1967

773. The essence of good foreign policy is constant re-examination.
— David Halberstom,
The Best and the Brightest, 1969

774. The first requirement of a statesman is that he be dull.
— Dean Acheson, in *Observer*,
June 21, 1970

775. Most foreign policies that history has marked highly, in whatever country, have been originated by leaders who were opposed by experts.
— Henry Kissinger,
Years of Upheaval, 1982

776. The foreign policy adopted by our government is to do justice to all, and to submit to wrong by none.
— Andrew Jackson, inaugural address, March 4, 1833

777. Tranquillity at home and peaceful relations abroad constitute the true permanent policy of our country.
— James K. Polk, message to Congress, December 5, 1848

778. The foreign policy of America can best be described by one word — peace.
— Calvin Coolidge, speech,
August 14, 1924

779. Our foreign policy has one primary object, and that is peace.
— Herbert Hoover, speech,
August 11, 1928

780. In the field of foreign policy I would dedicate this nation to the policy of the good neighbor.
— Franklin D. Roosevelt, speech,
July 2, 1932

781. A foreign policy is not difficult to state. We are for peace, first, last and always, for very simple reasons. We know that it is only in a peaceful atmosphere, a peace with justice, one in which we can be confident, that America can prosper as we have known prosperity in the past.
— Dwight D. Eisenhower, remark, May 1, 1957

782. Human rights is the soul of our foreign policy, because human rights is the very soul of our sense of nationhood.
— Jimmy Carter, in *New York Times*, December 7, 1978

783. Americans tend to think of foreign policy in terms of sporting events that allow for unambiguous results. Either the team wins or it loses; the game is over within a reasonable period of time, and everybody can go back to doing something else.
— Lewis H. Lapham, in *Harper's*, March, 1991

784. Foreign policy is really domestic policy with its hat on.
— Hubert H. Humphrey, speech, June 29, 1966

785. We cannot play innocents abroad in a world that is not innocent.
— Ronald Reagan, speech, February 6, 1985

786. War is not the continuation of policy. It is the breakdown of policy.
— Hans von Secckt, *Thoughts of a Soldier*, 1929

787. We are handicapped by policies based on old myths rather than current realities.
— J. William Fulbright, speech, March 27, 1964

788. The American foreign policy trauma of the sixties and seventies was caused by applying valid principles to unsuitable conditions.
— Henry Kissinger, in *Guardian*, December 16, 1992

789. The purpose of foreign policy is not to provide an outlet for our own sentiments of hope or indignation; it is to shape real events in a real world.
— John F. Kennedy, speech, September 26, 1963

790. International incidents should not govern policy, but foreign policy, incidents.
— Napoleon Bonaparte, *Maxims*, 1804–15

791. Ultimately, the danger is not that military spending no longer is the adjunct of foreign policy, but that foreign policy becomes the adjunct of military spending.
— Norman Cousins, *Pathology of Power*, 1987

792. The statesman must weigh the rewards of success against the penalties of failure. And he is permitted only one guess.
— Henry Kissinger, in *Newsweek*, October 22, 1990

793. You can always survive a mistake in domestic affairs, but you can get killed by one made in foreign policy.
— John F. Kennedy, in *Saturday Review*, March 7, 1964

794. This is the devilish thing about foreign affairs: they are foreign and will not always conform to our whim.
— James Reston, in *New York Times*, December 16, 1964

795. In statesmanship there are predicaments from which it is impossible to escape without some wrongdoing.
— Napoleon Bonaparte, *Maxims*, 1804–15

796. Limited policies inevitably are defensive policies, and defensive policies inevitably are losing policies.
— John Foster Dulles, *War or Peace*, 1950

797. Every nation determines its policies in terms of its own interests.
— John F. Kennedy, speech, September 26, 1963

798. Protectionism is the ally of isolationism, and isolationism is the Dracula of American foreign policy.
— William G. Hyland, speech,
May 17, 1987

799. Whatever it is that the government does, sensible Americans would prefer that the government do it to somebody else. This is the idea behind foreign policy.
— P. J. O'Rourke,
Parliament of Whores, 1991

800. No foreign policy — no matter how ingenious — has any chance of success if it is born in the minds of a few and carried out in the hearts of none.
— Henry Kissinger, speech,
August 2, 1973

801. Watching foreign affairs is sometimes like watching a magician; the eye is drawn to the hand performing the dramatic flourishes, leaving the other hand — the one doing the important job — unnoticed.

— David K. Shipler, in
New York Times, March 15, 1987

802. A Foreign Secretary ... is forever poised between the cliché and the indiscretion.
— Harold Macmillan, remark,
July 27, 1955

803. A foreign minister who waited until everyone agreed with him would have no foreign policy at all.
— A. J. P. Taylor,
The Trouble Makers, 1957

804. The statesman's duty is to bridge the gap between his nation's experience and his vision.
— Henry Kissinger,
Years of Upheaval, 1982

805. In foreign policy you have to wait twenty-five years to see how it comes out.
— James Reston, in
International Herald Tribune,
November 18, 1991

Freedom

See also Causes of War; Revolution; Slavery; Tyranny

806. The cause of Freedom is the cause of God!
— William Lisle Bowles, *The Right Honorable Edmund Burke*, 1791

807. If ever there was a holy war, it was that which saved our liberties and gave us independence.
— Thomas Jefferson, letter,
November 6, 1813

808. Yes, we'll rally round the flag, boys, we'll rally once again, / Shouting the battle cry of Freedom.
— George F. Root,
The Battle Cry of Freedom, 1863

809. The cost of freedom is always high, but Americans have always paid it.
— John F. Kennedy, speech,
October 12, 1962

810. Liberty and democracy become unholy when their hands are dyed with innocent blood.
— Mohandas K. Gandhi,
Non-Violence in Peace and War,
1948

811. Liberation is not deliverance.
— Victor Hugo,
Les Misérables, 1862

812. Freedom is not something that anybody can be given. Freedom is something people take.
— James Baldwin,
Nobody Knows My Name, 1961

813. Freedom is never voluntarily given by the oppressor; it must be demanded by the oppressed.
— Martin Luther King, Jr.,
Why We Can't Wait, 1963

814. To know how to free oneself is nothing; the arduous thing is to know what to do with one's freedom.
— André Gide, *The Immoralist*, 1902

815. A man who has nothing which he is willing to fight for, nothing which he cares more about than he does about his personal safety, is a miserable creature who has no chance of being free, unless made and kept so by the exertions of better men than himself.
— John Stuart Mill, in *Fraser's Magazine*, February, 1862

816. Freedom can't be bought for nothing. If you hold her precious, you must hold all else of little worth.
— Seneca, *Letters to Lucilius*, 1st c.

817. We gain freedom when we have paid the full price for our right to live.
— Rabindranath Tagore, *Fireflies*, 1928

818. Freedom is a hard-bought thing.
— Paul Robeson, *Here I Stand*, 1958

819. The history of free men is never really written by chance but by choice — their choice.
— Dwight D. Eisenhower, speech, October 9, 1956

820. Man is free the moment he wants to be.
— Voltaire, *Brutus*, 1748

821. Men are created different; they lose their social freedom and their individual autonomy in seeking to become like each other.
— David Riesman, *The Lonely Crowd*, 1950

822. Is life so dear or peace so sweet as to be purchased at the price of chains and slavery? Forbid it, Almighty God. I know not what course others may take, but as for me, give me liberty or give me death!
— Patrick Henry, speech, March 23, 1775

823. Men are never really willing to die except for the sake of freedom: therefore they do not believe in dying completely.
— Albert Camus, *The Rebel*, 1951

824. No cause is left but the most ancient of all, the one, in fact, that from the beginning of our history has determined the very existence of policies, the cause of freedom versus tyranny.
— Hannah Arendt, *On Revolution*, 1963

825. God grants liberty only to those who love it, and are always ready to guard and defend it.
— Daniel Webster, remark, June 3, 1834

826. Those who expect to reap the blessings of freedom must, like men, undergo the fatigue of supporting it.
— Thomas Paine, in *The American Crisis*, 1776–83

827. Let every nation know, whether it wishes us well or ill, that we shall pay any price, bear any burden, meet any hardship, support any friend, oppose any foe, to assure the survival and the success of liberty.
— John F. Kennedy, inaugural address, January 20, 1961

828. Free people, remember this: You may acquire liberty, but once lost it is never regained.
— Jean-Jacques Rousseau, *The Social Contract*, 1762

829. Freedom suppressed and again regained bites with keener fangs than freedom never endangered.
— Cicero, *De Officiis*, 44 B.C.

830. There is no substitute for a militant freedom.
— Calvin Coolidge, speech, April 27, 1922

831. The history of liberty is a history of resistance.
— Woodrow Wilson, speech, September 9, 1912

832. No man is entitled to the blessings of freedom, unless he be vigilant in its preservation.
— Douglas MacArthur, speech,
May 3, 1948

833. Eternal vigilance is the price of liberty.
— John Philpot Curran, speech,
July 10, 1790

834. The price of eternal vigilance is indifference.
— Marshall McLuhan,
Understanding Media, 1964

835. We do not profess to be the champions of liberty, and then consent to see liberty destroyed.
— Woodrow Wilson, speech,
September 4, 1919

836. Freedom always entails danger.
— W. E. B. DuBois, in
Midwest Journal, Winter, 1949

837. The only thing about liberty that I love is the fight for it; I care nothing about the possession of it.
— Henrik Ibsen, letter,
February 17, 1871

838. All those who seek to destroy the liberties of a democratic nation ought to know that war is the surest and the shortest means to accomplish it. This is the first axiom of the science.
— Alexis de Tocqueville,
Democracy in America, 1835

839. Unless a man has the talents to make something of himself, freedom is an irksome burden.
— Eric Hoffer,
The True Believer, 1951

840. Too little liberty brings stagnation, and too much brings chaos.
— Bertrand Russell,
Authority and the Individual,
1949

841. We prate of freedom; we are in deadly fear of life.
— Learned Hand, speech,
March 20, 1930

842. When liberty becomes license, some form of one-man power is not far distant.
— Theodore Roosevelt,
Works, 1887

843. Freedom is not worth fighting for if it means no more than license for everyone to get as much as he can for himself.
— Dorothy Canfield Fisher,
Seasoned Timber, 1939

844. None can love freedom but good men; the rest love not freedom but license, which never hath more scope than under tyrants.
— John Milton,
Tenure of Kings and Magistrates,
1649

845. The deadliest form of democracy is not autocracy but liberty frenzied.
— Otto Kahn, speech,
January 14, 1918

846. Liberty! O liberty! What crimes are committed in thy name!
— Marie-Jeanne Roland, in A. de Lamartine, *Historie des Girondins*,
1847

847. O freedom, what liberties are taken in thy name!
— Daniel George,
The Perpetual Pessimist, 1963

848. There is nothing with which it is so dangerous to take liberties as liberty itself.
— André Breton,
Surrealism and Painting, 1928

849. Man in general, if reduced to himself, is too wicked to be free.
— Joseph de Maistre,
Four Chapters on Russia, 1859

850. Liberty does not always have clean hands.
— André Malraux, speech,
November 12, 1966

851. The boisterous sea of liberty is never without a wave.
— Thomas Jefferson, letter,
October 20, 1820

852. The enemies of Freedom do not argue; they shout and shoot.
— William Ralph Inge,
End of an Age, 1948

853. Human history begins with man's acts of disobedience which is at the very same time the beginning of his freedom and development of his reason.
— Erich Fromm,
Psychoanalysis and Religion, 1950

854. Men are freest when they are most unconscious of freedom. The shout is a rattling of chains, always was.
— D. H. Lawrence,
Studies in Classic American Literature, 1924

855. What country can preserve its liberties, if its rulers are not warned from time to time, that this people preserve the spirit of resistance?
— Thomas Jefferson, letter,
November 13, 1787

856. It is harder to preserve than to obtain liberty.
— John Calhoun, speech,
January, 1848

857. Keep a check upon your rulers. Do this, and liberty is safe.
— William Henry Harrison,
speech, 1840

858. While the state exists there is no freedom; when there is freedom there will be no state.
— Lenin,
The State and Revolution, 1917

859. A hungry man is not a free man.
— Adlai Stevenson, speech,
September 6, 1952

860. It has been well said that a hungry man is more interested in four sandwiches than four freedoms.
— Henry Cabot Lodge Jr., in
New York Times, March 29, 1955

861. The poor man is never free; he serves in every country.
— Voltaire, *Les Guèbres*, 1769

862. We believe that the only whole man is a free man.
— Franklin D. Roosevelt, speech,
September 2, 1940

863. When truth is no longer free, freedom is no longer real: the truths of the police are the truths of today.
— Jacques Prévert, *Spectacle*, 1951

864. The truth which makes men free is for the most part the truth which men prefer not to hear.
— Herbert Agar,
A Time for Greatness, 1942

865. The truth is found when men are free to pursue it.
— Franklin D. Roosevelt, speech,
February 22, 1936

866. Freedom is a very great reality. But it means, above all things, freedom from lies.
— D. H. Lawrence,
Pornography and Obscenity, 1930

867. The spirit of truth and the spirit of freedom — they are the pillars of society.
— Henrik Ibsen,
Pillars of Society, 1877

868. I would rather belong to a poor nation that was free than to a rich nation that had ceased to be in love with liberty.
— Woodrow Wilson, speech,
October 27, 1913

869. A man is either free or he is not. There cannot be any apprenticeship for freedom.
— LeRoi Jones, in *Kulcher*,
Spring, 1962

870. True liberty acknowledges and defends the equal rights of all men, and all nations.
— Gerrit Smith, speech,
June 27, 1854

871. Liberty is precious — so precious that it must be rationed.
— Lenin, in S. Webb and B. Webb,
Soviet Communism, 1936

872. Liberty is never out of bounds or off limits; it spreads wherever it can capture the imagination of men.
— E. B. White,
The Points of My Compass, 1960

873. Freedom is the most contagious virus known to man.
— Hubert H. Humphrey, speech,
October 29, 1964

874. I was born to know you / To give you your name / Freedom.
— Paul Éluard,
Poésie et Vérité, 1942

875. There's something contagious about demanding freedom.
— Robin Morgan,
Sisterhood is Powerful, 1970

876. Liberty is its own reward.
— Woodrow Wilson, speech,
September 12, 1912

877. You should never have your best trousers on when you go out to fight for freedom and truth.
— Henrik Ibsen,
An Enemy of the People, 1882

Futility of War

See also Cost of War; Horrors of War; Vietnam

878. The Gulf War was like teenage sex. We got in too soon and out too soon.
— Tom Harkin, in *Independent on Sunday*, September 29, 1991

879. The Falklands thing was a fight between two bald men over a comb.
— Jorge Luis Borges, in *Time*,
February 14, 1983

880. With supreme irony, the war to "make the world safe for democracy" ended by leaving democracy more unsafe in the world than at any time since the collapse of the revolutions of 1848.
— James H. Robinson,
The Human Comedy, 1937

881. After each war there is a little less democracy to save.
— Brooks Atkinson,
Once Around the Sun, 1951

882. Even a successful war doesn't guarantee a blissful peace.
— Robert J. Samuelson, in *Newsweek*, March 18, 1991

883. You can no more win a war than you can win an earthquake.
— Jeanette Rankin, in H. Josephson, *Jeanette Rankin: First Lady in Congress*, 1974

884. Against war it may be said that it makes the victor stupid and the vanquished revengeful.
— Friedrich Wilhelm Nietzsche,
Human, All Too Human, 1878

885. A war, even the most victorious, is a national misfortune.
— Helmuth von Moltke,
letter, 1880

886. All victories breed hate, and that over your superior is foolish or fatal.
— Baltasar Gracián,
The Art of Worldly Wisdom, 1647

887. The art of war is like the art of the courtesan — indeed, they might be called sisters, since both are the slaves of desperation.
— Pietro Aretino, letter,
November 28, 1537

888. One is left with the horrible feeling now that war settles nothing; that to win a war is as disastrous as to lose one!
— Agatha Christie,
An Autobiography, 1977

889. In modern war there is no such thing as victor and vanquished ... there is only a loser and that loser is mankind.
— U Thant, speech, 1963

890. When man meets an obstacle he can't destroy, he destroys himself.
— Ryszard Kapuscinski, in *Granta*, 1985

891. War springs from unseen and generally insignificant causes.
— Thucydides, *History of the Peloponnesian War*, 431–413 B.C.

892. Every war is its own excuse.
— Karl Shapiro, *The Bourgeois Poet*, 1964

893. I have come to hate war not only because it kills off the flower of every nation, but because it destroys spiritual as well as material values.
— Ilya Ehrenburg, in *Saturday Review*, September 30, 1967

894. Women's rights, men's rights — human rights — are all threatened by the ever-present specter of war, so destructive now of human material and moral value as to render victory indistinguishable from defeat.
— Rosika Schwimmer, speech at Seneca Falls Convention, July, 1948

895. Far from establishing liberty throughout the world, war has actually encouraged and built up the development of dictatorships and has only restored liberty in limited areas at the cost of untold hardships, of human suffering, of death and destruction beyond the conception of our fathers.
— Robert A. Taft, *A Foreign Policy for Americans*, 1951

896. There was only one catch and that was Catch-22, which specified that a concern for one's own safety in the face of dangers that were real and immediate was the process of a rational mind ... Orr would be crazy to fly more missions and sane if he didn't, but if he was sane he had to fly them. If he flew them he was crazy and didn't have to; but if he didn't want to he was sane and had to.
— Joseph Heller, *Catch-22*, 1955

897. The worst thing about war was the sitting around and wondering what you were doing morally.
— Paul Fussell, in *Times*, November 28, 1991

898. History shows that wars are divided into two kinds, just and unjust. All wars that are progressive are just, and all wars that impede progress are unjust.
— Mao Zedong, "On Protracted War," May, 1938

899. I have many times asked myself whether there can be more potent advocates of peace upon earth through the years to come than this massed multitude of silent witnesses to the desolation of war.
— George V, message, May 13, 1922

900. War nourishes war.
— Johann Friedrich von Schiller, *Die Piccolomini*, 1799

901. For what can war, but endless war still breed?
— John Milton, "On the Lord General Fairfax at the Siege of Colchester," 1648

902. I hate war. War destroys individuals and whole generations. It throws civilization into the dark ages.
— Harry S Truman, in W. Hillman, *Mr. President*, 1952

903. I hate war as only a soldier who has lived it can, only as one who has seen its brutality, its futility, its stupidity.
— Dwight D. Eisenhower, speech, January 10, 1946

904. Violence seldom accomplishes permanent and desired results. Herein lies the futility of war.
— A. Philip Randolph, *The Truth About Lynching*, ca. 1922

Glory

See also the Dead; Honor; Resolve; Soldiers

905. War is divine in the mysterious glory that surrounds it and in the no less inexplicable attraction that draws us to it.
— Joseph de Maistre,
Les Soirées de Saint-Pétersbourg,
1821

906. Military glory — the attractive rainbow that rises in showers of blood.
— Abraham Lincoln, speech,
January 12, 1848

907. Of arms and the man I sing.
— Virgil, *Aeneid,* 19 B.C.

908. Sing, my tongue, of the battle in the glorious struggle.
— Venantius Fortunatus, 6th c.

909. All of us who served in one war or another know very well that all wars are the glory and the agony of the young.
— Gerald R. Ford, speech,
August 19, 1974

910. Glory is only given to those who have always dreamed of it.
— Charles DeGaulle,
Vers l'armée de métier, 1934

911. O sacred hunger of ambitious minds.
— Edmund Spenser,
The Faerie Queene, 1596

912. We are all motivated by a keen desire for praise, and the better a man is, the more he is inspired by glory.
— Cicero, *Pro Archia,* 62 B.C.

913. Of all the affections which attend human life, the love of glory is the most ardent.
— Richard Steele, in *Spectator,*
August 9, 1711

914. Popularity? It is glory's small change.
— Victor Hugo, *Ruy Blas,* 1838

915. Glory is largely a theatrical con-

cept. There is no striving for glory without a vivid awareness of an audience.
— Eric Hoffer,
The True Believer, 1951

916. The desire for glory clings even to the best man longer than any other passion.
— Cornelius Tacitus,
Histories, ca. 100

917. The glory of a great man ought always to be estimated by the means used to acquire it.
— François La Rochefoucauld,
Maxims, 1665

918. The deed is all, the glory nothing.
— Johann Wolfgang von Goethe,
Faust, 1832

919. Hasty glory goes out in a snuff.
— Thomas Fuller, *Gnomologia,*
1732

920. The paths of glory lead but to the grave.
— Thomas Gray,
Elegy Written in a Country Churchyard, 1751

921. To the ashes of the dead glory comes too late.
— Martial, *Epigrams,* 86 A.D.

922. Oh how quickly the glory of the world passes away!
— Thomas à Kempis,
Imitation of Christ, ca. 1420

923. You may my glories and my state depose, / But not my griefs; still I am king of those.
— William Shakespeare,
Richard II, 1595

924. If men cease to believe that they will one day become gods then they will surely become worms.
— Henry Miller,
The Colossus of Maroussi, 1941

Good and Evil

See also Conflict; Enemies; Justice; Tyranny

925. Morality is contraband in war.
— Mohandas K. Gandhi, *Non-Violence in Peace and War*, 1948

926. The end excuses any evil.
— Sophocles, *Electra*, ca. 414 B.C.

927. No man is justified in doing evil on the ground of expediency.
— Theodore Roosevelt, *The Strenuous Life: Essays and Addresses*, 1900

928. The state employs evil weapons to subjugate evil, and is alike contaminated by the objects with which it deals, and the means by which it works.
— Herbert Spencer, *Social Statics*, 1851

929. Every political good carried to the extreme must be productive of evil.
— Mary Wollstonecraft, *The French Revolution*, 1794

930. The difference between a good man and a bad one is the choice of the cause.
— William James, letter, December 24, 1895

931. All history treats almost exclusively of wicked men who, in the course of time, have come to be looked upon as good men. All progress is the result of successful crime.
— Friedrich Wilhelm Nietzsche, *The Dawn*, 1861

932. War is evil, but it is often the lesser evil.
— George Orwell, *Looking Back on the Spanish War*, 1945

933. When you choose the lesser of two evils, always remember that it is still an evil.
— Max Lerner, *Actions and Passions*, 1949

934. War is an unmitigated evil. But it certainly does one good thing. It drives away fear and brings bravery to the surface.
— Mohandas K. Gandhi, *Non-Violence in Peace and War*, 1948

935. As long as war is regarded as wicked, it will always have its fascination. When it is looked upon as vulgar, it will cease to be popular.
— Oscar Wilde, *The Critic as Artist*, 1891

936. The only thing necessary for the triumph of evil is for good men to do nothing.
— Edmund Burke, attributed

937. He who accepts evil without protesting against it is really cooperating with it.
— Martin Luther King, Jr., *Stride Toward Freedom*, 1958

938. Standing for right when it is unpopular is a true test of moral character.
— Margaret Chase Smith, speech, June 7, 1953

939. Who will condemn the hatred of evil that springs from the love of what is good and just?
— Menachem Begin, *The Revolt*, 1951

940. In battling evil, excess is good; for he who is moderate in announcing the truth is presenting half-truth. He conceals the other half out of fear of the people's wrath.
— Kahlil Gibran, *Thoughts and Meditations*, 1960

941. And out of good still to find means of evil.
— John Milton, *Paradise Lost*, 1667

942. One evil flows from another.
— Terence, *Eunuchus*, ca. 165 B.C.

943. Let us do evil, that good may come.
— Bible, *Romans 3:8*

944. There is this of good in real evils; they deliver us, while they last, from the petty despotism of all that were imaginary.
— Charles Caleb Colton,
Lacon, 1820–22

945. Yield not to evils, but attack all the more boldly.
— Virgil, *Aeneid*, 19 B.C.

946. Be not overcome of evil, but overcome evil with good.
— Bible, *Romans 12:21*

947. The chain reaction of evil — hate begetting hate, wars producing more wars — must be broken, or we shall be plunged into the dark abyss of annihilation.
— Martin Luther King, Jr.,
Strength to Love, 1963

948. Nature, in her indifference, makes no distinction between good and evil.
— Anatole France,
Crainquebille, 1916

949. There is no explanation for evil. It must be looked upon as a necessary part of the order of the universe. To ignore it is childish; to bewail it senseless.
— W. Somerset Maugham,
The Summing Up, 1938

950. The belief in a supernatural source of evil is not necessary; men alone are quite capable of every wickedness.
— Joseph Conrad,
Under Western Eyes, 1911

951. Our greatest evils flow from ourselves.
— Jean-Jacques Rousseau,
Émile, 1762

952. It is the evil that lies in ourselves that is ever least tolerant of the evil that dwells within others.
— Maurice Maeterlinck, *Wisdom and Destiny*, 1898

953. The evil best known is the most tolerable.
— Livy, *History of Rome*, ca. 10

954. What we call evil is simply ignorance bumping its head in the dark.
— Henry Ford, in *Observer*,
March 16, 1930

955. Ignorance of good and evil is the most upsetting fact of human life.
— Cicero, *De Finibus*, ca. 45 B.C.

956. Only among people who think no evil can Evil monstrously flourish.
— Logan Pearsall Smith,
Afterthoughts, 1931

957. All the evil in the world is the fault of the self-styled pure in heart, a result of their eagerness to unearth secrets and expose them to the light of the sun.
— Jean Giraudoux, *Electra*, 1937

958. *Good* and *evil* are names that signify our appetites and aversions.
— Thomas Hobbes,
Leviathan, 1651

959. A man is not good or bad for one action.
— Thomas Fuller,
Gnomologia, 1732

960. No notice is taken of a little evil, but when it increases it strikes the eye.
— Aristotle, *Politics*, 4th c. B.C.

961. There are in every man, at every hour, two simultaneous postulations, one towards God, the other towards Satan.
— Charles Baudelaire,
Mon Coeur Mis à Nu, 1887

962. Man must vanquish himself, must do himself violence, in order to perform the slightest action untainted by evil.
— E. M. Cioran,
The New Gods, 1969

963. There is hardly a man clever enough to recognize the full extent of the evil he does.
— François La Rochefoucauld,
Maxims, 1665

964. This is the seal of the absolute and sublime destiny of man — that he knows what is good and what is evil; that his destiny *is* his very ability to will either good or evil.
— Georg Wilhelm Friedrich Hegel, *The Philosophy of History*, 1832

965. The sad truth is that most evil is done by people who never make up their minds to be either good or evil.
— Hannah Arendt, in *New Yorker*, December 5, 1977

966. Our deeds determine us, as much as we determine our deeds.
— George Eliot, *Adam Bede*, 1859

967. The wicked flee when no man pursueth: but the righteous are bold as a lion.
— Bible, *Proverbs* 28:1

968. Virtue is bold, and goodness never fearful.
— William Shakespeare, *Measure for Measure*, 1604

969. Do not seek evil gains: evil gains are the equivalent of disaster.
— Hesiod, *Works and Days*, ca. 700 B.C.

970. It is by its promise of a sense of power that evil often attracts the weak.
— Eric Hoffer, *The Passionate State of Mind*, 1954

971. No man chooses evil because it is evil; he only mistakes it for happiness, the good he seeks.
— Mary Wollstonecraft, *A Vindication of the Rights of Men*, 1790

972. Men never do evil so completely and cheerfully as when they do it from religious conviction.
— Blaise Pascal, *Pensées*, 1670

973. When evil acts in the world it always manages to find instruments who believe that what they do is not evil but honorable.
— Max Lerner, *The Unfinished Country*, 1959

974. Evil is easy, and has infinite forms.
— Blaise Pascal, *Pensées*, 1670

975. The face of "evil" is always the face of total need.
— William S. Burroughs, *The Naked Lunch*, 1959

976. As the saying is, *homo solus aut deus, aut daemon*: a man alone is either a saint or a devil.
— Robert Burton, *The Anatomy of Melancholy*, 1621

977. I have seen the wicked in great power, and spreading himself like a green bay tree.
— Bible, *Psalms* 37:35

978. Evil men by their own nature cannot ever prosper.
— Euripedes, *Ion*, ca. 417 B.C.

979. Often an entire city has suffered because of an evil man.
— Hesiod, *Works and Days*, ca. 700 B.C.

980. Much of the most important evils that mankind have to consider are those which they inflict upon each other through stupidity or malevolence or both.
— Bertrand Russell, *Unpopular Essays*, 1950

981. Those who set in motion the forces of evil cannot always control them afterwards.
— Charles W. Chestnutt, *The Marrow of Tradition*, 1901

982. Evils draw men together.
— Aristotle, *Rhetoric*, 4th c. B.C.

983. He who is bent on doing evil can never want occasion.
— Publilius Syrus, *Moral Sayings*, 1st c. B.C.

984. Evil alone has oil for every wheel.
— Edna St. Vincent Millay, *Mine the Harvest*, 1954

985. We believe no evil till the evil's done.
— Jean de La Fontaine, *Fables*, 1668

986. There is no peace, saith the Lord, unto the wicked.
— Bible, *Isaiah* 48:22

987. The evil that men do lives after them, / The good is oft interred with their bones.
— William Shakespeare, *Julius Caesar*, 1599

Greatness

See also Glory; History; Honor; Military Command; Rulers

988. The privilege of the great is to see catastrophes from the terrace.
— Jean Giraudoux, *Tiger at the Gates*, 1935

989. Nothing so comforts the military mind as the maxim of a great but dead general.
— Barbara Tuchman, *The Guns of August*, 1962

990. To know the great men dead is compensation for having to live with the mediocre.
— Elbert Hubbard, *The Note Book*, 1927

991. Men do not shape destiny. Destiny produces the man for the hour.
— Fidel Castro, in *This Week*, May 24, 1959

992. Some are born great, some achieve greatness, and some have greatness thrust upon them.
— William Shakespeare, *Twelfth Night*, 1601

993. Though men pride themselves on their great actions, often they are not the result of any great design but of chance.
— François La Rochefoucauld, *Maxims*, 1665

994. Great offices will have great talents.
— William Cowper, *The Task*, 1785

995. Great men are the guideposts and landmarks in the state.
— Edmund Burke, speech, April 19, 1774

996. Great men hallow a whole people, and lift up all who live in their time.
— Sydney Smith, in S. Holland, *Memoir*, 1855

997. He is greatest who is most often in men's good thoughts.
— Samuel Butler, *Note-Books*, 1912

998. Lives of great men all remind us / We can make our lives sublime, / And, departing, leave behind us / Footprints on the sands of time.
— Henry Wadsworth Longfellow, "A Psalm of Life," 1839

999. A great man's greatest good luck is to die at the right time.
— Eric Hoffer, *The Passionate State of Mind*, 1954

1000. No man is truly great who is great only in his lifetime. The test of greatness is the page of history.
— William Hazlitt, *Table Talk*, 1821–22

1001. Great men have great faults.
— Proverb

1002. Great men are not always wise.
— Bible, *Job* 32:9

1003. Great minds tend toward banality.
— André Gide, *Pretexts*, 1903

1004. A great man's failures to understand define him.
— André Gide, *Pretexts*, 1903

1005. Great men are rarely isolated

mountain peaks; they are the summits of ranges.
— Thomas W. Higginson,
Atlantic Essays, 1871

1006. Every great man inevitably resents a partner in greatness.
— Lucan, *On the Civil War*, 1st c.

1007. Great men are but life-sized. Most of them, indeed, are rather short.
— Max Beerbohm,
And Even Now, 1920

1008. To be great is to be misunderstood.
— Ralph Waldo Emerson,
Essays, First Series, 1841

1009. Ignobly vain, and impotently great.
— Alexander Pope, in J. Addison,
Cato, 1713

1010. In a narrow sphere great men are blunderers.
— Napoleon Bonaparte,
Maxims, 1804–15

1011. Great men can't be ruled.
— Ayn Rand,
The Fountainhead, 1943

1012. So long as men worship the Caesars and Napoleons, Caesars and Napoleons will duly rise and make them miserable.
— Aldous Huxley,
Ends and Means, 1937

1013. Do not despise the bottom rung on the ascent to greatness.
— Publilius Syrus,
Moral Sayings, 1st c. B.C.

1014. All rising to great place is by a winding stair.
— Francis Bacon, *Essays*, 1625

1015. No sadder proof can be given by a man of his own littleness than disbelief in great men.
— Thomas Carlyle,
Heroes and Hero Worship, 1840

1016. No man was ever great by imitation.
— Samuel Johnson, *Rasselas*, 1759

1017. He who comes up to his own idea of greatness must always have had a very low standard of it in his head.
— William Hazlitt, in
Plain Speaker, 1826

1018. I distrust Great Men. They produce a desert of uniformity around them and often a pool of blood too, and I always feel a little man's pleasure when they come a cropper.
— E. M. Forster,
Two Cheers for Democracy, 1951

1019. The bravest sight in the world is to see a great man struggling against adversity.
— Seneca, *De Providentia*, 1st c.

1020. None think the great unhappy but the great.
— Edward Young,
Love of Fame, 1728

1021. Great men with great truths have seldom had much support from their associates.
— Philip Wylie,
Generation of Vipers, 1942

1022. To have a great man for a friend seems pleasant to those who have never tried it; those who have, fear it.
— Horace, *Epistles*, 13 B.C.

1023. Danger, the spur of all great minds.
— George Chapman,
The Revenge of Bussy D'Ambois,
1613

1024. In the face of great danger, salvation can only come through greatness.
— Charles DeGaulle,
Mémoires de guerre: L'Appel, 1955

1025. All greatness is unconscious, or it is little and naught.
— Thomas Carlyle,
Critical and Miscellaneous Essays,
1827

1026. No really great man ever thought himself so.
— William Hazlitt, in
Plain Speaker, 1826

1027. The world cannot live at the level of its great men.
— James G. Frazer, *The Golden Bough*, 1922

1028. No great thing is created suddenly.
— Epictetus, *Discourses*, 2nd c.

1029. A great man does enough for us when he refrains from doing us harm.
— Pierre de Beaumarchais, *The Barber of Seville*, 1775

1030. The abuse of greatness is when it disjoins / Remorse from power.
— William Shakespeare, *Julius Caesar*, 1599

1031. The search after the great men is the dream of youth, and the most serious occupation of manhood.
— Ralph Waldo Emerson, *Representative Men*, 1850

1032. I would sooner fail than not be among the greatest.
— John Keats, letter, October 8, 1818

1033. Greatness knows itself.
— William Shakespeare, *Henry IV, Part I*, 1597

1034. Whom the gods wish to destroy they first call promising.
— Cyril Connolly, *Enemies of Promise*, 1938

1035. Desire of greatness is a godlike sin.
— John Dryden, *Absalom and Achitophel*, 1681

1036. Let us never forget that the greatest man is never more than an animal disguised as a god.
— Francis Picabia, in *La Vie Moderne*, February 25, 1923

1037. We shall never resolve the enigma of the relation between the negative foundations of greatness and that greatness itself.
— Jean Baudrillard, *America*, 1986

1038. The greatest man in history was the poorest.
— Ralph Waldo Emerson, *Society and Solitude*, 1870

1039. All great deeds and all great thoughts have a ridiculous beginning.
— Albert Camus, *The Myth of Sisyphus*, 1942

1040. Great actions are not always true sons / Of great and mighty resolutions.
— Samuel Butler, *Hudibras*, 1663

1041. It is in times of difficulty that great nations, like great men, display the whole energy of their character, and become an object of admiration to posterity.
— Napoleon Bonaparte, *Maxims*, 1804–15

1042. There is no such thing as a *little war* for a great nation.
— Arthur Wellesley, Duke of Wellington, speech, January 16, 1838

1043. There was never a nation great until it came to the knowledge that it had nowhere in the world to go for help.
— Charles Dudley Warner, *Studies in the South and West with Comments on Canada*, 1889

1044. Great men, great nations, have not been boasters and buffoons, but perceivers of the terror of life.
— Ralph Waldo Emerson, *The Conduct of Life*, 1860

Heroes

See also Courage; Resolve; Soldiers

1045. The ordinary man is involved in action, the hero acts. An immense difference.
— Henry Miller,
The Books in My Life, 1951

1046. Heroism ... is endurance for one moment more.
— George F. Kennan, letter,
July 25, 1921

1047. The poetry of heroism appeals irresistibly to those who don't go to a war, and even more to those whom the war is making enormously wealthy. It's always so.
— Louis-Ferdinand Céline,
Journey to the End of the Night,
1932

1048. I gave my life for freedom — This I know: / For those who bade me fight had told me so.
— William Norman Ewer,
"Five Souls," 1917

1049. A hero is a man who does what he can.
— Romain Rolland,
Jean Christophe, 1904–12

1050. It was the nation and the race dwelling all round the globe that had the lion's heart. I had the luck to be called upon to give the roar.
— Winston S. Churchill, speech,
November 30, 1954

1051. What is a society without a heroic dimension?
— Jean Baudrillard, *America*, 1986

1052. A hero cannot be a hero unless in an heroic world.
— Nathaniel Hawthorne,
Journals, May 7, 1850

1053. Unlucky the country that needs a hero.
— Bertolt Brecht,
Leben des Galilei, 1943

1054. What with making their way and enjoying what they have won, heroes have no time to think. But the sons of heroes — ah, they have all the necessary leisure.
— Aldous Huxley,
"Vulgarity in Literature," 1930

1055. To have no heroes is to have no aspiration to live on the momentum of the past, to be thrown back upon routine, sensuality, and the narrow self.
— Charles Horton Cooley,
*Human Nature and the Social
Order*, 1902

1056. The opportunities for heroism are limited in this kind of world: the most people can do is sometimes not to be as weak as they've been at other times.
— Angus Wilson, in
Writers at Work, 1958

1057. History selects its heroes and its villains, and few of us resist participation either at the parade or at the guillotine.
— William F. Buckley, Jr.,
The Jeweler's Eye, 1968

1058. Heroes are created by popular demand, sometimes out of the scantiest materials, or none at all.
— Gerald White Johnson,
*American Heroes and Hero-
Worship*, 1943

1059. Fame is the perfume of heroic deeds.
— Proverb

1060. The fame of heroes owes little to the extent of their conquests and all to the success of the tributes paid to them.
— Jean Genet,
Prisoner of Love, 1986

1061. Heroes are very human, most of them; very easily touched by praise.
— Max Beerbohm,
And Even Now, 1920

1062. Every hero becomes a bore at last.
— Ralph Waldo Emerson,
Representative Men, 1850

1063. Heroism is the brilliant triumph of the soul over the flesh — that is to say, over fear: fear of poverty, of suffering, of calumny, of sickness, of isolation, and of death. There is no serious piety without heroism. Heroism is the dazzling and glorious concentration of courage.
— Henri Frédéric Amiel,
Amiel's Journal, 1883

1064. The heroic man does not pose; he leaves that for the man who wishes to be thought heroic.
— Elbert Hubbard,
The Note Book, 1927

1065. It is more difficult to be an honorable man for a week than to be a hero for fifteen minutes.
— Jules Renard, *Journal*, 1907

1066. Greater love hath no man than this, that a man lay down his life for his friends.
— Bible, *John* 15:13

1067. Deeds of heroism are but offered to those who, for many long years, have been heroes in obscurity and silence.
— Maurice Maeterlinck,
Wisdom and Destiny, 1898

1068. While he felt like a victim, he acted like a hero.
— Horace Walpole, *Memoirs of the Reign of King George II*, 1846

1069. Israel has created a new image of the Jew in the world — the image of a working and an intellectual people, of a people that can fight with heroism.
— David Ben Gurion, in
Time, June 9, 1967

1070. Heroism feels and never reasons, and therefore is always right.
— Ralph Waldo Emerson,
Essays, First Series, 1841

1071. Children demand that their heroes should be fleckless, and easily believe them so: perhaps a first discovery to the contrary is less revolutionary shock to the passionate child than the threatened downfall of habitual beliefs which makes the world seem to totter for us in maturer life.
— George Eliot,
Daniel Deronda, 1876

1072. Heroism does not require spiritual maturity.
— Abel Hermant,
Xavier ou les entretiens sur la grammaire française, 1923

1073. Show me a hero and I will write you a tragedy.
— F. Scott Fitzgerald,
The Crack-Up, 1945

Historians

See also History; History Is ...

1074. Man is a history-making creature who can neither repeat his past nor leave it behind.
— W. H. Auden,
The Dyer's Hand, 1962

1075. History repeats itself. Historians repeat each other.
— Philip Guedalla,
Supers and Supermen, 1920

1076. The writers of universal history will only prove themselves of real value when they are able to answer the essential question of history: "What is power?"
— Leo Tolstoy, *War and Peace*,
1865–69

1077. Even the gods cannot change history.
— Agathon, in Aristotle,
Nicomachean Ethics, 4th c. B.C.

1078. The first law for the historian is that he shall never dare utter an untruth. The second is that he shall suppress nothing that is true.
— Cicero, *De Oratore*, 55 B.C.

1079. Whosoever, in writing a modern history, shall follow truth too near the heels, it may haply strike out his teeth.
— Walter Ralegh,
History of the World, 1614

1080. Truth is a torch that gleams through the fog without dispelling it.
— Claud-Adrian Helvétius,
De l'Esprit, 1758

1081. We owe respect to the living; to the dead we owe only truth.
— Voltaire, *Oeuvres*, 1785

1082. Truth is the only merit that gives dignity and worth to history.
— John E. E. Dalberg, *The History of Freedom and Other Essays*, 1907

1083. Historians ought to be precise, faithful, and unprejudiced, and neither interest nor fear, hatred nor affection, should make them swerve from the way of truth, whose mother is history, the rival of time, the depository of great actions, the witness of the past, example of the present, and monitor of the future.
— Miguel de Cervantes,
Don Quixote, 1605–15

1084. All the historical books which contain no lies are extremely tedious.
— Anatole France,
The Crime of Sylvestre Bonnard,
1881

1085. The historian must not try to know what is truth, if he values his honesty; for, if he cares for his truths, he is certain to falsify his facts.
— Henry Brooks Adams,
The Education of Henry Adams,
1907

1086. The talent of historians lies in their creating a true ensemble out of facts which are but half true.
— Ernest Renan, *La Vie de Jésus*,
1863

1087. What makes a good writer of history is a guy who is suspicious. Suspicion marks the real difference between the man who wants to write honest history and the one who'd rather write a good story.
— Jim Bishop, in
New York Times, February 5, 1955

1088. The historian, essentially, wants more documents than he can really use; the dramatist only wants more liberties than he can really take.
— Henry James,
The Aspern Papers, 1909

1089. Tell me the acts, O historian, and leave me to reason upon them as I please; away with your reasoning and your rubbish! All that is not action is not worth reading.
— William Blake,
A Descriptive Catalogue, 1809

1090. Historians are the biggest liars in the world ... When the exceptional historian comes along, you have a poet.
— Melvin B. Tolson, in
Washington Tribune,
January 29, 1938

1091. Historian — An unsuccessful novelist.
— H. L. Mencken,
A Mencken Chrestomathy, 1949

1092. Every journey into the past is complicated by delusions, false memories, false naming of real events.
— Adrienne Rich,
Of Women Born, 1976

1093. The historian's job is to aggrandize, promoting accident to inevitability and innocuous circumstance to portent.
— Peter Conred,
The Art of the City, 1984

1094. Events in the past may be roughly divided into those which probably never happened and those which do not matter. This is what makes the trade of historian so attractive.
— William Ralph Inge,
Assessments and Anticipations,
1929

1095. History must always be taken with a grain of salt. It is, after all, not a science but an art.
— Phyllis McGinley,
Saint Watching, 1969

1096. The historian is a prophet in reverse.
— Friedrich von Schlegel,
Athenaeum, 1798–1800

1097. The chief duty of the historian is to judge the actions of men, so that the good may meet with the reward due to virtue and pernicious citizens may be deterred by the condemnation that awaits evil deeds at the tribunal of posterity.
— Cornelius Tacitus, *Annals*,
ca. 115–116

1098. The historian's first duties are sacrilege and the locking of false gods. They are his indispensable instruments for establishing the truth.
— Jules Michelet,
Historie de France, 1833–67

1099. The one duty we owe to history is to rewrite it.
— Oscar Wilde,
The Critic as Artist, 1891

1100. The historian who fails in his duty deceives the reader and wrongs the dead.
— Norman Douglas,
South Wind, 1917

1101. History can be well written only in a free country.
— Voltaire, letter,
May 27, 1737

1102. If Germany, thanks to Hitler and his successors, were to enslave the European nations and destroy most of the treasures of their past, future historians would certainly pronounce that she had civilized Europe.
— Simone Weil, in
Selected Essays, 1962

History

See also Greatness; History Is … ; Revolution; Rulers

1103. History shows that there are no invincible armies.
— Joseph Stalin, radio broadcast,
July 3, 1941

1104. That's the worst of a war — you have to go on hearing about it so long.
— Susan Glaspell, *Inheritors*, 1921

1105. There is no history of mankind, there are only many histories of all kinds of aspects of human life. And one of these is the history of political power. This is elevated into the history of the world.
— Karl Popper, *The Open Society
and Its Enemies*, 1945

1106. The whole history of civilization is strewn with creeds and institutions which were invaluable at first, and deadly afterwards.
— Walter Bagehot,
The English Constitution, 1867

1107. The bases for historical knowledge are not empirical facts but written texts, even if these texts masquerade in the guise of wars or revolution.
— Paul De Man, lecture,
September, 1969

1108. The vengeance of history is more terrible than the vengeance of the most powerful General Secretary.
— Leon Trotsky, *Stalin*, 1946

1109. Regarding history as the slaughter-bench at which the happiness of peoples, the wisdom of states, and the virtue of individuals have been victimized — the question inevitably arises — to what principle, to what final aim these enormous sacrifices have been offered.
— Georg Wilhelm Friedrich
Hegel, *The Philosophy of History*,
1832

1110. History teaches perhaps few clear lessons. But surely one such lesson learned by the world at great cost is that aggression unopposed becomes a contagious disease.
— Jimmy Carter, speech,
January 4, 1980

1111. The knowledge of what has gone before affords the best instruction for the direction and guidance of human life.
— Polybius, *History*, ca. 125 B.C.

1112. In a word, we may gather out of history a policy no less wise than eternal; by the comparison and application of other men's forepassed miseries with our own like errors and ill deservings.
— Walter Ralegh,
History of the World, 1614

1113. History, by putting crisis in perspective, supplies the antidote to every generation's illusion that its own problems are uniquely oppressive.
— Arthur M. Schlesinger, Jr.,
in *New York Times Magazine*,
July 27, 1986

1114. Only through history does a nation become completely conscious of itself. Accordingly, history is to be regarded as the national conscience of the human race.
— Arthur Schopenhauer, *The World as Will and Idea*, 1819

1115. To know one's origins is to know one's present and to be able to create one's future.
— William Henry Schubert,
Curriculum Books, 1980

1116. No progress of humanity is possible unless it shakes off the yoke of authority and tradition.
— André Gide, *Journals*,
March 17, 1931

1117. Tradition is a great retarding force, the *vis inertiae of history*.
— Friedrich Engels,
Anti-Dühring, 1878

1118. Tradition means giving votes to the most obscure of all classes, our ancestors. It is the democracy of the dead.
— Gilbert K. Chesterton,
Orthodoxy, 1908

1119. As soon as tradition has come to be recognized as tradition, it is dead.
— Allan Bloom,
The Closing of the American Mind, 1987

1120. Tradition is a guide and not a jailer.
— W. Somerset Maugham,
The Summing Up, 1938

1121. We have need of history in its entirety, not to fall back into it, but to see if we can escape from it.
— José Ortega y Gasset,
The Revolt of the Masses, 1930

1122. Custom is despot of mankind.
— Alexander Pushkin,
Eugene Onegin, 1823

1123. But to *explain* history is to depict the passions of mankind, the genius, the active powers, that play their part on the great stage.
— Georg Wilhelm Friedrich Hegel, *The Philosophy of History*, 1832

1124. What has once happened, will invariably happen again, when the same circumstances which combined to produce it, shall again combine in the same way.
— Abraham Lincoln, speech,
December 26, 1839

1125. What experience and history teach is this — that people and governments never have learned anything from history, or acted on principles deduced from it.
— Georg Wilhelm Friedrich Hegel, *The Philosophy of History*, 1832

1126. We learn from history that we learn nothing from history.
— George Bernard Shaw,
Man and Superman, 1903

1127. That men do not learn very much from the lessons of history is the most important of all the lessons of history.
— Aldous Huxley,
Collected Essays, 1959

1128. The lesson of history is rarely learned by the actors themselves.
— James A. Garfield, in W. R. Balch, *Maxims of James Abram Garfield*, 1880

1129. Does history repeat itself, the first time as tragedy, the second time as farce? No, that's too grand, too considered a process. History just burps, and we taste again that raw-onion sandwich it swallowed centuries ago.
— Julian Barnes, *A History of the World in 10½ Chapters*, 1989

1130. Those who cannot remember the past are condemned to repeat it.
— George Santayana,
The Life of Reason, 1905–06

1131. The hasty reformer who does not remember the past will find himself condemned to repeat it.
— John Buchan,
The Nations of Today, 1923

1132. There is no reason to repeat bad history.
— Eleanor Holmes Norton, in R. Morgan, *Sisterhood is Powerful*, 1970

1133. English history is all about men liking their fathers, and American history is all about men hating their fathers and trying to burn down everything they ever did.
— Malcolm Bradbury,
Stepping Westward, 1965

1134. American history is longer, larger more various, more beautiful, and more terrible than anything anyone has ever said about it.
— James Baldwin,
"A Talk to Teachers,"
October 16, 1963

1135. Human history becomes more and more a race between education and catastrophe.
— H. G. Wells,
The Outline of History, 1920

1136. Only the history of free people is worth our attention; the history of men under a despotism is merely a collection of anecdotes.
— Sébastien-Roch Nicholas de Chamfort, *Maxims*, 1796

1137. History does not long entrust the care of freedom to the weak or the timid.
— Dwight D. Eisenhower,
inaugural address,
January 20, 1953

1138. The very ink in which history is written is merely fluid prejudice.
— Mark Twain,
Following the Equator, 1897

1139. I don't know much about history, and I wouldn't give a nickel for all the history in the world. History is more or less bunk.
— Henry Ford, in J. Leonard,
The Tragedy of Henry Ford, 1932

1140. Happy the people whose annals are blank in history books!
— Thomas Carlyle,
Life of Frederick the Great, 1860

1141. We live in a world where amnesia is the most wished-for state. When did history become a bad word?
— John Guare, in
International Herald Tribune,
June 13, 1990

1142. There is no inevitability in history except as men make it.
— Felix Frankfurter, in
Saturday Review,
October 30, 1954

1143. If past history was all there was to the game, the richest people would be librarians.
— Warren Buffett, in
Washington Post, April 17, 1988

1144. The only thing new in the world is the history you don't know.
—Harry S Truman, in M. Miller,
Plain Speaking: An Oral Biography of Harry S Truman, 1974

1145. Human blunders usually do more to shape history than human wickedness.
—A. J. P. Taylor,
The Origins of the Second World War, 1961

1146. Difficulty is the excuse history never accepts.
—Edward R. Murrow, comment, October 19, 1959

1147. Nothing changes more constantly than the past; for the past that influences our lives does not consist of what actually happened, but of what men believe happened.
—Gerald White Johnson,
American Heroes and Hero-Worship, 1943

1148. The past is never dead. It's not even past.
—William Faulkner,
Requiem for a Nun, 1951

1149. History knows no resting places and no plateaus.
—Henry Kissinger,
White House Years, 1979

1150. The game of history is usually played by the best and the worst over the heads of the majority in the middle.
—Eric Hoffer,
The True Believer, 1951

1151. *Tout, passe, tout casse, tout lasse.* (Everything passes, everything perishes, everything palls.)
—Proverb

1152. History, most often, is recorded with a great amount of undeniable and systematic distortion.
—Edward Teller,
The Pursuit of Simplicity, 1980

1153. The past is the only dead thing that smells sweet.
—Cyril Connolly, in D. Pryce-Jones,
Journal and Memoir, 1983

1154. The dead govern the living.
—Auguste Comte,
Catéchisme Positiviste, 1852

1155. Why doesn't the past decently bury itself, instead of sitting waiting to be admired by the present?
—D. H. Lawrence,
St. Mawr, 1925

1156. History, that excitable and lying old lady.
—Guy de Maupassant,
On the Water, 1888

1157. Many falsehoods are passing into uncontradicted history.
—Samuel Johnson, letter, October 27, 1779

1158. Time dissipates to shining ether the solid angularity of facts.
—Ralph Waldo Emerson,
Essays, First Series, 1841

1159. History, sir, will tell lies as usual.
—George Bernard Shaw,
The Devil's Disciple, 1901

1160. Man, at bottom, is not entirely guilty, since he did not begin history, nor entirely innocent, since he continues it.
—Albert Camus,
Notebooks 1935–1942, 1962

1161. That great dust-heap called history.
—Augustine Birrell,
Obiter Dicta, 1884

1162. Into the dustbin of history!
—Leon Trotsky,
The History of the Russian Revolution, 1933

1163. I tell you the past is a bucket of ashes.
—Carl Sandburg,
Cornhuskers, 1918

History Is ...

See also History

1164. History, *n.* An account mostly false, of events mostly unimportant, which are brought about by rulers mostly knaves, and soldiers mostly fools.
— Ambrose Bierce,
The Devil's Dictionary, 1906

1165. History is the transformation of tumultuous conquerors into silent footnotes.
— Paul Eldridge,
Maxims for a Modern Man, 1965

1166. History is past politics, and politics is present history.
— E. A. Freeman,
Methods of Historical Study, 1886

1167. Human history is in essence a history of ideas.
— H. G. Wells,
The Outline of History, 1920

1168. The history of the world is but the biography of great men.
— Thomas Carlyle,
Heroes and Hero Worship, 1840

1169. The history of the world is the world's court of justice.
— Johann Friedrich von Schiller,
lecture, May 26, 1789

1170. History is philosophy teaching by example.
— Dionysius of Halicarnassus,
De Arte Rhetorica, ca. 20 B.C.

1171. History is the witness that testifies to the passing of time; it illumines reality, vitalizes memory, provides guidance in daily life, and brings us tidings of antiquity.
— Cicero, *De Oratore*, 55 B.C.

1172. History is the torch that is meant to illuminate the past to guard us against the repetition of our mistakes of other days. We cannot join in the rewriting of history to make it conform to our comfort and convenience.
— Claude G. Bowers, in F. J. Taylor, *The United States and the Spanish Civil War*, 1956

1173. History is a hill or high point of vantage, from which alone men see the town in which they live or the age in which they are living.
— Gilbert K. Chesterton,
All I Survey, 1933

1174. History is in a manner a sacred thing, so far as it contains truth.
— Miguel de Cervantes,
Don Quixote, 1605–15

1175. History is a better guide than good intentions.
— Jeane J. Kirkpatrick, in
Commentary, November, 1979

1176. The history of the world is none other than the progress of the consciousness of freedom.
— Georg Wilhelm Friedric Hegel,
The Philosophy of History, 1832

1177. History is the myth, the true myth, of man's fall made manifest in time.
— Henry Miller, *Plexus*, 1949

1178. History is a relay of revolutions.
— Saul Alinsky,
Rules for Radicals, 1971

1179. History is, strictly speaking, the study of questions; the study of answers belongs to anthropology and sociology.
— W. H. Auden,
The Dyer's Hand, 1962

1180. History is a vast early warning system.
— Norman Cousins, in
Saturday Review, April 15, 1978

1181. History is a realm in which human freedom and natural necessity are curiously intermingled.
— Reinhold Niebuhr,
The Structure of Nations and Empires, 1959

1182. All history is only one long story to this effect: men have struggled for power over their fellow men in order that they might win the joys of earth at the expense of others, and might shift the burdens of life from their own shoulders upon those of others.
— William Graham Sumner,
The Forgotten Man, 1883

1183. History is full of ignominious getaways by the great and famous.
— George Orwell,
"Who Are the War Criminals?,"
1943

1184. History is after all nothing but a pack of tricks which we play upon the dead.
— Voltaire, in J. Morley,
Voltaire, 1828

1185. History is no more than the portrayal of crimes and misfortunes.
— Voltaire, *L'Ingénu*, 1767

1186. History ... is, indeed, little more than a register of the crimes, follies, and misfortunes of mankind.
— Edward Gibbon, *The Decline and Fall of the Roman Empire*,
1776–88

1187. History is a bath of blood.
— William James,
Memories and Studies, 1911

1188. History is the study of other people's mistakes.
— Philip Guedalla,
Supers and Supermen, 1920

1189. History is nothing but a procession of false absolutes, a series of temples raised to pretexts, a degradation of the mind before the improbable.
— E. M. Cioran,
A Short History of Decay, 1949

1190. History, Stephen said, is a nightmare from which I am trying to awake.
— James Joyce, *Ulysses*, 1922

1191. The history of the world is a farce.
— Gustave Flaubert, *Intimate Notebook, 1840–1841*, 1967

1192. History is a gallery of pictures in which there are few originals and many copies.
— Alexis de Tocqueville,
The Old Regime and the French Revolution, 1856

1193. History is only a confused heap of facts.
— Philip Stanhope, letter,
February 5, 1750

1194. Universal history is the history of a few metaphors.
— Jorge Luis Borges,
Pascal's Sphere, 1951

1195. History is principally the inaccurate narration of events which ought not to have happened.
— Ernest Albert Hooten,
Twilight of Man, 1939

1196. History is littered with the wars which everybody knew would never happen.
— Enoch Powell, speech,
October 19, 1967

1197. History is a distillation of rumor.
— Thomas Carlyle, *History of the French Revolution*, 1837

1198. All history is modern history.
— Wallace Stevens, *Opus Posthumous*, 1957

1199. History is always written wrong, and so always needs to be rewritten.
— George Santayana,
The Life of Reason, 1905–06

1200. History is the present. That's why every generation writes it anew. But what most people think of as history is its end product, myth.
— E. L. Doctorow, in
Writers at Work, 1988

1201. "History" is not a divine force; it is the instrument of those who make it.
— J. William Fulbright,
Old Myths and New Realities,
1964

1202. The history of most countries has been that of majorities — mounted

majorities, clad in iron, armed with death, treading down the tenfold more numerous minorities.
— Oliver Wendell Holmes, Sr.,
speech, May 30, 1860

1203. History is the propaganda of the victors.
— Ernst Toller, attributed

1204. History is written by the winners.
— Alex Haley, interview,
April 20, 1972

1205. The history of the world is the history of a privileged few.
— Henry Miller,
Sunday after the War, 1944

1206. The best history is but like the art of Rembrandt; it casts a vivid light on

certain selected causes, on those which were best and greatest; it leaves all the rest in shadow and unseen.
— Walter Bagehot,
Physics and Politics, 1872

1207. What is history after all? History is facts which become lies in the end; legends are lies which become history in the end.
— Jean Cocteau, in *Observer,*
September 22, 1957

1208. History is the crystallization of popular beliefs.
— Donn Piatt, *Memories of Men
Who Saved the Union,* 1887

1209. The past is a foreign country; they do things differently there.
— L. P. Hartley,
The Go-Between, 1953

Honor

See also Duty; Glory; Greatness; Soldiers

1210. Of men who have a sense of honor, more come through alive than are slain, but from those who flee comes neither glory nor any help.
— Homer, *The Iliad,* ca. 700 B.C.

1211. There is no question what the roll of honor in America is. The roll of honor consists of the names of men who have squared their conduct by ideals of duty.
— Woodrow Wilson, speech,
February 27, 1916

1212. He is the fountain of honor.
— Francis Bacon,
An Essay of a King, 1642

1213. Honor shows the man.
— Proverb

1214. In the arena of human life the honors and rewards fall to those who show their good qualities in action.
— Aristotle,
Nicomachean Ethics, 325 B.C.

1215. What is left when honor is lost?
— Publilius Syrus,
Moral Sayings, 1st c. B.C.

1216. A good death does honor to a whole life.
— Petrarch,
To Laura in Death, 14th c.

1217. Set honor in one eye and death I' the other / And I will look on both indifferently.
— William Shakespeare,
Julius Caesar, 1599

1218. Honor has come back, as a king, to earth.
— Rupert Brooke,
"The Dead," 1914

1219. The Difference between a moral man and a man of honor is that the latter regrets a discreditable act even when it has worked out and he has not been caught.
— H. L. Mencken,
Prejudices, Fourth Series, 1924

1220. Leave not a stain in thine honor.
— Bible, *Ecclesiasticus* 33:22

1221. When you have to kill a man it costs nothing to be polite.
— Winston S. Churchill, statement, December 8, 1941

1222. Better die with honor than live with shame.
— Proverb

1223. Dishonor will not trouble me, once I am dead.
— Euripedes, *Alcestis*, 438 B.C.

1224. If we heed the teachings of history, we shall not forget that in the life of every nation emergencies may arise when a resort to arms can alone save it from dishonor.
— Chester A. Arthur, message to Congress, December 6, 1881

1225. A really great people, proud and high-spirited, would face all the disasters of war rather than purchase that base prosperity which is bought at the price of national honor.
— Theodore Roosevelt, speech, February 23, 1907

1226. We would rather starve than sell our national honor.
— Indira Gandhi, in *New York Times*, January 23, 1967

1227. There are things a man must not do even to save a nation.
— Murray Kempton, *America Comes of Middle Age*, 1963

1228. A nation reveals itself not only by the men it produces but also by the men it honors, the men it remembers.
— John F. Kennedy, speech, October 26, 1963

1229. To us is given the honor of striking a blow for freedom which will live in history, and in the better days that lie ahead men will speak with pride of our doings.
— Bernard Montgomery, message on the eve of the D-Day invasion, June 5, 1944

1230. By heaven methinks it were an easy leap / To pluck bright honor from the pale-faced moon, / Or dive into the bottom of the deep, / Where fathom-line could never touch the ground, / And pluck up drowned honor by the locks.
— William Shakespeare, *Henry IV, Part I*, 1597

1231. If we are marked to die, we are enow / To do our country loss; and if to live, / The fewer men, the greater share of honor.
— William Shakespeare, *Henry V*, 1599

1232. Never in the field of human conflict was so much owed by so many to so few.
— Winston S. Churchill, praising the Royal Air Force, August 20, 1940

1233. An honorable Peace is and always was my first wish! I can take no delight in the effusion of human Blood; but, if this War should continue, I wish to have the most active part of it.
— John Paul Jones, letter, September 2, 1782

1234. If peace cannot be maintained with honor, it is no longer peace.
— John Russell, speech, September 19, 1853

1235. Peace with honor.
— Richard M. Nixon, slogan concerning the Vietnam War, ca. 1972

1236. A medal glitters, but it also casts a shadow.
— Winston S. Churchill, speech, March 22, 1944

1237. When neither their property nor their honor is touched, the majority of men live content.
— Niccolò Machiavelli, *The Prince*, 1513

1238. War, he sung, is toil and trouble; / Honor but an empty bubble.
— John Dryden, *Alexander's Feast*, 1697

1239. Duty, honor! We make these words say whatever we want, the same as we do with parrots.

— Alfred Capus,
Mariage bourgeois, 1898

1240. The louder he talked of his honor, the faster we counted our spoons.

— Ralph Waldo Emerson,
The Conduct of Life, 1860

Horrors of War

See also Civilians; Death; Futility of War

1241. War involves in its progress such a train of unforeseen and unsupposed circumstances that no human wisdom can calculate the end.

— Thomas Paine,
Prospects on the Rubicon, 1787

1242. When war begins, then hell opens.

— Proverb

1243. Accurst be he that first invented war.

— Christopher Marlowe,
Tamburlaine the Great, 1587

1244. He who is the author of a war lets loose the whole contagion of hell and opens a vein that bleeds a nation to death.

— Thomas Paine, in
The American Crisis, 1776–83

1245. Whoever fights monsters should see to it that in the process he does not become a monster.

— Friedrich Wilhelm Nietzsche,
Beyond Good and Evil, 1886

1246. To walk through the ruined cities of Germany is to feel an actual doubt about the continuity of civilization.

— George Orwell, in
Observer, April 8, 1945

1247. It was through the Second World War that most of us suddenly appreciated for the first time the power of man's concentrated efforts to understand and control the forces of nature. We were appalled by what we saw.

— Vannevar Bush,
Science is Not Enough, 1967

1248. In the arts of life man invents nothing; but in the arts of death he outdoes Nature herself, and produces by chemistry and machinery all the slaughter of plague, pestilence, and famine.

— George Bernard Shaw,
Man and Superman, 1903

1249. Speaking in terms of evolution, we find that war is not a permanent institution of mankind ... The chaotic brawls, the internecine fighting of the lowest savages have nothing in common with the institution of war.

— Bronislaw Malinowski, speech,
September 17, 1936

1250. When men are inhuman, take care not to feel towards them as they do towards other humans.

— Marcus Aurelius,
Meditations, 2nd c.

1251. Nature has, herself, I fear, imprinted in man a kind of instinct to inhumanity.

— Michel de Montaigne,
Essays, 1580

1252. Man's inhumanity to man / makes countless thousands mourn.

— Robert Burns,
"Man Was Made to Mourn," 1786

1253. Wild animals never kill for sport. Man is the only one to whom the torture and death of his fellow-creatures is amusing in itself.

— James A. Froude, *Oceana*, 1886

1254. Don't cheer, men; those poor devils are dying.

— Jack Philip, order at the battle
of Santiago, July 4, 1898

1255. What passing-bells for these who die as cattle? / Only the monstrous anger of the guns.
— Wilfred Owen,
"Anthem for Doomed Youth,"
1917

1256. Anyone who has ever looked into the glazed eyes of a soldier dying on the battlefield will think hard before starting a war.
— Otto von Bismarck, speech,
August, 1867

1257. The purple testament of bleeding war.
— William Shakespeare,
Richard II, 1595

1258. The greatness of war is just what at first sight seems to be its horror — that for the sake of their country men will overcome the natural feelings of humanity, that they will slaughter their fellow men who have done them no injury, nay whom they perhaps respect as chivalrous foes.
— Heinrich von Treitschke,
Politics, 1897–98

1259. Yes; quaint and curious war is! / You shoot a fellow down / You'd treat if met where any bar is, / Or help to half-a-crown.
— Thomas Hardy,
The Man He Killed, 1902

1260. We hear war called murder. It is not: it is suicide.
— Ramsey MacDonald, in
Observer, May 4, 1930

1261. Ugly deeds are taught by ugly deeds.
— Sophocles, *Electra*, ca. 414 B.C.

1262. I believe that all wars are blasphemy. I do not believe that wars can be glorious, and surely not holy. War means death, and death is ugly.
— Elie Wiesel, in
Washington Post, April 11, 1991

1263. War is sweet to them that know it not.
— Proverb

1264. Take my word for it, if you had seen but one day of war you would pray to Almighty God that you might never see such a thing again.
— Arthur Wellesley,
Duke of Wellington, attributed

Imperialism *see* Expansion

International Relations

See also Alliances; the Cold War; Diplomacy;
Nationalism; Treaties

1265. There is but one sure way of ending war and that is the establishment, by common consent, of a central control which shall have the last word in any conflict of interests.
— Sigmund Freud, in
Free World, 1933

1266. During the time men live without a common power to keep them all in awe, they are in that condition which is called war; and such a war, as is of every man, against every man.
— Thomas Hobbes, *Leviathan*, 1651

1267. There is nothing more difficult to take in hand, more perilous to conduct, or more uncertain in its success, than to take the lead in the introduction of a new order of things.
— Niccolò Machiavelli,
The Prince, 1513

1268. Peace with all nations, and the right which that gives us with respect to all nations, are our object.
— Thomas Jefferson, letter,
March 24, 1793

1269. We do not covet anything from any nation except their respect.
— Winston S. Churchill, radio
broadcast, October 21, 1940

1270. We only want that which is given naturally, to all peoples of the world, to be masters of our own fate, only of our fate, not of others, and in cooperation and friendship with others.
— Golda Meir, speech,
March 25, 1946

1271. Only a peace between equals can last. Only a peace the very principle of which is equality and a common participation in a common benefit.
— Woodrow Wilson, speech,
January 22, 1917

1272. International crises have their advantages. They frighten the weak but stir and inspire the strong.
— James Reston,
Sketches in the Sand, 1967

1273. Every government is in some respects a problem for every other government, and it will always be this way so long as the sovereign state, with its supremely self-centered rationale remains the basis of international life.
— George F. Kennan,
*Russia and the West under Lenin
and Stalin*, 1961

1274. The only alternative to coexistence is codestruction.
— Jawaharlal Nehru, in
Observer, August 29, 1954

1275. A policy that can be accurately, though perhaps not prudently, defined as one of "peaceful coexistence."
— J. William Fulbright, speech,
March 27, 1964

1276. These are our aims ... to see to it that change shall take place in Ger-many's relations to Poland, which will ensure a peaceful coexistence of the two powers.
— Adolf Hitler, in G. Stein,
Hitler, 1967

1277. One hopes to achieve the zero option, but in the absence of that we must achieve balanced numbers.
— Margaret Thatcher,
regarding nuclear missiles, in
New York Times, January 20, 1983

1278. The balance of power.
— Robert Walpole, speech,
February 13, 1741

1279. The management of a balance of power is a permanent undertaking, not an exertion that has a foreseeable end.
— Henry Kissinger,
White House Years, 1979

1280. If this phrase of the "balance of power" is to be always an argument for war, the pretext for war will never be wanting, and peace can never be secure.
— John Bright, speech,
March 31, 1854

1281. There must be, not a balance of power, but a community of power; not organized rivalries, but an organized common peace.
— Woodrow Wilson, speech,
January 22, 1917

1282. A state worthy of the name has no friends — only interests.
— Charles DeGaulle, in
Newsweek, October 1, 1962

1283. What a country calls its vital economic interests are not the things which enable its citizens to live, but the things which enable it to make war. Gasoline is much more likely than wheat to be a cause of international conflict.
— Simone Weil,
The Need for Roots, 1949

1284. If you wish to avoid foreign collision, you had better abandon the ocean.
— Henry Clay, speech,
January 22, 1812

1285. It is but seldom that any one overt act produces hostilities between the nations; there exists, more commonly, a previous jealousy and ill will, a predisposition to take offense.
— Washington Irving,
The Sketch Book, 1819–20

1286. If ever there is another war in Europe, it will come out of some damned silly thing in the Balkans.
— Otto von Bismarck, in
Hansard, August 16, 1945

1287. Whoever lights the torch of war in Europe can wish for nothing but chaos.
— Adolf Hitler, speech,
May 21, 1935

1288. Of all nations, those submit to civilization with the most difficulty which habitually live by the chase.
— Alexis de Tocqueville,
Democracy in America, 1835

1289. The awful truth is that the use of violence for political gain has become more, not less widespread in the last decade.
— Ronald Reagan, speech,
September 26, 1983

1290. What we call foreign affairs is no longer foreign affairs. It's a local affair. Whatever happens in Indonesia is important to Indiana.
— Dwight D. Eisenhower, speech,
June 12, 1959

1291. Am I my brother's keeper?
— Bible, *Genesis* 4:9

1292. I am not willing to risk the lives of German soldiers for countries whose names we cannot spell properly.
— Volker Rühe, in *Independent*,
August 28, 1992

1293. How horrible, fantastic, incredible it is that we should be digging trenches and trying on gas masks here because of a quarrel in a faraway country between people of whom we know nothing.
— Neville Chamberlain, radio
broadcast, September 27, 1938

1294. Only when a menaced country has the whole-hearted support of its people and the will to resist to the limit of its resources should we consider an appeal for help.
— J. Lawton Collins,
*War in Peacetime: The History
and Lessons of Korea*, 1969

1295. It is doubtful if the oppressed ever fight for freedom. They fight for pride and power — power to oppress others. The oppressed want above all to imitate their oppressors; they want to retaliate.
— Eric Hoffer,
The True Believer, 1951

1296. I have always given it as my decided opinion that no nation has a right to intermeddle in the internal concerns of another.
— George Washington, letter,
August 25, 1796

1297. No nation is wise enough to rule another.
— Helen Keller,
Let Us Have Faith, 1940

1298. No man is good enough to govern another man without that other's consent.
— Abraham Lincoln, speech,
October 16, 1854

1299. No man is good enough to be another man's master.
— George Bernard Shaw,
Major Barbara, 1905

1300. A government is not legitimate merely because it exists.
— Jeane J. Kirkpatrick, in
Time, June 17, 1985

1301. The great nations have always acted like gangsters, and the small nations like prostitutes.
— Stanley Kubrick, in
Guardian, June 5, 1963

1302. I asked Tom if countries always apologized when they had done wrong, and he says: "Yes; the little ones does."
— Mark Twain,
Tom Sawyer Abroad, 1894

1303. Poor nations are hungry, and rich nations are proud; and pride and hunger will ever be at variance.
— Jonathan Swift,
Gulliver's Travels, 1726

1304. The right of conquest has no foundation other than the right of the strongest.
— Jean-Jacques Rousseau,
The Social Contract, 1762

1305. In every particular state of the world, those nations which are strongest tend to prevail over the others; and in certain marked peculiarities the strongest tend to be the best.
— Walter Bagehot,
Physics and Politics, 1872

1306. The responsibility of the great states is to serve and not to dominate the world.
— Harry S Truman, message to Congress, April 16, 1945

1307. Men and nations must use their power with the purpose of making it an instrument of justice and a servant of interests broader than their own.
— Reinhold Niebuhr,
The Irony of American History, 1952

1308. Let us call a truce to terror, let us invoke the blessings of peace. And, as we build an international capacity to keep peace, let us join in dismantling the national capacity to wage war.
— John F. Kennedy, speech,
September 25, 1961

1309. No country has suffered so much

from the ruins of war while being at peace as the Americans.
— Edward Dahlberg,
Alms for Oblivion, 1964

1310. The United States is not a nation to which peace is a necessity.
— Grover Cleveland, message to Congress, December 7, 1896

1311. Any man and any nation that seeks peace — and hates war — and is willing to fight the good fight against hunger and disease and ignorance and misery will find the United States of America by their side, willing to walk with them — walk with them every step of the way.
— Lyndon B. Johnson, speech,
December 17, 1963

1312. Today our potential foreign obligations are almost unlimited. We have moved from a position of isolation and rejection of world responsibility to a position of isolated, almost singular responsibility for the whole world.
— Eugene J. McCarthy,
The Limits of Power, 1967

1313. We did not choose to be the guardians of the gate, but there is no one else.
— Lyndon B. Johnson, speech,
July 28, 1964

1314. There were two kinds of sanctions, effective and ineffective. To apply the latter was provocative and useless. If we were to apply the former, we ran the risk of war, and it would be dangerous to shut our eyes to the fact.
— Anthony Eden,
Facing the Dictators, 1962

Justice

See also Freedom; Good and Evil; Revolution; Tyranny

1315. Justice is better served in conferences of peace than in conflicts at arms.
— Warren G. Harding, speech,
February 6, 1922

1316. The Law speaks too softly to be heard amid the din of arms.
— Gaius Marius, statement,
ca. 92 B.C.

1317. War is a dreadful thing, and unjust war is a crime against humanity. But it is such a crime because it is unjust, not because it is war.
— Theodore Roosevelt, speech, April 23, 1910

1318. The Bible nowhere prohibits war.
— Henry Wager Halleck, *Elements of Military Art and Science*, 1859

1319. There are things worth fighting for. A world in which brutality and lawlessness are allowed to go unchecked isn't the kind of world we're going to want to live in.
— Walter E. Boomer, in *USA Today*, January 17, 1991

1320. The core of our defense is the faith we have in the institutions we defend.
— Franklin D. Roosevelt, speech, October 12, 1940

1321. If the world were just, there would be no need of valor.
— Agesilaus, in Plutarch, *Lives*, ca. 1st-2nd c.

1322. A just fear of an imminent danger, though there be no blow given, is a lawful cause of war.
— Francis Bacon, *Essays*, 1625

1323. Do not expect justice where might is right.
— Phaedrus, *Fables*, 1st c.

1324. Three things are required for any war to be just. The first is the authority of the sovereign on whose command war is waged ... Secondly, a just cause is required, namely that those who are attacked are attacked because they deserve it on account of some wrong they have done ... Thirdly, the right intention of those waging war is required, that is, they must intend to promote the good and to avoid evil.
— Thomas Aquinas, *Summa theologiae*, 1273

1325. The phrase "just war" is very ambiguous and causes a lot of confusion. In the weak sense, it means that war is permissible, it is not contrary to morality to fight the war. But, in the stronger sense, it means the war is obligatory, it is your moral duty to fight it.
— Douglas Lackey, in *Washington Post*, February 2, 1991

1326. A "just war" is hospitable to every self-deception on the part of those waging it, none more than the certainty of virtue under whose shelter every abomination can be committed with a clear conscience.
— Alexander Cockburn, in *New Statesman and Society*, February 8, 1991

1327. Truth never damages a cause that is just.
— Mohandas K. Gandhi, *Non-violence in Peace and War*, 1948

1328. The only true and lasting peace [is] based on justice and right.
— Calvin Coolidge, radio broadcast, December 10, 1923

1329. The people should fight for their law as for a wall.
— Heraclitus, *On the Universe*, 5th c. B.C.

1330. National injustice is the surest road to national downfall.
— William E. Gladstone, speech, 1878

1331. If we justify war, it is because all peoples always justify the traits of which they find themselves possessed, not because war will bear an objective examination of its merits.
— Ruth Benedict, *Patterns of Culture*, 1934

1332. If you kick a man he kicks you back. Therefore never be too angry to combat injustice.
— Bertolt Brecht, *The Threepenny Opera*, 1928

1333. It is better to have a war for justice than peace in injustice.
— Charles Péguy,
Basic Verities, 1943

1334. Equal and exact justice should characterize all our intercourse with foreign countries.
— James K. Polk, inaugural
address, March 4, 1845

1335. No nation is fit to sit in judgment upon any other nation.
— Woodrow Wilson, speech,
April 20, 1915

1336. It is easier to fight for principles than to live up to them.
— Alfred Adler,
Problems of Neurosis, 1929

1337. Absolute freedom mocks at justice. Absolute justice denies freedom.
— Albert Camus, *The Rebel*,
1951

1338. During war we imprison the rights of man.
— Jean Giraudoux,
Tiger at the Gates, 1935

Leadership

See also Duty; Greatness; Military Command; Rulers

1339. The leader is a stimulus, but he is also a response.
— Edward C. Lindeman,
Social Discovery, 1924

1340. A leader is a dealer in hope.
— Napoleon Bonaparte,
Maxims, 1804–15

1341. The genius of a good leader is to leave behind him a situation which common sense, without the grace of genius, can deal with successfully.
— Walter Lippmann, in
New York Herald Tribune,
April 14, 1945

1342. A leader is best / When people barely know that he exists.
— Witter Bynner,
*The Way of Life According to
Laotzu*, 1944

1343. A constitutional statesman is in general a man of common opinions and uncommon abilities.
— Walter Bagehot,
Biographical Studies, 1907

1344. The main essentials of a successful prime minister ... sleep and a sense of history.
— Harold Wilson,
The Governance of Britain, 1977

1345. A councilor ought not to sleep the whole night through, a man to whom the populace is entrusted, and who has many responsibilities.
— Homer, *The Iliad*, ca. 700 B.C.

1346. In times of peace the people look most to their representatives; but in war, to the executive solely.
— Thomas Jefferson, letter,
February 10, 1810

1347. A disposition to preserve, and an ability to improve, taken together, would be my standard of a statesman.
— Edmund Burke,
*Reflections on the Revolution in
France*, 1790

1348. A great statesman is he who knows when to depart from traditions, as well as when to adhere to them.
— John Stuart Mill,
Representative Government, 1861

1349. There are men who, by their sympathetic attractions, carry nations with them, and lead the activity of the human race.
— Ralph Waldo Emerson,
The Conduct of Life, 1860

1350. The men who have changed the universe have never accomplished it by

changing officials but always by inspiring the people.
— Napoleon Bonaparte,
Maxims, 1804–15

1351. The secret of a leader lies in the tests he has faced over the whole course of his life and the *habit of action* he develops in meeting those tests.
— Gail Sheehy, *Gorbachev*, 1991

1352. You know what makes leadership? It is the ability to get men to do what they don't want to do, and like it.
— Harry S Truman, in
Time, November 8, 1976

1353. The real leader has no need to lead — he is content to point the way.
— Henry Miller,
The Wisdom of the Heart, 1941

1354. People are more easily led than driven.
— David Harold Fink,
Release from Nervous Tension,
1943

1355. Leadership should be born out of the understanding of the needs of those who would be affected by it.
— Marian Anderson, in
New York Times, July 22, 1951

1356. All of the great leaders have had one characteristic in common: it was the willingness to confront unequivocally the major anxiety of their people in their time. This, and not much else, is the essence of leadership.
— John Kenneth Galbraith,
The Age of Uncertainty, 1977

1357. No man is great enough or wise enough for any of us to surrender our destiny to. The only way in which anyone can lead us is to restore to us the belief in our own guidance.
— Henry Miller,
The Wisdom of the Heart, 1941

1358. The final test of a leader is that he leaves behind him in other men the conviction and the will to carry on.
— Walter Lippmann, in

New York Herald Tribune,
April 14, 1945

1359. Leadership in today's world requires far more than a large stock of gunboats and a hard fist at the conference table.
— Hubert H. Humphrey, speech,
October 20, 1966

1360. The great leaders have always stage managed their effects.
— Charles DeGaulle,
Le Fil de l'épée, 1934

1361. Charlatanism of some degree is indispensable to effective leadership.
— Eric Hoffer,
The True Believer, 1951

1362. The trick of statesmanship is to turn the inevitable to one's own advantage.
— Christopher Layne, in
Atlantic Monthly, June, 1989

1363. A statesman should be possessed of good sense, a primary political quality; and its fortunate possessor needs a second quality — the courage to show that he has it.
— Adolphe Thiers, speech,
May 6, 1834

1364. The leader must know, must know that he knows, and must be able to make it abundantly clear to those about him that he knows.
— Clarence B. Randall,
Making Good in Management,
1964

1365. A man is not as big as his belief in himself; he is as big as the number of persons who believe in him.
— Woodrow Wilson, speech,
October 3, 1912

1366. The followers of a great man often put their eyes out, so that they may be better able to sing his praise.
— Friedrich Wilhelm Nietzsche,
*Miscellaneous Maxims and
Opinions*, 1879

1367. There are some whom the applause of the multitude has deluded into the belief that they are really statesmen.

— Plato, *The Republic,*
ca. 370 B.C.

1368. The leader is always alone in times of doom.

— Charles DeGaulle,
Mémoires de guerre: L'Appel, 1955

1369. It is seldom that statesmen have the option of choosing between a good and an evil.

— Charles Caleb Colton,
Lacon, 1820–22

1370. If an individual wants to be a leader and isn't controversial, that means he never stood for anything.

— Richard M. Nixon, in
Dallas Times-Herald,
December 10, 1978

1371. He that would govern others, first should be / Master of himself.

— Philip Massinger,
The Bondman, 1624

1372. All ambitions are lawful except those which climb upward on the miseries or credulities of mankind.

— Joseph Conrad,
A Personal Record, 1912

1373. The efficiency of the truly national leader consists primarily in preventing the division of the attention of a people, and always in concentrating it on a single enemy.

— Adolf Hitler,
Mein Kampf, 1924

1374. When statesmen forsake their own conscience for the sake of their public duties ... they lead their country by a short route to chaos.

— Robert Bolt,
A Man for All Seasons, 1968

1375. A conquering army on the border will not be halted by the power of eloquence.

— Otto von Bismarck, speech,
September 24, 1867

1376. I don't think that a leader can control to any great extent his destiny. Very seldom can he step in and change the situation if the forces of history are running in another direction.

— Richard M. Nixon, in E. Mazo,
*Richard Nixon: A Political and
Personal Portrait,* 1959

1377. But methought it lessened my esteem of a king, that he should not be able to command the rain.

— Samuel Pepys,
Diary, July 19, 1962

Liberty *see* Freedom

Losing *see* Defeat

Militarism

See also Aggression, Duty; Military Command;
Nationalism

1378. To delight in war is a merit in the soldier, a dangerous quality in the captain, and a positive crime in the statesman.

— George Santayana,
The Life of Reason, 1905–06

1379. We must train and classify the whole of our male citizens, and make military instruction a regular part of collegiate education.

— Thomas Jefferson, letter,
June 18, 1813

1380. Let me have war, say I; it exceeds peace as far as day does night; it's spritely, waking, audible, and full of vent. Peace is a very apoplexy, lethargy: mulled, dead, sleepy, insensible; a getter of more bastard children than war's a destroyer of men.
— William Shakespeare,
Coriolanus, 1608

1381. The inevitableness, the idealism, and the blessing of war, as an indispensable and stimulating law of development, must be repeatedly emphasized.
— Friedrich von Berndardi,
Germany and the Next War, 1912

1382. The trouble with military rule is that every colonel or general is soon full of ambition. The navy takes over today and the army tomorrow.
— Yakubu Gowon, in
Chicago Daily News,
August 29, 1970

1383. The army is a nation within the nation; it is a vice of our time.
— Alfred de Vigny, *Servitude et grandeur militaires*, 1835

1384. Ambition, / The soldier's virtue.
— William Shakespeare,
Antony and Cleopatra, 1606–07

1385. What millions died that Caesar might be great!
— Thomas Campbell,
Pleasures of Hope, 1799

1386. Hero-worship is strongest where there is least regard for human freedom.
— Herbert Spencer,
Social Statics, 1851

1387. You cannot organize civilization around the core of militarism and at the same time expect reason to control human destinies.
— Franklin D. Roosevelt,
radio address, October 26, 1938

1388. Where the state is weak, the army rules.
— Napoleon Bonaparte, remark,
January 9, 1808

1389. The weaknesses of the many make the leader possible.
— Elbert Hubbard,
The Note Book, 1927

1390. The outcome of the war is in our hands; the outcome of words is in the council.
— Homer, *The Iliad*, ca. 700 B.C.

1391. A handful of soldiers is always better than a mouthful of arguments.
— G. C. Lichtenberg,
Aphorisms, 1765–99

1392. A warlike spirit, which alone can create and civilize a state, is absolutely essential to national defense and to national perpetuity.
— Douglas MacArthur, in
Infantry Journal, March, 1927

1393. So long as war is the main business of nations, temporary despotism — despotism during the campaign — is indispensable.
— Walter Bagehot,
Physics and Politics, 1872

1394. It is well that war is so terrible — lest we should grow too fond of it.
— Robert E. Lee, letter,
December 13, 1862

1395. I have a deep sympathy with war, it so apes the gait and bearing of the soul.
— Henry David Thoreau,
Journal, 1906

1396. The enthusiasm for war, and the predatory temper of which it is the index, prevails in the largest measure among the upper classes, especially among the hereditary leisure class.
— Thorstein Veblen,
The Theory of the Leisure Class,
1899

1397. I have never understood this liking for war. It panders to instincts already catered for within the scope of any respectable domestic establishment.
— Alan Bennett,
Forty Years On, 1969

1398. Men love war because it allows them to look serious. Because it is the one thing that stops women laughing at them.
— John Fowles, *The Magus*, 1965

1399. I have met with men who loved stamps, and stones, and snakes, but I could not imagine any man loving war.
— Margot Asquith, *The Autobiography of Margot Asquith*, 1922

1400. The military caste did not originate as a party of patriots, but as a party of bandits.
— H. L. Mencken, *Minority Report*, 1956

1401. Mankind is composed of two sorts of men — those who love and create, and those who hate and destroy.
— José Martí, *Letter to a Cuban Farmer*, 1893

1402. People who are vigorous and brutal often find war enjoyable, provided that it is a victorious war and that there is not too much interference with rape and plunder. This is a great help in persuading people that wars are righteous.
— Bertrand Russell, *Unpopular Essays*, 1950

1403. Physical violence is the basis of authority.
— Leo Tolstoy, *The Kingdom of God is Within You*, 1893

1404. When the military man approaches, the world locks up its spoons and packs off its womankind.
— George Bernard Shaw, *Man and Superman*, 1903

1405. To call war the soil of courage and virtue is like calling debauchery the soil of love.
— George Santayana, *The Life of Reason*, 1905–06

1406. The pitifulest thing out is a mob; that's what an army is — a mob; they don't fight with courage that's born in them, but with courage that's borrowed from their mass, and from their officers.

— Mark Twain, *Huckleberry Finn*, 1884

1407. A man in armor is his armor's slave.
— Robert Browning, *Herakles*, 1871

1408. Whoso sheddeth man's blood, by man shall his blood be shed.
— Bible, *Genesis* 9:6

1409. All they that take the sword shall perish with the sword.
— Bible, *Matthew* 26:52

1410. The empire of the warrior, built by the sword, perishes by the sword.
— Robert Briffault, *Rational Evolution*, 1930

1411. The sword is the axis of the world and its power is absolute.
— Charles DeGaulle, *Vers l'Armée de Métier*, 1934

1412. The people are always in the wrong when they are faced by the armed forces.
— Napoleon Bonaparte, letter, October 2, 1810

1413. I love the majesty of human suffering.
— Alfred de Vigny, *La Maison du Berger*, 1844

1414. I love war …Peace will be hell for me.
— George S. Patton, on *CBS TV*, July 23, 1963

1415. We don't thrive on military acts. We do them because we have to, and thank God we are efficient.
— Golda Meir, regarding Israel, in *Vogue*, July, 1969

1416. Death loves a shining mark, a signal blow.
— Edward Young, *Night Thoughts*, 1742–45

1417. All the gods are dead except the god of war.
— Eldridge Cleaver, *Soul on Ice*, 1968

1418. We look on the world as a whole. We cannot be weak anywhere without creating danger everywhere.
— John Foster Dulles, in A. Berding, *Dulles on Diplomacy*, 1965

1419. In the councils of government, we must guard against the acquisition of unwarranted influence, whether sought or unsought, by the military-industrial complex. The potential for the disastrous rise of misplaced power exists and will persist.
— Dwight D. Eisenhower, farewell address, January 17, 1961

1420. The Army will hear nothing of politics from me, and in return I expect to hear nothing of politics from the Army.
— Herbert Asquith, speech, April 4, 1914

1421. If there is one basic element in our Constitution, it is civilian control of the military.
— Harry S Truman, *Memoirs*, 1955–56

1422. It is called the Army of the Potomac but it is only McClennan's bodyguard ... If McClennan is not using the army, I should like to borrow it for a while.

— Abraham Lincoln, statement, April 9, 1862

1423. To place any dependence upon militia, is, assuredly, resting upon a broken staff.
— George Washington, letter, September 24, 1776

1424. Military intelligence is a contradiction in terms.
— Groucho Marx, in *San Francisco Chronicle*, January 29, 1978

1425. The military mind is indeed a menace. Old-fashioned futurity that sees only men fighting and dying is smoke and fire; hears nothing more civilized than a cannonade; scents nothing but the stink of battle wounds and blood.
— Sean O'Casey, *Sunset and Evening Star*, 1954

1426. Militarism ... is fetish worship. It is the prostration of men's souls and the laceration of their bodies to appease an idol.
— R. H. Tawney, *The Acquisition Society*, 1921

1427. Strike the tent.
— Robert E. Lee, last words, October 12, 1870

Military Command

See also Leadership; Militarism; Rulers; Soldiers

1428. It is not well that there should be many masters; one man must be supreme.
— Homer, *The Iliad*, ca. 700 B.C.

1429. To do great things is difficult; but to command great things is more difficult.
— Friedrich Wilhelm Nietzsche, *Thus Spake Zarathustra*, 1883–92

1430. It is much safer to obey than to govern.
— Thomas à Kempis, *Imitation of Christ*, ca. 1420

1431. If it moves, salute it; if it doesn't move, pick it up; if you can't pick it up, paint it.
— Anonymous, guidelines for soldiers

1432. Nothing is easy in war.
— Dwight D. Eisenhower, in *Infantry School Quarterly*, 1953

1433. 'Tis a dainty thing to command, though 'twere but a flock of sheep.
— Miguel de Cervantes, *Don Quixote*, 1605–15

1434. The superior man is easy to serve and difficult to please.
— Confucius, *Analects*, ca. 480 B.C.

1435. The professional military mind is by necessity an inferior and unimaginative mind; no man of high intellectual quality would willingly imprison his gifts in such a calling.
— H. G. Wells, *The Outline of History*, 1920

1436. There is no merit without rank, but there is no rank without some merit.
— François La Rochefoucauld, *Maxims*, 1665

1437. He is the best general who makes the fewest mistakes.
— Proverb

1438. A man's name, title, and rank are artificial and impermanent; they do nothing to reveal what he really is, even to himself.
— Jean Giraudoux, *Siegfried*, 1928

1439. Men are of no importance. What counts is who commands.
— Charles DeGaulle, in *New York Times*, May 12, 1968

1440. The only prize much cared for by the powerful is power. The prize of the general is not a bigger tent, but command.
— Oliver Wendell Holmes, Jr., *Law and the Court*, 1913

1441. It is an interesting question how far men would retain their relative rank if they were divested of their clothes.
— Henry David Thoreau, *Walden*, 1854

1442. At the age of four with paper hats and wooden swords we're all Generals. Only some of us never grow out of it.
— Peter Ustinov, *Romanoff and Juliet*, 1956

1443. The man who commands efficiently must have obeyed others in the past, and the man who obeys dutifully is worthy of being some day a commander.
— Cicero, *De Legibus*, ca. 52 B.C.

1444. Learn to obey before you command.
— Solon, in Diogenes Laertius, *Lives and Opinions of Eminent Philosophers*, 3rd c.

1445. The man who obeys is nearly always better than the man who commands.
— Ernest Renan, *Dialogues et fragments philosophiques*, 1876

1446. He that cannot obey, cannot command.
— Benjamin Franklin, *Poor Richard's Almanack*, August, 1734

1447. If you command wisely, you'll be obeyed cheerfully.
— Thomas Fuller, *Gnomologia*, 1732

1448. It's the orders you disobey that make you famous.
— Douglas MacArthur, in *Time*, September 11, 1978

1449. The only real training for leadership is leadership.
— Antony Jay, *Management and Machiavelli*, 1968

1450. The most important quality in a leader is that of being acknowledged as such. All leaders whose fitness is questioned are clearly lacking in force.
— André Maurois, *The Art of Living*, 1939

1451. Authority must be accompanied by prestige, and prestige comes only from distance.
— Charles DeGaulle, *Le Fil de l'épée*, 1934

1452. Authority is never without hate.
— Euripedes, *Ion*, ca. 417 B.C.

1453. I've known a lot of generals who were war lovers. They scare the living hell out of me, and they're also not very good generals, not by my measure. Custer loved war, and look at what he accomplished.
— Norman Schwarzkopf, in *New York Times*, February 5, 1991

1454. The worst calamity after a stupid general is an intelligent general.
— Charles DeGaulle,
The Words of the General, 1962

1455. I am convinced that the best service a retired general can perform is to turn in his tongue along with his suit, and to mothball his opinions.
— Omar Bradley, in
New York Times, May 17, 1959

1456. To know when to retreat; and to dare to do it.
— Arthur Wellesley,
Duke of Wellington, reply
when asked how to recognize a
great general, in W. Fraser,
Words on Wellington, 1889

1457. In the Soviet army it takes more courage to retreat than to advance.
— Joseph Stalin, conversation,
September, 1941

1458. The general who advances without coveting fame and retreats without fearing disgrace, whose only thought is to protect his country and do good service for his sovereign, is the jewel of the kingdom.
— Sun Tzu, *The Art of War*,
ca. 500 B.C.

1459. The highest form of vanity is love of fame.
— George Santayana,
The Life of Reason, 1905–06

1460. Humility must always be the portion of any man who receives acclaim earned in the blood of his followers and the sacrifices of his friends.
— Dwight D. Eisenhower, speech,
July 12, 1945

1461. Fame usually comes to those who are thinking about something else.
— Oliver Wendell Holmes, Sr.,
*The Autocrat of the Breakfast
Table*, 1858

1462. The most terrible warfare is to be a second lieutenant leading a platoon when you are on the battlefield.

— Dwight D. Eisenhower,
remark, March 17, 1954

1463. The sergeant is the army.
— Dwight D. Eisenhower, in *New
York Times*, December 24, 1972

1464. A soldier is a slave — he does what he is told to do — everything is possible for him — his head is a superfluity. He is only a stick used by men to strike other men; and he is often tossed to Hell without a second thought.
— Elbert Hubbard, *The Roycroft
Dictionary and Book of Epigrams*,
1923

1465. The defeats and victories of the fellows at the top aren't always defeats or victories for the fellows at the bottom.
— Bertolt Brecht,
Mother Courage, 1939

1466. Victory shifts from man to man.
— Homer, *The Iliad*, ca. 700 B.C.

1467. A leader should not get too far in front of his troops or he will be shot in the ass.
— Joseph Clark, in
Washingtonian, November, 1979

1468. A chief is a man who assumes responsibility. He says, "I was beaten." He does not say, "My men were beaten."
— Antoine de Saint-Exupéry,
Piloto de guerre, 1942

1469. A general is just as good or just as bad as the troops under his command make him.
— Douglas MacArthur, speech,
August 16, 1962

1470. In this country it is considered wise to kill an admiral from time to time in order to encourage the others.
— Voltaire, *Candide*, 1759

1471. The height of ability in the least able consists in knowing how to submit to the good leadership of others.
— François La Rochefoucauld,
Maxims, 1665

1472. Every French soldier carries a marshal's baton in his knapsack.
— Napoleon Bonaparte, attributed

1473. An army of stags led by a lion would be more formidable than one of lions led by a stag.
— Proverb

1474. Lions led by donkeys.
— Max Hoffman, describing British soldiers in the First World War, in A. Clark, *The Donkeys*, 1961

1475. Tell me what brand of whiskey that Grant drinks. I would like to send a barrel of it to my other generals.
— Abraham Lincoln, response to questions about Grant's drinking, in *New York Herald*, November 26, 1863

Morale

See also Battle Cries; Battle Dispatches and Reports; Heroes; Nationalism; Patriotism

1476. Morale is the state of mind. It is steadfastness and courage and hope. It is confidence and zeal and loyalty. It is élan, *esprit de corps* and determination.
— George C. Marshall, in *Military Review*, October, 1948

1477. The spirit of a nation is what counts — the look in its eyes.
— Jean Giraudoux, *Electra*, 1937

1478. I venture to say no war *can* be long carried on against the will of the people.
— Edmund Burke, *Letters on a Regicide Peace*, 1797

1479. A nation which makes the final sacrifice for life and freedom does not get beaten.
— Kemal Atatürk, in M. M. Mousharrafa, *Atat Fürk*, 1944

1480. The more warlike the spirit of the people, the less need for a large standing army.
— Douglas MacArthur, in *Infantry Journal*, March, 1927

1481. What counts is not necessarily the size of the dog in the fight — it's the size of the fight in the dog.
— Dwight D. Eisenhower, speech, January 31, 1958

1482. It is not enough to fight. It is the spirit which we bring to the fight that decides the issue. It is morale that wins the victory.
— George C. Marshall, in *Military Review*, October, 1948

1483. The most vital quality a soldier can possess is self-confidence, utter, complete and bumptious.
— George S. Patton, letter, June 6, 1944

1484. I feel an army in my fist.
— Johann Friedrich von Schiller, *The Robbers*, 1781

1485. War rhetoric is a moral rhetoric. People are not willing to die unless there's some kind of a moral goal or value that transcends private interest.
— Theodore Windt, Jr., in *Christian Science Monitor*, January 15, 1991

1486. It is essential to persuade the soldier that those he is being urged to massacre are bandits who do not deserve to live; before killing other good, decent fellows like himself, his gun would fall from his hands.
— André Gide, *Journals*, February 10, 1943

1487. To be able to destroy with good conscience, to be able to behave badly and call your bad behavior "righteous indignation" — this is the height of psycholog-

ical luxury, the most delicious of moral treats.
— Aldous Huxley,
Crome Yellow, 1921

1488. People do not want words — they want the sound of battle.
— Gamal Abdel Nasser, speech,
January 20, 1969

1489. The sound of the drum drives out thought; for that very reason it is the most military of instruments.
— Joseph Joubert, *Pensées*, 1842

1490. How good bad music and bad reasons sound when one marches against an enemy!
— Friedrich Wilhelm Nietzsche,
The Dawn, 1861

1491. So, as you go into battle, remember your ancestors and remember your descendants.
— Cornelius Tacitus,
Agricola, ca. 98

1492. Think of it, soldiers; from the summit of these pyramids, forty centuries look down upon you.
— Napoleon Bonaparte, speech
before the battle of the Pyramids,
July 21, 1798

1493. You write to me that it's impossible; the word is not French.
— Napoleon Bonaparte, letter,
July 9, 1813

1494. Our greatest foes, and whom we must chiefly combat, are within.
— Miguel de Cervantes,
Don Quixote, 1605–15

1495. It's not whether you win or lose, but how you place the blame.
— John Peers,
1,001 Logical Laws, 1979

1496. Humilities are piled on a soldier ... so in order that he may, when the time comes, be not too resentful of the final humility — a meaningless and dirty death.
— John Steinbeck,
East of Eden, 1952

1497. There are no atheists in foxholes.
— William T. Cummings,
sermon at Bataan, 1942

1498. "Why me?" That is the soldier's first question, asked each morning as the patrols go out and each evening as the night settles around the foxholes.
— William Broyles, Jr.,
in *New York Times*,
May 26, 1986

1499. It is the savor of bread broken with comrades that makes us accept the values of war.
— Antoine de Saint-Exupéry,
Wind, Sand, and Stars, 1939

1500. There is a strength in the union even of very sorry men.
— Homer, *The Iliad*, ca. 700 B.C.

1501. Conscription may have been good for the country, but it damn near killed the army.
— Richard Hull, in A. Sampson,
Anatomy of Britain Today, 1965

1502. An army without culture is a dull-witted army, and a dull-witted army cannot defeat the enemy.
— Mao Zedong,
"The United Front in Cultural
Works," October 30, 1944

1503. No army has done so much with so little.
— Douglas MacArthur,
referring to the U.S. Army and
the fall of Bataan, in
New York Times,
April 11, 1942

1504. War educates the senses, calls into action the will, perfects the physical constitution, brings men into such swift and close collision in critical moments that man measures man.
— Ralph Waldo Emerson,
Miscellanies, 1884

1505. Nothing in life is so exhilarating as to be shot at without result.
— Winston S. Churchill,
The Malakand Field Force, 1898

Mottoes *see* Slogans and Mottoes

Nationalism

See also Causes of War; Expansion; Patriotism

1506. Patriotism is when love of your own people comes first; nationalism, when the hate for people other than your own comes first.
— Charles DeGaulle, in
Life, May 9, 1969

1507. That kind of patriotism which consists in hating all other nations.
— Elizabeth Gaskell,
Sylvia's Lovers, 1863

1508. Patriotism is a lively sense of responsibility. Nationalism is a silly cock crowing on its own dunghill.
— Richard Aldington,
The Colonel's Daughter, 1931

1509. The nationalist has a broad hatred and a narrow love. He cannot stifle a predilection for dead cities.
— André Gide, *Journals*, 1918

1510. Nationalism is our form of incest, is our idolatry, is our insanity. "Patriotism" is its cult.
— Erich Fromm,
The Sane Society, 1955

1511. It is sad that being a good patriot often means being the enemy of the rest of mankind.
— Voltaire,
Philosophical Dictionary, 1764

1512. I realize that patriotism is not enough. I must have no hatred or bitterness towards anyone.
— Edith Cavell, last words,
October 12, 1915

1513. War springs from the love and loyalty which should be offered to God being applied to some God substitute, one of the most dangerous being nationalism.
— Robert Runcie, sermon, July
26, 1982

1514. God and Country are an unbeatable team; they break all records for oppression and bloodshed.
— Luis Buñuel,
My Last Sigh, 1983

1515. We Germans fear God, but nothing else in the world.
— Otto von Bismarck, speech,
February 6, 1888

1516. Nationalism has two fatal charms for its devotees: it presupposes local self-sufficiency, which is a pleasant and desirable condition, and it suggests, very subtly, a certain personal superiority by reason of one's belonging to a place which is definable and familiar, as against a place which is strange, remote.
— E. B. White,
One Man's Meat, 1944

1517. I believe that we could without any degree of egotism, single-handed lick any nation in the world.
— Will Rogers, in P. McSpadden
Love, *The Will Rogers Book*, 1972

1518. Nationalism is an infantile disease. It is the measles of mankind.
— Albert Einstein, letter, 1921

1519. Nations, like men, have their infancy.
— Henry St. John,
Letters on the Study of History,
1752

1520. The disasters of the world are due to its inhabitants not being able to grow old simultaneously. There is always a raw and intolerant nation eager to destroy the tolerant and mellow.
— Cyril Connolly,
The Unquiet Grave, 1944

1521. Altogether, national hatred is

something peculiar. You will always find it strongest and most violent where there is the lowest degree of culture.
— Johann Wolfgang von Goethe, in J. Eckermann, *Conversations with Goethe*, March 14, 1830

1522. Nationalist pride, like other variants of pride, can be a substitute for self-respect.
— Eric Hoffer, *The Passionate State of Mind*, 1954

1523. Nationalism is power hunger tempered by self-deception.
— George Orwell, *Notes on Nationalism*, 1945

1524. We are all tattooed in our cradles with the beliefs of our tribe; the record may seem superficial, but it is indelible. You cannot educate a man wholly out of the superstitious fears which were implanted in his imagination, no matter how utterly his reason may reject them.
— Oliver Wendell Holmes, Sr., *The Poet at the Breakfast Table*, 1872

1525. The chief cause of human error is to be found in prejudices picked up in childhood.
— René Descartes, *Principles of Philosophy*, 1644

1526. If all Americans understood the nature of battle, they might be vulnerable to truth. But the myths of warfare are embedded deep in our ancestral memories. By the time children have reached the age of awareness, they regard uniforms, decorations and Sousa marches as exalted, and those who argue otherwise are regarded as unpatriotic.
— William Manchester, in *New York Times Magazine*, June 14, 1987

1527. Intellectually I know that America is no better than any other country; emotionally I know she is better than every other country.
— Sinclair Lewis, interview, December 29, 1930

1528. It is natural anywhere that people like their own kind, but it is not necessarily natural that their fondness for their own kind should lead them to the subjection of whole groups of other people not like them.
— Pearl S. Buck, *What America Means to Me*, 1943

1529. It is a most mistaken way of teaching men to feel they are brothers, by imbuing their mind with perpetual hatred.
— William Godwin, *An Enquiry concerning the Principles of Political Justice*, 1793

1530. In individuals insanity is rare, but in groups, parties, nations and epochs it is the rule.
— Friedrich Wilhelm Nietzsche, *Beyond Good and Evil*, 1886

1531. When a whole nation is roaring Patriotism at the top of its voice, I am fain to explore the cleanness of its hands and purity of its heart.
— Ralph Waldo Emerson, *Journals*, 1824

1532. The people arose as one man.
— Bible, *Judges* 20:8

1533. At bottom, every state regards another as a gang of robbers who will fall upon it as soon as there is an opportunity.
— Arthur Schopenhauer, *Parerga and Paralipomena*, 1851

1534. Nations hate other nations for the evil which is in themselves.
— George W. Russell, *The National Being*, 1917

1535. All nations have present, or past, or future reasons for thinking themselves incomparable.
— Paul Valéry, *Selected Writings*, 1964

1536. My toast would be, may our country be always successful, but whether successful or otherwise, always right.
— John Quincy Adams, letter, August 1, 1816

1537. Our country! In her intercourse with foreign nations, may she always be in the right; but our country, right or wrong.
— Stephen Decatur, toast,
April, 1816

1538. Our country, right or wrong! When right, to be kept right; when wrong, to be put right.
— Carl Schurz, speech,
October, 1899

1539. It seems that American patriotism measures itself against an outcast group. The right Americans are the right Americans because they're not like the wrong Americans, who are not really Americans.
— Eric Hobsbawm, in
Marxism Today, January, 1988

1540. A nation is a historical group of men of recognizable cohesion, held together by a common enemy.
— Theodore Herzl,
The Jewish State, 1896

1541. Everything belongs to the fatherland when the fatherland is in danger.
— Georges Jacques Danton,
speech, August 28, 1792

1542. A nation will not count the sacrifice it make, if it supposes it is engaged in a struggle for its fame, its influence and its existence.
— Benjamin Disraeli, speech,
May 24, 1855

1543. What is the German fatherland? Wherever the German tongue is heard.
— Ernst Moritz Arndt,
Was Ist des Deutschen Vaterland,
1813

1544. Our true nationality is mankind.
— H. G. Wells,
The Outline of History, 1920

1545. The nation must learn to consider as national whatever is true.
— Dionysios Solomos,
Table Talk, ca. 1850

1546. A country losing touch with its own history is like an old man losing his glasses, a distressing sight, at once vulnerable, unsure, and easily disoriented.
— George Walden, in
Times, December 20, 1986

1547. The driving force of a nation lies in its spiritual purpose, made effective by free, tolerant but unremitting national will.
— Franklin D. Roosevelt, message
to Congress, April 14, 1938

Navy

See also Battle Cries; Military Command

1548. No big modern war has been won without preponderant sea power; and, conversely, very few rebellions of maritime provinces have succeeded without acquiring sea power.
— Samuel Eliot Morison,
*The Oxford History of the
American People*, 1965

1549. He that commands the sea is at great liberty, and may take as much and as little of the war as he will.
— Francis Bacon, *Essays*, 1625

1550. The navy of the United States is the right arm of the United States and is emphatically the peacekeeper.
— Theodore Roosevelt, in
New York Times,
November 22, 1914

1551. A good navy is not a provocative of war. It is the surest guaranty of peace.
— Theodore Roosevelt,
message to Congress,
December 2, 1902

1552. A modern navy can not be improvised. It must be built and in existence when the emergency arises.
— William Howard Taft, inaugural address, March 4, 1909

1553. You gentlemen of England / Who live at home at ease, / How little do you think / On the dangers of the sea.
— Martin Parker, "The Valiant Sailors," ca. 1650

1554. The sea hates a coward!
— Eugene O'Neill, *Mourning Becomes Electra,* 1931

1555. There is nothing more enticing, disenchanting, and enslaving than the life at sea.
— Joseph Conrad, *Lord Jim,* 1900

1556. Death, old captain, it is time! raise the anchor.
— Charles Baudelaire, *Les Fleurs de Mal,* 1861

1557. Don't talk to me about naval tradition. It's nothing but rum, sodomy, and the lash.
— Winston S. Churchill, in P. Gretton, *Former Naval Person,* 1968

1558. Only one military organization can hold and gain ground in war — a ground army supported by tactical aviation with supply lines guarded by the navy.
— Omar Bradley, in *Military Review,* September, 1951

Neutrality

See also Appeasement; Diplomacy; Foreign Relations; International Relations

1559. Even to observe neutrality you must have a strong government.
— Alexander Hamilton, speech, June 29, 1787

1560. In the judgment of this government, loans by American bankers to any foreign nation at war are inconsistent with the true spirit of neutrality.
— William Jennings Bryan, statement, August 15, 1914

1561. We have stood apart, studiously neutral.
— Woodrow Wilson, message to Congress, December 7, 1915

1562. America cannot be an ostrich with its head in the sand.
— Woodrow Wilson, speech, February 1, 1916

1563. Armed neutrality is ineffectual enough at best.
— Woodrow Wilson, speech, April 2, 1917

1564. As long as Europe prepares for war, America must prepare for neutrality.
— Walter Lippmann, in *New York Herald Tribune,* May 17, 1934

1565. There are two things that a democratic people will always find very difficult, to begin a war and to end it.
— Alexis de Tocqueville, *Democracy in America,* 1835

1566. The nation is a power hard to rouse, but when roused harder still and more hopeless to resist.
— William E. Gladstone, speech, April 2, 1880

1567. Democracies are indeed slow to make war, but once embarked upon a martial venture are equally slow to make peace and reluctant to make a tolerable, rather than a vindictive, peace.
— Reinhold Niebuhr, *The Structure of Nations and Empires,* 1959

1568. It isn't the oceans which cut us off from the world — it's the American way of looking at things.
— Henry Miller, *The Air-Conditioned Nightmare,* 1945

Oppression *see* Tyranny

Pacifism

See also Appeasement; Peace; Peace Is ... ;
War and Peace

1569. War will cease when men refuse to fight.
— Anonymous

1570. Sometime they'll give a war and nobody will come.
— Carl Sandburg, *The People, Yes*, 1936

1571. What if someone gave a war and Nobody came?
— Allen Ginsburg, "Graffiti," 1972

1572. And the combat ceased for want of combatants.
— Pierre Corneille, *Le Cid*, 1636

1573. There is no way to peace. Peace is the way.
— A. J. Muste, in *New York Times*, November 16, 1967

1574. It takes twenty years or more of peace to make a man; it takes only twenty seconds of war to destroy him.
— Baudouin I, King of Belgium, speech, May 12, 1959

1575. It is long and hard and painful to create life: it is short and easy to steal the life others have made.
— George Bernard Shaw, *Back to Methuselah*, 1921

1576. We must conquer war, or war will conquer us.
— Ely Culbertson, *Must We Fight Russia?* 1946

1577. Mankind must put an end to war or war will put an end to mankind.
— John F. Kennedy, speech, September 25, 1961

1578. If man does find the solution for world peace it will be the most revolutionary reversal of his record we have ever known.
— George C. Marshall, *Biennial Report of the Chief of Staff, United States Army*, September 1, 1945

1579. So long as governments set the example of killing their enemies, private individuals will occasionally kill theirs.
— Elbert Hubbard, *Contemplations*, 1902

1580. I know war as few other men now living know it, and nothing to me is more revolting. I have long advocated its complete abolition, as its very destructiveness on both friend and foe has rendered it useless as a method of settling international disputes.
— Douglas MacArthur, speech, April 19, 1951

1581. War contains so much folly, as well as wickedness, that much is to be hoped from the progress of reason; and if any thing is to be hoped, every thing ought to be tried.
— James Madison, in *National Gazette*, February 2, 1792

1582. Our knowledge of science has already outstripped our capacity to control it. We have many men of science, too few men of God.
— Omar Bradley, speech, November 10, 1948

1583. We kill because we're afraid of our own shadow, afraid that if we used a little common sense we'd have to admit that our glorious principles were wrong.
— Henry Miller, *The Wisdom of the Heart*, 1941

1584. Non-violence is not a garment to be put on and off at will. Its seat is in the heart, and it must be an inseparable part of our very being.
— Mohandas K. Gandhi,
Non-Violence in Peace and War,
1948

1585. I will not by the noise of bloody wars and the dethroning of kings advance you to glory: but by the gentle ways of peace and love.
— Thomas Traherne,
Centuries, ca. 1672

1586. There is such a thing as a man being too proud to fight.
— Woodrow Wilson, speech,
May 10, 1915

1587. Passive resistance is a sport for gentlemen (and ladies) — just like the pursuit of war, a heroic enterprise for the ruling classes but a grievous burden on the rest.
— Kenneth Kaunda,
Kaunda on Violence, 1980

1588. I believe that a man is the strongest soldier for daring to die unarmed.
— Mohandas K. Gandhi, speech,
August 12, 1920

1589. Among other evils which being unarmed brings you, it causes you to be despised.
— Niccolò Machiavelli,
The Prince, 1513

1590. The peace of the man who has forsworn the use of the bullet seems to me not quite peace, but a canting impotence.
— Ralph Waldo Emerson,
Journals, 1839

1591. Love hath no fury like a non-combatant.
— C. E. Montague,
Disenchantment, 1922

1592. The only thing that's been a worse flop than the organization of non-violence has been the organization of violence.
— Joan Baez, *Daybreak*, 1968

1593. The war that will end war.
— H. G. Wells, title of book, 1914

1594. War can be abolished only through war, and in order to get rid of the gun it is necessary to take up the gun.
— Mao Zedong,
"Problems of War and Strategy,"
November 6, 1938

1595. The pacifist is as surely a traitor to his country and to humanity as it is the most brutal wrongdoer.
— Theodore Roosevelt, speech,
July 27, 1917

1596. It sometimes happens that he who would not hurt a fly will hurt a nation.
— Henry Taylor,
The Statesman, 1836

1597. Passivity is fatal to us. Our goal is to make the enemy passive.
— Mao Zedong, in *Time*,
December 18, 1950

1598. They shall beat their swords into plowshares, and their spears into pruning-hooks; nation shall not lift up sword against nation, neither shall they learn war any more.
— Bible, *Isaiah* 2:4

1599. It would now be technically possible to unify the world, abolish war and poverty altogether, if men desired their own happiness more than the misery of their enemies.
— Bertrand Russell,
Portraits from Memory, 1956

1600. The State calls its own violence law, but that of the individual crime.
— Max Stirner,
The Ego and His Own, 1845

1601. The day will come when a nation that lifts up the sword against a nation will be put in the same felon category as the man who strikes his brother in anger.
— David Lloyd George, speech,
April 21, 1908

1602. I devoutly believe in the reign of peace and in the gradual advent of some

sort of socialistic equilibrium. The fatalistic view of the war-function is to me nonsense ... And when whole nations are the armies, and the science of destruction vies in intellectual refinement with the sciences of production, I see that war becomes absurd and impossible from its own monstrosity.
—William James,
Memories and Studies, 1911

1603. To establish any mode to abolish war, however advantageous it might be to nations, would be to take from such government the most lucrative of its branches.

—Thomas Paine,
The Rights of Man, 1791

1604. I like to believe that people, in the long run, are going to do more to promote peace than our governments. Indeed, I think that people want peace so much that one of these days governments had better get out of the way and let them have it.
—Dwight D. Eisenhower,
radio address, August 31, 1959

1605. A government without the power of defense! It is a solecism.
—James Wilson, statement,
December 11, 1787

Patriotism

See also Freedom; Nationalism; Rebellion

1606. The patriot, volunteer, fighting for country and his rights, makes the most reliable soldier on earth.
—Thomas J. ("Stonewall")
Jackson, in H. McGuire,
Stonewall Jackson: An Address,
1897

1607. It is sweet and honorable to die for one's country.
—Horace, *Odes,* 23 B.C.

1608. What a pity it is / That we can die but once to save our country!
—Joseph Addison, *Cato,* 1713

1609. I only regret that I have but one life to lose for my country.
—Nathan Hale, last words,
September 22, 1776

1610. Martyred many times must be / Who would keep his country free.
—Edna St. Vincent Millay,
Make Bright the Arrows, 1940

1611. You're not here to die for your country. You're here to make those so-and-so's die for theirs.
—John H. ("Iron Mike")
Michaels, in *Time,*
November 11, 1985

1612. They died to save their country and they only saved the world.
—Gilbert K. Chesterton,
"English Graves," 1922

1613. I would die for my country, but I could never let my country die for me.
—Neil Kinnock, speech,
September 30, 1986

1614. He who loves not his home and country, which he has seen, how shall he love humanity in general which he has not seen?
—William Ralph Inge,
Outspoken Essays, First Series,
1919

1615. Such is the patriot's boast, where'er we roam, / His first, best country ever is at home.
—Oliver Goldsmith,
The Traveler, 1764

1616. Be England what she will, / With all her faults, she is my country still.
—Charles Churchill,
The Farewell, 1764

1617. The love of Americans for their country is not an indulgent, it is an exacting and chastising love; they cannot tolerate its defects.

— Jacques Maritain,
Reflections on America, 1958

1618. To make us love our country, our country ought to be lovely.

— Edmund Burke, *Reflections on the Revolution in France*, 1790

1619. It is not the function of our government to keep the citizen from falling into error; it is the function of the citizen to keep the government from falling into error.

— Robert H. Jackson, *American Communications Association v Douds*, May, 1950

1620. What we need are critical lovers of America — patriots who express their faith in their country by working to improve it.

— Hubert H. Humphrey,
Beyond Civil Rights: A New Day of Equality, 1968

1621. What do we mean by patriotism in the context of our times? I venture to suggest ... a patriotism which is not short, frenzied outbursts of emotion, but the tranquil and steady dedication of a lifetime.

— Adlai Stevenson, speech,
August 27, 1952

1622. When were the good and the brave ever in a majority?

— Henry David Thoreau,
A Plea for Captain John Brown, 1859

1623. In the beginning of a change, the patriot is a scarce man, and brave, and hated and scorned. When his cause succeeds, the timid join him, for then it costs nothing to be a patriot.

— Mark Twain, *Notebook*, 1935

1624. These are the times that try men's souls. The summer soldier and the sunshine patriot will, in this crisis, shrink from the service of their country; but he that stands it *now*, deserves the love and thanks of men and women.

— Thomas Paine, in
The American Crisis, 1776–83

1625. Patriotism is just loyalty to friends, people, families.

— Robert Santos, in A. Santoli,
Everything We Had, 1981

1626. Who serves his country well has no need of ancestors.

— Voltaire, *Mérope*, 1743

1627. My kind of loyalty was loyalty to one's country, not to its institutions or its office holders.

— Mark Twain, *A Connecticut Yankee at King Arthur's Court*, 1889

1628. No one loves his country for its size or eminence, but because it's his own.

— Seneca, *Letters to Lucilius*, 1st c.

1629. I think patriotism is like charity — it begins at home.

— Henry James,
The Portrait of a Lady, 1881

1630. Patriotism itself is a necessary link in the golden chains of our affections and virtues.

— Samuel Taylor Coleridge,
The Friend, 1818

1631. To strike freedom of the mind with the fist of patriotism is an old and ugly subtlety.

— Adlai Stevenson, speech,
August 27, 1952

1632. Talking of patriotism, what humbug it is; it is a word which always commemorates a robbery. There isn't a foot of land in the world which doesn't represent the ousting and re-ousting of a long line of successive owners.

— Mark Twain, *Notebook*, 1935

1633. Of all ennobling sentiments, patriotism may be the most easily manipulated ... Among its toxic fruits are intolerance, belligerence and blind obedience, perhaps because it blooms more luxuriantly during times of war.

— Nancy Gibbs, in *Time*,
February 11, 1991

1634. Patriotism is the last refuse of a scoundrel.
— Samuel Johnson, letter,
April 7, 1775

1635. In Dr. Johnson's famous dictionary patriotism is defined as the last resort of a scoundrel. With all due respect to an enlightened but inferior lexicographer, I beg to submit that it is the first.
— Ambrose Bierce,
The Devil's Dictionary, 1906

1636. When Dr. Johnson defined patriotism as the last refuge of a scoundrel, he ignored the enormous possibilities of the word reform.
— Roscoe Conkling, in D. Jordan,
Roscoe Conkling of New York, 1971

1637. No matter that patriotism is too often the refuge of scoundrels. Dissent, rebellion, and all-around hell-raising remain the true duty of patriots.
— Barbara Ehrenreich,
The Worst Years of Our Lives, 1991

1638. You'll never have a quiet world till you knock the patriotism out of the human race.
— George Bernard Shaw,
O'Flaherty V.C., 1919

1639. Conceit, arrogance, and egotism are the essentials of patriotism.
— Emma Goldman,
Anarchism, 1917

1640. At its worst, American patriotism degenerates into a coarse form of national self-congratulation.
— Lance Morrow,
Fishing in the Tiber, 1988

1641. Never was patriot yet, but was a fool.
— John Dryden,
Absalom and Achitophel, 1681

1642. A patriot is a fool in ev'ry age.
— Alexander Pope,
Imitations of Horace, 1733–38

1643. Patriotism is a pernicious, psychopathic form of idiocy.
— George Bernard Shaw,
in *L'Esprit Français*, 1932

1644. Do you wish men to be virtuous? Then let us begin by making them love their country.
— Jean-Jacques Rousseau, *A Discourse in Political Economy*, 1758

1645. Whenever you hear a man speak of his love for his country it is a sign that he expects to be paid for it.
— H. L. Mencken,
A Mencken Chrestomathy, 1949

1646. The citizen who criticizes his country is paying it an implied tribute.
— J. William Fulbright, speech,
April 28, 1966

1647. Love of our country is another of those specious illusions, which have been invented by impostors in order to render the multitude the blind instruments of their crooked designs.
— William Godwin,
*An Enquiry concerning the
Principles of Political Justice*, 1793

1648. When a nation is filled with strife, then do patriots flourish.
— Lao-Tzu, *Tao-te-ching*,
6th c. B.C.

1649. Patriotism is easy to understand in America. It means looking out for yourself by looking out for your country.
— Calvin Coolidge, speech,
May 30, 1923

1650. In time of war the loudest patriots are the greatest profiteers.
— August Bebel, speech,
November, 1870

1651. Protectionism and patriotism are reciprocal.
— John Calhoun, speech,
December 12, 1811

1652. Patriotism is often an arbitrary veneration of real estate above principles.
— George Jean Nathan,
Testament of a Critic, 1931

1653. So to be patriots as not to forget we are gentlemen.
— Edmund Burke,
*Thoughts on the Cause of the
Present Discontents*, 1770

1654. Patriotism is an ephemeral motive that scarcely ever outlasts the particular threat to society that aroused it.
— Denis Diderot, *Observations on the Drawing Up of Laws*, 1774

1655. The love of country is the first virtue in a civilized man.
— Napoleon Bonaparte, speech, July 14, 1812

1656. What this country needs — what every country needs occasionally — is a good hard bloody war to revive the view of patriotism on which its existence as a nation depends.
— Ambrose Bierce, letter, February 15, 1911

1657. We have achieved the most amazing things, a few million people opening up half a continent. But we have not yet found a Canadian soul except in time of war.
— Lester B. Pearson, in *Time*, May 5, 1967

1658. The single best augury is to fight for one's country.
— Homer, *The Iliad*, ca. 700 B.C.

1659. It is a well-known fact that we always recognize our homeland when we are about to lose it.
— Albert Camus, *Nuptials*, 1939

1660. Patriotism is in political life what faith is in religion.
— John E. E. Dalberg, in *The Home and Foreign Review*, July, 1862

1661. The good die young.
— Proverb

1662. Let us therefore brace ourselves to our duties and so bear ourselves that if the British Empire and its Commonwealth last for a thousand years men will still say, "This was their finest hour."
— Winston S. Churchill, speech, June 18, 1940

1663. War is an ugly thing, but not the ugliest of things: the decayed and degraded state of moral and patriotic feeling which thinks nothing *worth* a war, is worse.
— John Stuart Mill, *Dissertations and Discussions*, 1859

Peace

See also Neutrality; Pacifism; War and Peace

1664. First keep the peace within yourself, then you can also bring peace to others.
— Thomas à Kempis, *Imitation of Christ*, ca. 1420

1665. A peace above all earthly dignities, / A still and quiet conscience.
— William Shakespeare, *Henry VIII*, 1613

1666. Rendering oneself unarmed when one had been the best-armed, out of a height of feeling — that is the means to real peace, which must always rest on a peace of mind.
— Friedrich Wilhelm Nietzsche, *The Wanderer and His Shadow*, 1880

1667. Mark the perfect man, and behold the upright; for the end of that man is peace.
— Bible, *Psalms* 37:37

1668. "Pax vobiscum" will answer all queries.
— Walter Scott, *Ivanhoe*, 1819

1669. I would rather have peace in the world than be president.
— Harry S Truman, message, December 24, 1948

1670. Let us have peace.
— Ulysses S. Grant, upon accepting the nomination for president, May 29, 1868

1671. What hast thou to do with peace? Turn thee behind me.
— Bible, *II Kings* 9:18

1672. Our ultimate goal is a world without war. A world made safe for diversity, in which all good men, goods and ideas can freshly move across every border and every boundary.
— Lyndon B. Johnson,
State of the Union address,
January 8, 1964

1673. A peaceful world is a world in which differences are tolerated, and are not eliminated by violence.
— John Foster Dulles,
War or Peace, 1950

1674. Never before has the idea that peace is indivisible has been as true as it is now. Peace is not unity in similarity, but unity in diversity, in the juxtaposing and reconciling of differences.
— Mikhail Gorbachev, lecture,
June 5, 1991

1675. You may call for peace as loudly as you wish, but where there is no brotherhood there can in the end be no peace.
— Max Lerner,
Actions and Passions, 1949

1676. It is easier to love humanity than to love your neighbor.
— Eric Hoffer, interview on
CBS TV, November 14, 1967

1677. World peace, like community peace, does not require that each man love his neighbor — it requires only that they live together with mutual tolerance, submitting their disputes to a just and peaceful settlement.
— John F. Kennedy, speech,
June 10, 1963

1678. God and the politicians willing, the United States can declare peace upon the world, and win it.
— Ely Culbertson,
Must We Fight Russia? 1946

1679. If you have a nation of men who have risen to that height of moral culti-vation that they will not declare war or carry arms, for they have not so much madness left in their brains, you have a nation of lovers, of benefactors, of true, great and able men.
— Ralph Waldo Emerson,
Miscellanies, 1884

1680. It is not enough just to be for peace. The point is, what can we do about it?
— Richard M. Nixon, in
New York Times, March 10, 1971

1681. I take it that what all men are really after is some form or perhaps only some formula of peace.
— Joseph Conrad,
Under Western Eyes, 1911

1682. The Marshall Plan will go down in history as one of America's greatest contributions to the peace of the world.
— Harry S Truman,
Memoirs, 1955–56

1683. For peace, with justice and honor, is the fairest and most profitable of pos-sessions, but with disgrace and shameful cowardice it is the most infamous and harmful of all.
— Polybius, *History*, ca. 125 B.C.

1684. Armed peace.
— Friedrich von Logau,
Poetic Aphorisms, 1654

1685. [This is] an era of violent peace.
— James D. Watkins, in *New York Times*, December 7, 1986

1686. We keep a vigil of peace around the world.
— Lyndon B. Johnson, speech,
May 30, 1963

1687. Though peace be made, yet it is interest that keeps peace.
— Oliver Cromwell, speech,
September 4, 1654

1688. The secret wall of a town is peace.
— Proverb

1689. The pursuit of peace resembles the building of a great cathedral. It is the

work of a generation. In concept it requires a master-architect; in execution,
the labors of many.
 — Hubert H. Humphrey, remark,
February 17, 1965

1690. Peace and freedom do not come
cheap, and we are destined — all of us
here today — to live out most if not all of
our lives in uncertainty and challenge and
peril.

 — John F. Kennedy, speech,
October 12, 1961

1691. 'Tis not hard, I think / For men
so old as we to keep the peace.
 — William Shakespeare,
Romeo and Juliet, 1595

1692. A time to love, and a time to
hate; a time of war, and a time of peace.
 — Bible, *Ecclesiastes* 3:8

Peace Is ...

See also War and Peace; War Is ...

1693. Peace, *n.* In international
affairs, a period of cheating between two
periods of fighting.
 — Ambrose Bierce,
The Devil's Dictionary, 1906

1694. Peace: A monotonous interval
between fights.
 — Elbert Hubbard, *The Roycroft
Dictionary and Book of Epigrams*,
1923

1695. Peace / Is the temporary beautiful ignorance that War / Somewhere pro-
gresses.
 — Edna St. Vincent Millay,
Make Bright the Arrows, 1940

1696. Peace is an armistice in a war
that is continuously going on.
 — Thucydides, *History of the
Peloponnesian War*, 431–413 B.C.

1697. Peace is not an absence of war;
it is virtue, a state of mind, a disposition
for benevolence, confidence, justice.
 — Baruch Spinoza,
Theological-Political Treatise, 1670

1698. Peace is when time doesn't mat-
ter as it passes by.
 — Maria Schell, in *Time*,
March 3, 1958

1699. Peace is more the product of
our day-to-day living than of a spectac-
ular program, intermittently executed.

 — Dwight D. Eisenhower, speech,
March 23, 1950

1700. Peace is a daily, a weekly, a
monthly process, gradually changing
opinions, slowly ending old barriers, quietly building new structures.
 — John F. Kennedy, speech,
September 20, 1963

1701. Peace is indivisible.
 — Maxim Litvinov, message,
February 25, 1920

1702. Peace is a virtual, mute, sus-
tained victory of potential powers against
probable greeds.
 — Paul Valéry, *Reflections on the
World Today*, 1931

1703. Peace is much more precious
than a piece of land.
 — Anwar al-Sadat, speech,
March 8, 1978

1704. Peace is an unstable equilibrium, which can be preserved only by
acknowledged supremacy or equal power.
 — Will Durant,
The Lessons of History, 1968

1705. Peace is no more than a dream
as long as we need the comfort of the clan.
 — Peter Nichols, in *Independent*,
September 1, 1990

1706. Eternal peace is a dream, and
not even a beautiful one, and war is a part

of God's world order. In it are developed the noblest virtues of man, courage and abnegation, dutifulness and self-sacrifice at the risk of life. Without war the world would sink to materialism.
— Helmuth von Moltke, letter, December 11, 1880

1707. Fair peace is becoming to men; fierce anger belongs to beasts.
— Ovid, *The Art of Love*, ca. 8

1708. An unjust peace is better than a just war.
— Cicero, *Epistola ad Atticum*, 1st c. B.C.

1709. The only condition of peace in this world is to have no ideas, or, at least, not to express them.
— Oliver Wendell Holmes, Sr., *The Professor at the Breakfast Table*, 1860

1710. War makes rattling good history; but Peace is poor reading.
— Thomas Hardy, *The Dynasts*, 1904–08

Power

See also Power Corrupts; Strength; Tyranny; Tyrants; Weapons

1711. The fundamental concept in social science is Power, in the same sense in which Energy is the fundamental concept in physics.
— Bertrand Russell, *Power*, 1938

1712. The problem of power is how to achieve its responsible use rather than its irresponsible and indulgent use — of how to get men of power to live for the public rather than off the public.
— Robert F. Kennedy, *The Pursuit of Justice*, 1964

1713. Power without responsibility: the prerogative of the harlot throughout the ages.
— Rudyard Kipling, cited by Stanley Baldwin, speech, March 18, 1931

1714. Power tends to confuse itself with virtue and a great nation is peculiarly susceptible to the idea that its power is a sign of God's favor.
— J. William Fulbright, speech, April 21, 1966

1715. We thought, because we had power, we had wisdom.
— Stephen Vincent Benét, *Litany for Dictatorships*, 1935

1716. Few men are satisfied with less power than they are able to procure.
— William Henry Harrison, speech, 1840

1717. I hope our wisdom will grow with our power, and teach us, that the less we use our power the greater it will be.
— Thomas Jefferson, letter, June 12, 1815

1718. Power educates the potentate.
— Ralph Waldo Emerson, *The Conduct of Life*, 1860

1719. He who is firmly seated in authority soon learns to think security, and not progress, the highest lesson of statecraft.
— James Russell Lowell, *Among My Books*, 1870

1720. Who is all-powerful should fear everything.
— Pierre Corneille, *Cinna*, 1640

1721. He who has the greatest power put into his hands, will only become the more impatient of any restraint in the use of it.
— William Hazlitt, "On the Spirit of Monarchy," 1823

1722. Arbitrary power is the natural object of temptation to a prince.
— Jonathan Swift, *Thoughts on Various Subjects*, 1706

1723. In all supremacy of power, there is inherent a prerogative to pardon.
— Benjamin Whichcote, *Moral and Religious Aphorisms*, 1703

1724. Powerful men in particular suffer from the delusion that human beings have no memories. I would go so far as to say that the distinguishing trait of powerful men is the psychotic certainty that people forget acts of infamy as easily as their parents' birthdays.
— Stephen Vizinczey, in *Horizon*, October, 1976

1725. Isolation from reality is inseparable from the exercise of power.
— George Reedy, in A. Schlesinger, Jr., *The Imperial Presidency*, 1973

1726. We see men fall from high estate on account of the very faults through which they attained it.
— Jean de La Bruyère, *Characters*, 1688

1727. Those in possession of absolute power can not only prophesy and make their prophecies come true, but they can also lie and make their lies come true.
— Eric Hoffer, *The Passionate State of Mind*, 1954

1728. The arrogance of power.
— J. William Fulbright, title of book, 1967

1729. Power tires only those who do not have it.
— Giulio Andreotti, in *Independent on Sunday*, April 5, 1992

1730. Power when wielded by abnormal energy is the most serious of facts.
— Henry Brooks Adams, *The Education of Henry Adams*, 1907

1731. To know the pains of power, we must go to those who have it; to know its pleasure, we must go to those who are seeking it.
— Charles Caleb Colton, *Lacon*, 1820–22

1732. Lust for power is the most flagrant of all the passions.
— Cornelius Tacitus, *Annals*, ca. 115–116

1733. I love power. But it is as an artist that I love it. I love it as a musician loves his violin, to draw out its sounds and chords and harmonies.
— Napoleon Bonaparte, in H. Ellis, *The Dance of Life*, 1923

1734. An honest man can feel no pleasure in the exercise of power over his fellow citizens.
— Thomas Jefferson, letter, January 13, 1813

1735. It is when power is wedded to chronic fear that it becomes formidable.
— Eric Hoffer, *The Passionate State of Mind*, 1954

1736. Our sense of power is more vivid when we break a man's spirit than when we win his heart.
— Eric Hoffer, *The Passionate State of Mind*, 1954

1737. For some men the power to destroy life becomes the equivalent to the female power to create life.
— Myriam Miedzian, *Boys Will Be Boys*, 1991

1738. The impulse to mar and to destroy is as ancient and almost as nearly universal as the impulse to create. The one is an easier way than the other of demonstrating power.
— Joseph W. Krutch, *The Best of Two Worlds*, 1950

1739. Power takes as ingratitude the writhing of its victims.
— Rabindranath Tagore, *Stray Birds*, 1916

1740. The depository of power is always unpopular.
— Benjamin Disraeli,
Coningsby, 1844

1741. Political power, properly so called, is merely the organized power of one class for oppressing another.
— Karl Marx,
The Communist Manifesto, 1848

1742. Power should not be concentrated in the hands of so few, and powerlessness in the hands of so many.
— Maggie Kuhn, in *Ms.*,
June, 1975

1743. The arts of power and its minions are the same in all countries and in all ages. It marks its victim: denounces it; and excites the public odium and the public hatred, to conceal its own abuses and encroachments.
— Henry Clay, speech,
March 14, 1834

1744. In every community there is a class of people profoundly dangerous to the rest. I don't mean the criminals. For them we have punitive sanctions. I mean the leaders. Invariably, the most dangerous people seek the power.
— Saul Bellow, *Herzog*, 1964

1745. Power-worship blurs political judgment because it leads, almost unavoidably, to the belief that present trends will continue. Whoever is winning at the moment will always seem to be invincible.
— George Orwell,
Shooting an Elephant, 1950

1746. Closeness to power heightens the dignity of all men.
— Theodore H. White,
The Making of the President 1960,
1961

1747. In my opinion, most of the great men of the past were only there for the beer — the wealth, prestige and grandeur that went with the power.
— A. J. P. Taylor, in P. Vansittart,
Voices 1870–1914, 1984

1748. A friend in power is a friend lost.
— Henry Brooks Adams,
The Education of Henry Adams,
1907

1749. We should keep silent about those in power; to speak well of them almost implies flattery; to speak ill of them while they are alive is dangerous, when they are dead is cowardly.
— Jean de La Bruyère,
Characters, 1688

1750. If you wish to know a man, give him authority.
— Proverb

1751. Corridors of power.
— Charles P. Snow,
title of book, 1965

1752. The wise become as the unwise in the enchanted chambers of power, whose lamps make every face the same color.
— Walter Savage Landor,
Imaginary Conversations,
1824–53

1753. Nothing doth more hurt in a state than that cunning men pass for wise.
— Francis Bacon, *Essays*, 1625

1754. We have, I fear, confused power with greatness.
— Stewart L. Udall, speech,
June 13, 1965

1755. People who have power respond simply. They have no minds but their own.
— Ivy Compton-Burnett,
The Mighty and Their Fall,
1961

1756. Intelligence is not all that important in the exercise of power, and is often, in point of fact, useless.
— Henry Kissinger, in
Esquire, June, 1975

1757. Men of power have no time to read; yet the men who do not read are unfit for power.
— Michael Foot,
Debts of Honor, 1980

1758. The fate of every nation rests in its own power.
— Helmuth von Moltke, speech, March 1, 1880

1759. The essence of government is power; and power, lodged as it must be in human hands, will ever be liable to abuse.
— James Madison, speech, December 2, 1829

1760. The first principle of a civilized state is that power is legitimate only when it is under contract.
— Walter Lippmann, *The Public Philosophy*, 1955

1761. Only he deserves power who every day justifies it.
— Dag Hammarskjöld, *Markings*, 1965

1762. Power must never be trusted without a check.
— John Adams, letter, February 2, 1816

1763. Power abdicates only under the stress of counter-power.
— Martin Buber, *Paths in Eutopia*, 1950

1764. Law is but a heathen word for power.
— Daniel Defoe, *The History of the Kentish Petition*, 1712–13

1765. All empire is no more than power in trust.
— John Dryden, *Absalom and Achitophel*, 1681

1766. Magnanimity in politics is not seldom the truest wisdom; and a great empire and little minds go ill together.
— Edmund Burke, *On Conciliation with America*, 1775

1767. He who has his thumb on the purse has the power.
— Otto von Bismarck, speech, May 21, 1869

1768. The exercise of power is determined by thousands of interactions between the world of the powerful and that of the powerless, all the more so because these worlds are never divided by a sharp line: everyone has a small part of himself in both.
— Václav Havel, *Disturbing the Peace*, 1986

1769. Power! Did you ever hear of men being asked whether other souls should have power or not? It is born in them.
— Olive Schreiner, *The Story of an African Farm*, 1883

1770. Life is a search after power.
— Ralph Waldo Emerson, *The Conduct of Life*, 1860

1771. I see here, Sir, what all the world desires to have — power.
— Matthew Boulton, in J. Boswell, *Life of Samuel Johnson*, March 22, 1776

1772. The will to power.
— Friedrich Wilhelm Nietzsche, title of book, 1888

1773. The secret of power is the will.
— Giuseppe Mazzini, letter, 1831

1774. When the will to power is wanting, there is decline.
— Friedrich Wilhelm Nietzsche, *The Anti-Christ*, 1888

1775. The concentration of power is what always precedes the destruction of human initiative, and, therefore of human energy.
— Woodrow Wilson, speech, September 4, 1912

1776. The need to exert power, when thwarted in the open fields of life, is the more likely to assert itself in trifles.
— Charles Horton Cooley, *Human Nature and the Social Order*, 1902

1777. He that fails in his endeavors after wealth or power will not long retain either honesty or courage.
— Samuel Johnson, in *Adventurer*, October 16, 1753

1778. The sole advantage of power is that you can do more good.
— Baltasar Gracián,
The Art of Worldly Wisdom, 1647

1779. You cannot have power for good without having power for evil too. Even mother's milk nourishes murderers as well as heroes.
— George Bernard Shaw,
Major Barbara, 1905

1780. When power feels itself totally justified and approved it immediately destroys whatever freedom we have left; and that is fascism.
— Luis Buñuel, in
New York Times Magazine,
March 11, 1973

1781. Concentrated power has always been the enemy of liberty.
— Ronald Reagan, in
New Republic, December 16, 1981

1782. People demand freedom only when they have no power.
— Friedrich Wilhelm Nietzsche,
The Will to Power, 1888

1783. Power is so apt to be insolent and Liberty to be saucy, that they are very seldom upon good terms.
— George Savile, *Political, Moral,
and Miscellaneous Thoughts and
Reflections*, 1750

1784. It is a strange desire to seek power and to lose liberty.
— Francis Bacon, *Essays*, 1625

1785. The love of liberty is the love of others; the love of power is the love of ourselves.
— William Hazlitt,
Table Talk, 1821–22

Power Corrupts

See also Power; Power Is ... ; Tyranny; Tyrants

1786. Historic responsibility has to make up for the want of legal responsibility. Power tends to corrupt and absolute power corrupts absolutely.
— John E. E. Dalberg, letter,
April 5, 1887

1787. It is not power itself, but the legitimation of the lust for power, which corrupts absolutely.
— R. H. S. Crossman, in
New Statesman, April 21, 1951

1788. Power corrupts the few, while weakness corrupts the many.
— Eric Hoffer,
The Passionate State of Mind,
1954

1789. Powerlessness frustrates; absolute powerlessness frustrates absolutely.
— Russell Baker, in
New York Times, May 1, 1969

1790. This is the bitterest pain among men, to have much knowledge but no power.
— Herodotus, *The History*,
ca. 450 B.C.

1791. Except our own thoughts, there is nothing absolutely in our power.
— René Descartes,
A Discourse on Method, 1637

1792. Anarchy always brings about absolute power.
— Napoleon Bonaparte, speech,
June 7, 1815

1793. If power corrupts, being out of power corrupts absolutely.
— Douglass Cater, in
Book Digest, December, 1979

1794. The king said, "Power does not corrupt. Fear corrupts, perhaps the fear of a loss of power."
— John Steinbeck, *The Short
Reign of Pippin IV*, 1957

1795. In the United States, though power corrupts, the expectation of power paralyzes.
— John Kenneth Galbraith,
A View from the Stands, 1986

1796. Those who have been once intoxicated with power, and have desired any kind of emolument from it, even though for but one year, can never willingly abandon it.
— Edmund Burke,
Letter to a Member of the National Assembly, 1791

1797. Power intoxicates men. It is never voluntarily surrendered. It must be taken from them.
— James F. Byrnes,
in *New York Times*,
May 15, 1956

1798. Great power, which incites / Great envy, hurls some men to destruction; they are drowned / In a long, splendid stream of honors.
— Juvenal, *Satires*, ca. 100

1799. The effect of power and publicity on all men is the aggravation of self, a sort of tumor that ends by killing the victim's sympathies.
— Henry Brooks Adams, *The Education of Henry Adams*, 1907

1800. Power will intoxicate the best hearts, as wine the strongest heads.
— Charles Caleb Colton,
Lacon, 1820–22

1801. Power, like the diamond, dazzles the beholder, and also the wearer; it dignifies meanness; it magnifies littleness; to what is contemptible, it gives authority; to what is low exaltation.
— Charles Caleb Colton,
Lacon, 1820–22

1802. All, or the greatest part of men that have aspired to riches or power, have attained thereunto either by force or fraud, and what they have by craft or cruelty gained, to cover the foulness of this fact, they call purchase, as a name more honest.
— Walter Ralegh,
The Cabinet Council, pub. 1751

1803. The greater the power, the more dangerous the abuse.
— Edmund Burke, speech, 1771

1804. Unlimited power is apt to corrupt the minds of those who possess it.
— William Pitt, speech,
January 9, 1770

1805. The possession of unlimited power will make a despot of almost any man. There is a possible Nero in the gentlest human creature that walks.
— Thomas B. Aldrich,
Pankapog Papers, 1903

1806. No man is wise enough nor good enough to be trusted with unlimited power.
— Charles Caleb Colton,
Lacon, 1820–22

1807. No one is fit to be trusted with power.
— Charles P. Snow,
The Light and the Dark,
1961

1808. I am more and more convinced that man is a dangerous creature; and that power, whether vested in many or a few, is ever grasping and, like the grave, cries, "Give, give!"
— Abigail Adams, letter,
November 27, 1775

1809. Power, like a desolating pestilence, / Pollutes whate'er it touches.
— Percy Bysshe Shelley,
Queen Mab, 1813

1810. Concentrated power is not rendered harmless by the good intentions of those who create it.
— Milton Friedman,
Capitalism and Freedom,
1962

1811. Goodness, armed with power, is corrupted; and pure love without power is destroyed.
— Reinhold Niebuhr,
Beyond Tragedy, 1938

Power Is ...

See also Power; Strength; Tyranny

1812. Power is the great aphrodisiac.
— Henry Kissinger, in
New York Times, January 19, 1971

1813. All power is a trust.
— Benjamin Disraeli,
Vivian Grey, 1826

1814. Power is the great regulator of the relations among states.
— René Albrecht-Carrié, *A Diplomatic History of Europe Since the Congress of Vienna*, 1958

1815. Power is not only what you have but what the enemy thinks you have.
— Saul Alinsky,
Rules for Radicals, 1971

1816. Political power grows out of the barrel of a gun.
— Mao Zedong,
Selected Works of Mao Zedong,
1965

1817. "Power may be at the end of a gun," but sometimes it's also at the end of the shadow or the image of a gun.
— Jean Genet,
Prisoner of Love, 1986

1818. Power and violence are opposites; where the one rules absolutely, the other is absent.
— Hannah Arendt,
Crisis of the Republic, 1972

1819. Power politics is the diplomatic name for the law of the jungle.
— Ely Culbertson,
Must We Fight Russia? 1946

1820. Power is not a means, it is an end. One does not establish a dictatorship in order to safeguard a revolution; one makes the revolution in order to establish the dictatorship.
— George Orwell, *1984*, 1949

1821. Power ... is an instrument that must be used toward an end.
— James Kirkpatrick, speech,
July 20, 1981

1822. Power is not an institution, and not a structure; neither is it a certain strength we are endowed with; it is the name that one attributes to a complex strategical situation in a particular society.
— Michel Foucault,
The History of Sexuality, 1976

1823. Power is what men seek, and any group that gets it will abuse it.
— Lincoln Steffens, in
Exposé, February, 1956

1824. Power is in inflicting pain and humiliation. Power is in tearing human minds to pieces and putting them together again in new shapes of our own choosing.
— George Orwell, *1984*, 1949

1825. Power is always charged with the impulse to eliminate human nature, the human variable, from the equation of action. Dictators do it by terror or by the inculcation of blind faith; the military do it by iron discipline; and the individual masters think they can do it by automation.
— Eric Hoffer,
The Temper of Our Time, 1967

1826. Power, whether exercised over matter or over men, is partial to simplification.
— Eric Hoffer,
The Ordeal of Change, 1964

1827. The least one can say of power is that a vocation for it is suspicious.
— Jean Rostand,
Pensées d'un Biologiste, 1939

1828. Power is evil; and everything that belongs to power belongs to the devil.
— Malcolm Muggeridge, on
ABC TV, March 19, 1968

1829. Power is not happiness.
— William Godwin,
*An Enquiry concerning the
Principles of Political Justice,*
1793

1830. Power? It's like a Dead Sea fruit.
When you achieve it, there is nothing there.
— Harold Macmillan, in
A. Sampson, *The New Anatomy
of Britain,* 1971

Predictions of War

See also Appeasement; Causes of War

1831. True wisdom consists not in seeing what is immediately before our eyes, but in foreseeing what is to come.
— Terence, *Adelphoe,* 160 B.C.

1832. I see wars, horrible wars, and the Tiber foaming with much blood.
— Virgil, *Aeneid,* 19 B.C.

1833. Ye shall hear of wars and rumors of wars.
— Bible, *Matthew* 24:6

1834. That war and rumors of war are the great threats to political stability and to liberty needs no demonstration. Total war means total subjection of the individual to the state.
— Robert H. Jackson,
*The Supreme Court in the
American System of Government,*
1955

1835. For nation shall rise against nation, and kingdom against kingdom.
— Bible, *Matthew* 24:7

1836. Ancestral voices prophesying war!
— Samuel Taylor Coleridge,
Kubla Khan, 1798

1837. As long as there are sovereign nations possessing great power, war is inevitable.
— Albert Einstein, in *Atlantic
Monthly,* November, 1945

1838. The immediate cause of World War III is the preparation of it.
— C. Wright Mills, in L. & A. Gordon, *American Chronicle,*
1987

1839. A war regarded as inevitable or even probable, and therefore much prepared for, has a very good chance of eventually being fought.
— George F. Keenan,
The Cloud of Danger, 1977

1840. I say that there's nothing to stop war from going on forever.
— Bertolt Brecht,
Mother Courage, 1939

1841. Wars will continue just the same until the force of circumstances renders them impossible.
— Alfred Nobel, statement, 1890

1842. To accept civilization *as it is* practically means accepting decay.
— George Orwell, *Inside the
Whale and Other Essays,* 1940

1843. There is nothing so subject to the inconstancy of fortune as war.
— Miguel de Cervantes,
Don Quixote, 1605–15

1844. The outcome of the greatest events is always determined by a trifle.
— Napoleon Bonaparte, letter,
October 7, 1797

1845. War will exist until that distant day when the conscientious objector enjoys the same reputation and prestige that the warrior does today.
— John F. Kennedy, in
A. Schlesinger, Jr., *A Thousand
Days: John F. Kennedy in the
White House,* 1979

1846. If war no longer occupied men's thoughts and energies, we could within a

generation, put an end to all serious poverty throughout the world.
— Bertrand Russell,
Unpopular Essays, 1950

1847. The wave of the future is not the conquest of the world by a single dogmatic creed but the liberation of the diverse energies of free nations and free men.
— John F. Kennedy, speech,
March 23, 1962

1848. We cannot accept the doctrine that war must be forever a part of man's destiny.
— Franklin D. Roosevelt, speech,
November 2, 1940

1849. If there is another war there will be no victors, only losers.
— Richard M. Nixon, in
New York Times, July 24, 1968

1850. The next World War will be fought with stones.
— Albert Einstein, in
Living Philosophies, 1949

1851. If the Third World War is fought with nuclear weapons, the fourth will be fought with bows and arrows.
— Louis Mountbatten,
in *Maclean's Magazine*,
November 17, 1975

1852. It's going to be a "come-as-you-are" war.
— Ralph Gauer, in
Newsweek, July 9, 1984

1853. Throughout human history, the apostles of purity, those who have claimed to possess a total explanation, have wrought havoc among mere mixed-up human beings.
— Salman Rushdie, in
Independent on Sunday,
February 4, 1990

1854. You have a row of dominoes set up; you knock over the first one, and what will happen to the last one is that it will go over very quickly.
— Dwight D. Eisenhower, the

"domino theory," speech,
April 7, 1954

1855. The lights are going out all over Europe; we shall not see them lit again in our lifetime.
— Edward Grey, comment,
August 3, 1914

1856. We are, to put it mildly, in a mess, and there is a strong chance that we shall have exterminated ourselves by the end of the century. Our only consolation will have to be that, as a species, we have had an exciting term of office.
— Desmond Morris,
The Naked Ape, 1967

1857. We don't want any more wars, but a man is a damn fool to think there won't be any more of them.
— Smedley D. Butler, in
New York Times, August 21, 1931

1858. The most persistent sound which reverberates through man's history is the beating of war drums.
— Arthur Koestler,
Janus: A Summing Up, 1978

1859. The moral climax of this, the culminating and final war for human liberty, has come.
— Woodrow Wilson, speech
regarding the First World War,
January 8, 1918

1860. I hope we may say that thus, this fateful morning, came to an end all wars.
— David Lloyd George, speech,
November 11, 1918

1861. I believe the last war was too much an educator for there ever to be another on a large scale.
— Henry Ford,
The American Scrap Book, 1928

1862. I seriously doubt if we will ever have another war. This is probably the very last one.
— Richard M. Nixon, in
New York Times,
March 10, 1971

1863. A Japanese attack on Pearl Harbor is a strategic impossibility.
— George Fielding Eliot,
"The Impossible War with Japan,"
September, 1938

1864. Pearl Harbor ... is one of the greatest, if not the very greatest, maritime fortress in the world ... It is the one sure sanctuary in the whole of the vast Pacific both for ships and men.
— John W. Vandercook, in *Vogue*,
January 1, 1941

1865. Hitler has missed the bus.
— Neville Chamberlain, speech,
April 4, 1940

1866. I have said this before, but I shall say it again and again: Your boys are not going to be sent into any foreign wars.
— Franklin D. Roosevelt, speech,
October 30, 1040

1867. We Americans know — although others appear to forget — the risk of spreading conflict. We still seek no wider war.
— Lyndon B. Johnson, statement

following conflict in the Gulf of Tonkin, August 4, 1964

1868. We are not about to send American boys nine or ten thousand miles away from home to do what Asian boys ought to be doing for themselves.
— Lyndon B. Johnson, speech,
October 21, 1964

1869. I believe there is a light at the end of what has been a long and lonely tunnel.
— Lyndon B. Johnson,
speech regarding Vietnam,
September 21, 1966

1870. We have reached an important point when the end begins to come into view.
— William C. Westmoreland,
speech, November 21, 1967

1871. Now this is not the end. It is not even the beginning of the end. But it is, perhaps, the end of the beginning.
— Winston S. Churchill, speech,
November 10, 1942

Preparation for War

See also Aggression; Expansion; Morale; Propaganda;
Public Opinion; Strength; Weapons

1872. Let him who desires peace prepare for war.
— Vegetius, *De Rei Militari*,
ca. 375

1873. Forewarned, forearmed; to be prepared is half the victory.
— Miguel de Cervantes,
Don Quixote, 1605–15

1874. An old and haughty nation proud in arms.
— John Milton, *Comus*, 1637

1875. To be always ready for war, said Mentor, is the surest way to avoid it.
— François Fénelon,
Télémaque, 1699

1876. One should always have one's boots on, and be ready to leave.
— Michel de Montaigne,
Essays, 1580

1877. I do not hold that we should rearm to fight. I hold that we should rearm in order to parley.
— Winston S. Churchill,
radio broadcast,
October 8, 1951

1878. If we desire to secure peace ... it must be known that we are at all times ready for war.
— George Washington, speech,
December 13, 1793

1879. We shall more certainly preserve peace when it is well understood that we are prepared for war.
— Andrew Jackson,
farewell address, March 4, 1837

1880. It is an unfortunate fact that we can secure peace only by preparing for war.
— John F. Kennedy, speech,
September 6, 1960

1881. Americans have been habitually unprepared for all of their major wars. A peace-loving people with nonaggressive tendencies is never ready.
— Thomas A. Bailey,
A Diplomatic History of the American People, 1958

1882. We may not be in the slightest danger of invasion, but if in an armed world we disarm, we shall count less and less in the councils of nations.
— Walter Lippmann, in
Metropolitan, February, 1915

1883. A drop of sweat on the drill ground will save many drops of blood on the battlefield.
— August Willich,
The Army: Standing Army or National Army? 1866

1884. The more you sweat in peace, the less you bleed in war.
— Hyman G. Rickover,
speech, 1983

1885. War: The sure result of the existence of armed men.
— Elbert Hubbard,
The Roycroft Dictionary and Book of Epigrams, 1923

1886. The possession of battle-ready troops, a well-filled treasury and a lively disposition, these were the real reasons which moved me to war.
— Frederick the Great,
A History of My Times, 1741

1887. Wars occur because people prepare for conflict, rather than for peace.
— Trygve Lie, in *Labor*,
September 6, 1947

1888. Are we so devoid of spiritual and moral force and intellectual ingenuity that we cannot possibly prevent war by any means other than military preparedness?
— Margaret Chase Smith,
in *Christian Science Monitor*,
January 15, 1952

1889. A self-respecting nation is ready for anything, including war, except for a renunciation of its option to make war.
— Simone Weil, in
Nouveaux Cahiers, April 1, 1937

1890. One believes in the coming of war if one does not sufficiently abhor it.
— Thomas Mann,
The Magic Mountain, 1924

1891. The grim fact is that we prepare for war like precocious giants and for peace like retarded pygmies.
— Lester B. Pearson,
news summaries,
March 15, 1955

1892. The world in arms is not spending money alone. It is spending the sweat of its laborers, the genius of its scientists, the hopes of its children.
— Dwight D. Eisenhower, speech,
April 16, 1953

1893. When Wall Street yells war, you may rest assured every pulpit in the land will yell war.
— Eugene V. Debs, speech,
June 16, 1918

1894. For God's sake, do not drag me into another war!
— Sydney Smith, letter,
February 19, 1823

1895. All wars are planned by old men / In council rooms apart.
— Grantland Rice,
"The Two Sides of War," 1955

1896. I don't think old men ought to promote wars for young men to fight. I don't like warlike old men.
— Walter Lippmann,
interview, May, 1961

1897. The military mind always imagines that the next war will be on the same lines as the last. That has never been the case and never will be.
— Ferdinand Foch, attributed

1898. Cry "Havoc!" and let slip the dogs of war.
— William Shakespeare,
Julius Caesar, 1599

1899. If the British went out by water, to show two lanterns in the North Church steeple; and if by land, one as a signal, for we were apprehensive it would be difficult to cross the Charles River or get over Boston Neck.
— Paul Revere, signal code,
April 16, 1775

1900. Once to every man and nation comes the moment to decide.
— James Russell Lowell,
"The Present Crisis," 1845

1901. Every one may begin a war at his pleasure, but cannot so finish it.
— Niccolò Machiavelli,
*Discourse on the First Ten Books
of Titus Livius*, 1513–17

1902. The chance of war.
— William Shakespeare,
Troilus and Cressida, 1602

1903. Put your trust in God, my boys, and keep your powder dry.
— Valentine Blacker, in E. Hayes,
Ballads of Ireland, 1856

1904. God is always with the strongest battalions.
— Frederick the Great, letter,
May 8, 1760

Preventing War

See also Futility of War; War and Peace

1905. We make war that we may live in peace.
— Aristotle, *Nicomachean Ethics*,
325 B.C.

1906. We best avoid wars by taking even physical action to stop small ones.
— Anthony Eden, speech,
November 1, 1956

1907. You have to take chances for peace, just as you must take chances in war. Some say that we were brought to the verge of war. The ability to get to the verge of war without getting into the war is the necessary art.
— John Foster Dulles, in
Life, January 11, 1956

1908. I have always been opposed even to the thought of fighting a "preventive war." There is nothing more foolish than to think that war can be stopped by war. You don't "prevent" anything by war except peace.
— Harry S Truman, *Memoirs*,
1955–56

1909. Unless they are immediate victims, the majority of mankind behaves as if war was an act of God which could not be prevented; or they behave as if war elsewhere was none of their business. It would be a bitter cosmic joke if we destroy ourselves due to atrophy of the imagination.
— Martha Gellhorn,
The Face of War, 1967

1910. This is the problem: Is there any way of delivering mankind from the menace of war?
— Albert Einstein, letter,
July 30, 1932

1911. We can best help you to prevent war not by repeating your words and following your methods but by finding new words and creating new methods.
— Virginia Woolf,
Three Guineas, 1938

1912. It isn't enough to talk about peace. One must believe in it. And it isn't enough to believe in it. One must work for it.

— Eleanor Roosevelt, radio
broadcast, November 11, 1951

1913. The work, my friend, is peace. More than an end to this war — an end to the beginnings of all war.

— Franklin D. Roosevelt,
undelivered speech scheduled for
April 13, 1945

1914. If we are not able to prevent a third world war, we shall go down in history — if history should survive — as the guilty generation, the generation which did nothing to prevent the annihilation of mankind itself.

— U Thant, in *New York Times*,
November 12, 1963

1915. I think we have no greater challenge or duty but to prevent war. I don't consider myself as a pacifist. I consider myself as actively committed to preventing wars.

— Ramsey Clark, in *USA Today*,
January 17, 1991

1916. Reluctance to use military force is an American military tradition. Since war is ultimately a political act, not a military act, give political tools the opportunity to work first.

— Colin Powell, speech,
September 28, 1993

1917. The way to prevent war is to bend every energy toward preventing it, not to proceed by the dubious indirection of preparing for it.

— Max Lerner, *Actions and
Passions*, 1949

1918. There is a homely adage which runs: "Speak softly and carry a big stick; you will go far."

— Theodore Roosevelt, speech,
April 2, 1903

1919. If our air forces are never used, they have achieved their finest goal.

— Nathan F. Twining, news
summaries, March 31, 1956

1920. One sword keeps another in the sheath.

— George Herbert,
Jacula Prudentum, 1651

1921. The sword within the scabbard keep, / And let mankind agree.

— John Dryden,
The Secular Masque, 1700

1922. Nations do not arm for war. They arm to keep themselves from war.

— Barry Goldwater,
Why Not Victory? 1962

1923. Clothe thee in war; arm thee in peace.

— Proverb

1924. 'Tis safest making peace with sword in hand.

— Proverb

1925. Weapons breed peace.

— Proverb

1926. A strong defense is the surest way to peace.

— Gerald R. Ford, speech,
August 12, 1974

1927. The surest way to prevent war is not to fear it.

— John Randolph, speech,
March 5, 1806

1928. We're eyeball to eyeball and I think the other fellow just blinked.

— Dean Rusk, in *Saturday
Evening Post*, December 8, 1962

1929. Some say it will bring war to the heavens, but its purpose is to deter war, in the heavens and on earth.

— Ronald Reagan, State of the
Union Address, concerning the
Strategic Defense Initiative,
February 6, 1985

1930. Our strategy is one of preventing war by making it self-evident to our enemies that they're going to get their clocks cleaned if they start one.

— John W. Vessey, Jr.,
in *New York Times*,
July 15, 1984

Propaganda

See also Civilians; Enemies; Nationalism;
Public Opinion

1931. Give me the writing of a nation's advertising and propaganda, and I care not who governs its politics.
— Hugh MacLennan,
in *Maclean's Magazine*,
November 5, 1960

1932. It is very dangerous to write the truth in war, and the truth is also very dangerous to come by.
— Ernest Hemingway, speech,
June 4, 1937

1933. Wherever books will be burned, men also, in the end, are burned.
— Heinrich Heine,
Almansor, 1823

1934. It is the absolute right of the State to supervise the formation of public opinion.
— Josef Göbbels, speech, 1923

1935. If you feed the people just with revolutionary slogans they will listen today, they will listen tomorrow, they will listen the day after tomorrow, but on the fourth day they will say, "To hell with you."
— Nikita Khrushchev, in *New York Times*, October 4, 1964

1936. Cities are taken by the ears.
— Proverb

1937. Whoever controls the language, the images, controls the race.
— Allen Ginsberg, in
New Yorker, August 24, 1968

1938. An unexciting truth may be eclipsed by a thrilling lie.
— Aldous Huxley,
Brave New World Revisited, 1958

1939. You furnish the pictures and I'll furnish the war.
— William Randolph Hearst,
cable to Frederick Remington,
March, 1898

1940. The press is not public opinion.
— Otto von Bismarck, speech,
September 30, 1862

1941. All propaganda must be so popular and so such an intellectual level, that even the most stupid of those towards whom it is directed will understand it.
— Adolf Hitler,
Mein Kampf, 1924

1942. A belief is not true because it is useful.
— Henri Frédéric Amiel,
Amiel's Journal, 1883

1943. Why is propaganda so much more successful when it stirs up hatred than when it tries to stir up friendly feeling?
— Bertrand Russell,
The Conquest of Happiness, 1930

1944. The effectiveness of political and religious propaganda depends upon the methods employed, not, on the doctrine taught. These doctrines may be true or false, wholesome or pernicious — it makes little or no difference.
— Aldous Huxley,
Brave New World Revisited,
1958

1945. Propaganda, to be effective, must be believed. To be believed, it must be credible. To be credible, it must be true.
— Hubert H. Humphrey, speech,
December 6, 1965

1946. The truth is rarely pure, and never simple.
— Oscar Wilde,
The Importance of Being Earnest,
1895

1947. One cannot fashion a credible deterrent out of an incredible action.
— Robert McNamara,
The Essence of Security, 1968

1948. Propaganda is that branch of the art of lying which consists in nearly deceiving your friends without quite deceiving your enemies.
— F. M. Cornford, in *New Statesman*, September 15, 1978

1949. Propaganda is a soft weapon; hold it in your hands too long, and it will move about like a snake, and strike the other way.
— Jean Anouilh, *The Lark*, 1955

1950. Eternal truths will be neither true nor eternal unless they have fresh meaning for every new social situation.
— Franklin D. Roosevelt, speech, September 20, 1940

1951. Disinformation is most effective in a very narrow context.
— Frank Snepp, in *Christian Science Monitor*, February 26, 1985

1952. The truth is often a terrible weapon of aggression. It is possible to lie, and even to murder for the truth.
— Alfred Adler, *Problems of Neurosis*, 1929

1953. A little inaccuracy sometimes saves tons of explanation.
— Saki, *The Square Egg*, 1924

1954. The most dangerous untruths are truths slightly distorted.
— G. C. Lichtenberg, *Aphorisms*, 1765–99

1955. There are three kinds of lies: lies, damned lies and statistics.
— Benjamin Disraeli, in M. Twain, *Autobiography*, 1924

1956. [The War Office maintained three sets of figures:] one to mislead the public, another to mislead the Cabinet, and the third to mislead itself.
— Herbert Asquith, in A. Horne, *Price of Glory*, 1962

1957. The real war will never get in the books.
— Walt Whitman, *Specimen Days*, 1882

1958. In our country [Russia] the lie has become not just a moral category but a pillar of the state.
— Alexander Solzhenitsyn, in *Observer*, December 29, 1974

1959. How is the world ruled and led to war? Diplomats lie to journalists and believe these lies when they see them in print.
— Karl Kraus, *Half-Truths and One-And-A-Half-Truths: Selected Aphorisms*, 1976

1960. In wartime, truth is so precious that she should always be attended by a bodyguard of lies.
— Winston S. Churchill, in *Time*, December 24, 1984

1961. When war is declared, truth is the first casualty.
— Arthur Ponsonly, *Falsehood in Wartime*, 1928

1962. The first casualty when war comes is truth.
— Hiram W. Johnson, attributed

1963. The appalling thing about war is that it kills all love of truth.
— Georg Brandes, letter, March, 1915

1964. Among the calamities of war, may be justly numbered the diminution of the love of truth, by the falsehoods which interest dictates, and credulity encourages.
— Samuel Johnson, in *The Idler*, November 11, 1758

1965. Everyone, when there's war in the air, learns to live in a new element: falsehood.
— Jean Giraudoux, *Tiger at the Gates*, 1935

1966. *Kommt der Krieg ins Land / Gibt's lügen wie Sand.* (When war enters a country / It produces lies like sand.)
— Anonymous saying, Germany, 1920s

1967. It is sometimes necessary to lie damnably in the interests of a nation.
— Hilaire Belloc, letter, December 12, 1917

1968. Propaganda does not deceive people; it merely helps them to deceive themselves.
— Eric Hoffer, *The Passionate State of Mind*, 1954

1969. Men willingly believe what they wish.
— Julius Caesar, *De Bello Gallico*, 1st c. B.C.

1970. As soon as by one's own propaganda even a glimpse of right on the other side is admitted, the cause for doubting one's own right is laid.
— Adolf Hitler, *Mein Kampf*, 1924

1971. The propagandist's purpose is to make one set of people forget that certain other sets of people are human.
— Aldous Huxley, *The Olive Tree*, 1937

1972. No one has ever succeeded in keeping nations at war except by lies.
— Salvador de Madariaga, *Anarchy or Hierarchy*, 1937

1973. Only the mob and the elite can be attracted by the momentum of totalitarianism itself. The masses have to be won by propaganda.
— Hannah Arendt, *The Origins of Totalitarianism*, 1951

1974. War is peace. Freedom is slavery. Ignorance is strength.
— George Orwell, *1984*, 1949

1975. Repetition does not transform a lie into a truth.
— Franklin D. Roosevelt, radio address, October 26, 1939

1976. What I tell you three times is true.
— Lewis Carroll, *The Hunting of the Snark*, 1876

Public Opinion

See also Causes of War; Enemies; Nationalism; Propaganda

1977. Public opinion wins wars.
— Dwight D. Eisenhower, statement, April 25, 1944

1978. It is tremendously to the people's interests that they should understand the causes of war — but it is very hard to get them interested in the subject.
— Kenneth Burke, *Permanence and Change*, 1935

1979. It is far more difficult to change the mentality of the people than it is to change a country's political order or even its economy.
— Ilya Ehrenburg, in *Saturday Review*, September 30, 1967

1980. American public opinion is like an ocean — it cannot be stirred by a teaspoon.
— Hubert H. Humphrey, speech, October 11, 1966

1981. Nothing is more dangerous in wartime than to live in the temperamental atmosphere of a Gallup Poll, always feeling one's pulse and taking one's temperature.
— Winston S. Churchill, speech, September 30, 1941

1982. A government is based on public opinion and must keep in step with what public opinion decides, which considers and calculates everything.
— Napoleon Bonaparte, letter, November 25, 1803

1983. In a democracy such as ours military policy is dependent on public opinion.
— George C. Marshall, in *Yank*, January 28, 1943

1984. All becomes easy when we follow the current of opinion; it is the ruler

of the world.
— Napoleon Bonaparte,
Maxims, 1804–15

1985. Its name is Public Opinion. It is held in reverence. It settles everything. Some think it is the voice of God.
— Mark Twain,
Europe and Elsewhere, 1925

1986. Public Opinion ... an attempt to organize the ignorance of the community, and to elevate it to the dignity of physical force.
— Oscar Wilde,
The Critic as Artist, 1891

1987. The basis of our government ... opinion of the people.
— Thomas Jefferson, letter,
January 16, 1787

1988. We are ruled by Public Opinion, not by Statute law.
— Elbert Hubbard,
The Note Book, 1927

1989. Public opinion's always in advance of the law.
— John Galsworthy,
Windows, 1922

1990. It is the besetting vice of democracies to substitute public opinion for law. This is the usual form in which the masses of men exhibit their tyranny.
— James Fenimore Cooper,
The American Democrat, 1838

1991. Public opinion sets bounds to every government, and is the real sovereign in every free one.
— James Madison, in
National Gazette,
December 19, 1791

1992. Public opinion is the most potent monarch this world knows.
— Benjamin Harrison, speech,
February 22, 1888

1993. Public opinion is stronger than the legislature, and nearly as strong as the Ten Commandments.
— Charles Dudley Warner,
My Summer in a Garden, 1870

1994. There is no group in America that can withstand the force of an aroused public opinion.
— Franklin D. Roosevelt,
statement, June 16, 1933

1995. A government can be no better than the public opinion which sustains it.
— Franklin D. Roosevelt, speech,
January 8, 1936

1996. A straw vote only shows which way the hot air blows.
— O. Henry, *Rolling Stones*, 1912

1997. Public sentiment is to public officers what water is to the wheel of the mill.
— Henry Ward Beecher,
Proverbs from Plymouth Pulpit,
1887

1998. In the modern world the intelligence of public opinion is the one indispensable condition of social progress.
— Charles William Eliot,
speech, 1869

1999. There's a kind of permission for war which can be given only by the world's mood and atmosphere, the feel of its pulse. It would be madness to undertake a war without that permission.
— Jean Giraudoux,
Tiger at the Gates, 1935

2000. That mysterious independent variable of political calculation, Public Opinion.
— T. H. Huxley,
Universities, Actual and Ideal,
1874

2001. Public opinion is the thermometer a monarch should constantly consult.
— Napoleon Bonaparte,
Maxims, 1804–15

2002. Public opinion in this country is everything.
— Abraham Lincoln, speech,
September 16, 1859

2003. The more opinions you have, the less you see.
— Wim Wenders, in
Evening Standard, April 25, 1990

2004. Opinion is that exercise of the human will which helps us to make a decision without information.
— John Erskine,
The Complete Life, 1943

2005. Public opinion exists only where there are no ideas.
— Oscar Wilde, in
Saturday Review,
November 17, 1894

2006. We accumulate our opinions at an age when our understanding is at its weakest.
— G. C. Lichtenberg,
Aphorisms, 1765–99

2007. Opinion is ultimately determined by the feelings, and not by the intellect.
— Herbert Spencer,
Social Statics, 1851

2008. What we call public opinion is generally public sentiment.
— Benjamin Disraeli, speech,
August 3, 1880

2009. Opinions have vested interests just as men have.
— Samuel Butler,
Note-Books, 1912

2010. The history of the world is the record of the weakness, frailty and death of public opinion.
— Samuel Butler,
Note-Books, 1912

2011. New opinions are always suspected, and usually opposed, without any other reason but because they are not always common.
— John Locke,
*An Enquiry Concerning
Human Understanding*,
1690

2012. I have grown tired of standing in the lean and lonely front line facing the greatest enemy that ever confronted man — public opinion.
— Clarence Darrow,
The Story of My Life, 1932

2013. We can never be sure that the opinion we are endeavoring to stifle is a false opinion; and even if we were sure, stifling it would be an evil still.
— John Stuart Mill,
On Liberty, 1859

2014. I am very fond of truth, but not at all of martyrdom.
— Voltaire, letter, February, 1776

2015. A plague of opinion! A man may wear it on both sides, like a leather jerkin.
— William Shakespeare,
Troilus and Cressida, 1602

2016. Public opinion is a permeating influence, and it exacts obedience to itself; it requires us to think other men's thoughts, to speak other men's words, to follow other men's habits.
— Walter Bagehot,
Biographical Studies, 1907

2017. In the United States today, we have more than our share of the nattering nabobs of negativism. They have formed their own 4-H club — the "hopeless, hysterical, hypochondriacs of history."
— Spiro Agnew, speech,
September 11, 1970

2018. One should respect public opinion in so far as is necessary to avoid starvation and to keep out of prison, but anything that goes beyond this is voluntary submission to an unnecessary tyranny.
— Bertrand Russell,
The Conquest of Happiness, 1930

2019. The idea of what the public will think prevents the public from ever thinking at all, and acts as a spell on the exercise of private judgment.
— William Hazlitt,
Table Talk, 1821–22

2020. Public opinion, the fear of losing public confidence, apprehension of

censure by the press make all men in power conservative and safe.
— Rutherford B. Hayes,
Diary, October 22, 1876

2021. There is nothing that makes more cowards and feeble men than public opinion.
— Henry Ward Beecher,
Proverbs from Plymouth Pulpit,
1887

2022. There are certain times when public opinion is the worst of all opinions.
— Sébastien-Roch Nicholas de Chamfort, *Maxims*, 1796

2023. A study of the history of opinion is a necessary preliminary to the emancipation of the mind.
— John Maynard Keynes,
The End of Laissez-Faire, 1926

2024. Public opinion, a vulgar, impertinent, anonymous tyrant who deliberately makes life unpleasant for anyone who is not content to be the average man.
— William Ralph Inge,
Outspoken Essays, First Series,
1919

2025. The world will only, in the end, follow those who have been despised as well as served it.
— Samuel Butler,
Note-Books, 1912

2026. Public opinion is the mixed result of the intellect of the community acting upon general feeling.
— William Hazlitt,
The Literary Examiner, 1823

2027. Difference of opinion leads to inquiry, and inquiry to truth.
— Thomas Jefferson, letter,
March 13, 1815

2028. The man who never alters his

opinion is like standing water, and breeds reptiles of the mind.
— William Blake,
The Marriage of Heaven and Hell,
1790

2029. The public buys its opinions as it buys its meat, or takes in its milk, on the principle that it is cheaper to do this than to keep a cow. So it is, but the milk is more likely to be watered.
— Samuel Butler,
Note-Books, 1912

2030. Thus to be independent of public opinion is the first formal condition of achieving anything great or rational whether in life or in science.
— Georg Wilhelm Friedrich Hegel, *The Philosophy of Right,*
1821

2031. Opinions are a private matter. The public has an interest only in judgments.
— Walter Benjamin, in
Frankfurter Zeitung, 1931

2032. The opinion of the strongest is always the best.
— Jean de La Fontaine,
Fables, 1668

2033. Public opinion is a weak tyrant compared with our own private opinion.
— Henry David Thoreau,
Walden, 1854

2034. Private opinion creates public opinion. Public opinion overflows eventually into national behavior and national behavior ... can make or mar the world. That is why private opinion, and private behavior, and private conversation are so terrifyingly important.
— Jan Struther,
A Pocketful of Pebbles, 1946

Rank *see* Military Command

Rebellion

See also Civil War; Revolution

2035. Rebellion lay in his way, and he found it.
— William Shakespeare,
Henry IV, Part I, 1597

2036. I hold it, that a little rebellion, now and then, is a good thing, and as necessary in the political world as storms in the physical.
— Thomas Jefferson, letter,
January 30, 1787

2037. It is not rebellion itself which is noble but the demands it makes upon us.
— Albert Camus,
The Plague, 1947

2038. No one can go on being a rebel too long without turning into an autocrat.
— Lawrence Durrell,
Balthazar, 1958

2039. If there is no right of rebellion against a state of things that no savage tribe would endure without resistance, then I am sure that it is better for men to fight and die without than to live in such a state of right as this.
— Roger Casement, speech,
June 29, 1916

2040. Every act of rebellion expresses a nostalgia for innocence and an appeal to the essence of being.
— Albert Camus, *The Rebel,* 1951

2041. As a dimension of man, rebellion actually defines him.
— Robert Lindner,
Must You Conform? 1956

2042. What is a rebel? A man who says no.
— Albert Camus, *The Rebel,* 1951

2043. This people hath a revolting and a rebellious heart.
— Bible, *Jeremiah* 5:23

Reform

See also Revolution

2044. An invasion of armies can be resisted; an invasion of ideas cannot be resisted.
— Victor Hugo,
Historie d'un crime, 1877

2045. A state without the means of some change is without the means of its conservation.
— Edmund Burke, *Reflections on the Revolution in France,* 1790

2046. Reform, that you may preserve.
— Thomas Babington, debate,
March 2, 1831

2047. Men must be capable of imagining and executing and insisting on social change if they are to reform or even maintain civilization, and capable too of furnishing the rebellion which is sometimes necessary if society is not to perish of immobility.
— Rebecca West,
The Meaning of Treason, 1949

2048. Every social war is a battle between the very few on both sides who care and who fire their shots across a crowd of spectators.
— Murray Kempton,
Part of Our Time, 1955

2049. Attempts at reform, when they fail, strengthen despotism, as he that struggles tightens those cords he does not succeed in breaking.
— Charles Caleb Colton,
Lacon, 1820–22

2050. Every reform, however necessary, will by weak minds be carried to an excess which will itself need reforming.
— Samuel Taylor Coleridge,
Biographia Literaria, 1817

2051. The lunatic fringe in all reform movements.
— Theodore Roosevelt,
Autobiography, 1913

2052. Every abuse ought to be reformed, unless the reform is more dangerous than the abuse itself.
— Voltaire,
Philosophical Dictionary, 1764

2053. A reform is a correction of abuses; a revolution is a transfer of power.
— Edward Bulwar-Lytton,
speech, 1866

2054. Beginning reform is beginning revolution.
— Arthur Wellesley,
Duke of Wellington, letter,
November 7, 1830

2055. Every man is a reformer until reform tramps on his toes.
— Edgar Watson Howe,
Country Town Sayings, 1911

2056. Unless the reformer can invent something which substitutes attractive virtues for attractive vices, he will fail.
— Walter Lippmann,
A Preface to Politics, 1913

2057. Every reform was once a private opinion, and when it shall be a private opinion again, it will solve the problem of the age.
— Ralph Waldo Emerson,
Essays, First Series, 1841

2058. It is one of the consolations of middle-aged reformers that the good they inculcate must live after them if it is to live at all.
— Saki, *Beasts and Super-Beasts*,
1914

2059. Nobody expects to find comfort and companionability in reformers.
— Heywood Broun, in *New York World*, February 6, 1928

2060. All reformers are bachelors.
— George Moore,
The Bending of the Bough, 1900

2061. The best reformers the world has ever seen are those who commence on themselves.
— George Bernard Shaw, in
E. Esar, *The Dictionary of Humorous Quotations*, 1949

2062. All Reformers, however strict their social conscience, live in houses just as big as they can pay for.
— Logan Pearsall Smith,
Afterthoughts, 1931

Resolve

See also Courage; Duty; Honor

2063. Not by speeches and majority decisions will the greatest problems of the time be decided ... but by Blood and Iron.
— Otto von Bismarck, speech,
September 30, 1862

2064. You ask what is our policy? I will say, it is to wage war by sea, land, and air, with all our might and with all the strength that God can give us.
— Winston S. Churchill, speech,
May 13, 1940

2065. It is not a field of a few acres of ground, but a cause, that we are defending, and whether we defeat the enemy in

one battle, or by degrees, the consequence will be the same.
— Thomas Paine, in
The American Crisis, 1776–83

2066. Americans never quit.
— Douglas MacArthur, in
New York Times, August 9, 1928

2067. A majority can do anything.
— Joseph G. Cannon, in
Baltimore Sun, March 4, 1923

2068. Germany will either be a world power or will not be at all.
— Adolf Hitler,
Mein Kampf, 1924

2069. Assassinate me you may; intimidate me you cannot.
— John Philpot Curran,
Defense of Rebels, 1798

2070. There is no working middle course in wartime.
— Winston S. Churchill,
speech, July 2, 1942

2071. The Egyptians could run to Egypt, the Syrians into Syria. The only place we could run was into the sea, and before we did that we might as well fight.
— Golda Meir, in *Life,*
October 3, 1969

2072. There is no longer a way out of our present situation except by forging a road toward our objective, violently and by force, over a sea of blood and under a horizon blazing with fire.
— Gamal Abdel Nasser, speech,
November 6, 1969

2073. I am sailing out along parallel 32.5 to stress that this is the Libyan border. This is the line of death where we shall stand and fight with our backs to the wall.
— Muammar Qaddafi,
challenge to the United States
Sixth Fleet, in *New York Times,*
January 26, 1986

2074. We shall go on to the end, we shall fight in France, we shall fight on the seas and oceans, we shall fight with growing confidence and growing strength in the air, we shall defend our island, whatever the cost may be, we shall fight on the beaches, we shall fight on the landing grounds, we shall fight in the fields and in the streets, we shall fight in the hills; we shall never surrender.
— Winston S. Churchill, speech,
June 4, 1940

Revolution

See also Rebellion; Revolution Is … ;
Revolutionaries

2075. In revolutions the occasions may be trifling but great interests are at stake.
— Aristotle, *Politics,* 4th c. B.C.

2076. Not actual suffering but the hope of better things incites people to revolt.
— Eric Hoffer,
The Ordeal of Change, 1964

2077. The seed of revolution is repression.
— Woodrow Wilson, message to
Congress, December 2, 1919

2078. The right of revolution is an inherent one. When people are oppressed by their government, it is a natural right they enjoy to relieve themselves of the oppression, if they are strong enough, whether by withdrawal from it, or by overthrowing it, and substituting a government more acceptable.
— Ulysses S. Grant,
Personal Memoirs, 1885

2079. The oppressed are always morally in the right.
— Robert Briffault,
Rational Evolution, 1930

2080. An oppressed people are authorized whenever they can to rise and break their fetters.
— Henry Clay, speech,
March 4, 1818

2081. Oppression that is clearly inexorable and invincible does not give rise to revolt but to submission.
— Simone Weil,
Factory Journal, 1934–35

2082. Those who make peaceful revolution impossible will make violent revolution inevitable.
— John F. Kennedy, speech,
March 12, 1962

2083. Great political and social changes begin to be possible as soon as men are not afraid to risk their lives.
— Thomas Masaryk, letter,
March 16, 1917

2084. To gain that which is worth having, it may be necessary to lose everything else.
— Bernadette Devlin McAliskey,
The Price of My Soul, 1969

2085. If a man hasn't discovered something that he will die for, he isn't fit to live.
— Martin Luther King, Jr.,
speech, June 23, 1963

2086. All successful revolutions are the kicking in of a rotten door. The violence of revolutions is the violence of men who charge into a vacuum.
— John Kenneth Galbraith,
The Age of Uncertainty, 1977

2087. You can never have a revolution in order to establish a democracy. You must have a democracy in order to have a revolution.
— Gilbert K. Chesterton,
Tremendous Trifles, 1909

2088. Clemency is also a revolutionary measure.
— Camille Desmoulins, speech,
July 14, 1789

2089. All civilization has from time to time become a thin crust over a volcano of revolution.
— Havelock Ellis, *Little Essays of Love and Virtue*, 1922

2090. All great movements are popular movements. They are the volcanic eruptions of human passions and emotions, stirred into activity by the ruthless Goddess of Distress or by the torch of the spoken word cast into the midst of the people.
— Adolf Hitler,
Mein Kampf, 1924

2091. A revolution only lasts fifteen years, a period which coincides with the effectiveness of a generation.
— José Ortega y Gasset,
The Revolt of the Masses, 1930

2092. States, like men, have their growth, their manhood, their decripitude, their decay.
— Walter Savage Landor,
Imaginary Conversations, 1824–53

2093. The main effect of a real revolution is perhaps that it sweeps away those who do not know how to wish and brings to the front men with insatiable appetites for action, power and all that the world has to offer.
— Eric Hoffer,
The Passionate State of Mind,
1954

2094. If there is one safe generalization in human affairs, it is that revolutions always destroy themselves.
— William Ralph Inge,
Outspoken Essays, First Series,
1919

2095. Make the Revolution a parent of settlement, and not a nursery of future revolutions.
— Edmund Burke, *Reflections on the Revolution in France*, 1790

2096. The main object of a revolution is the liberation of man ... not the interpretation and application of some transcendental ideology.
— Jean Genet,
Prisoner of Love, 1986

2097. The revolutionary spirit is mighty convenient in this, that it frees one from all scruples as regards ideas.
— Joseph Conrad,
A Personal Record, 1912

2098. The spirit of revolution, the spirit of insurrection, is a spirit radically opposed to liberty.
— François Guizot, speech,
December 29, 1830

2099. Revolutions conducted in the name of liberty more often than not refine new tools of authority.
— Henry Kissinger,
White House Years, 1979

2100. When the people contend for their liberty they seldom get anything by their victory but new masters.
— George Savile, *Political, Moral and Miscellaneous Thoughts and Reflections*, 1750

2101. Armed insurrection stands in the same relation to revolution as revolution as a whole does to evolution.
— Leon Trotsky,
The History of the Russian Revolution, 1933

2102. Insurrection — by means of guerrilla bands — is the true method of warfare for all nations desirous of emancipating themselves from a foreign yoke ...It is invincible, indestructible.
— Giuseppe Mazzini,
General Instructions for the Members of Young Italy, 1831

2103. The end justifies the means.
— Hermann Busenbaum,
Medulla Theologiae Moralis, 1650

2104. Assassination is the quickest way.
— Molière, *Le Sicilien*, 1668

2105. Assassination is the extreme form of censorship.
— George Bernard Shaw,
The Showing Up of Blanco Posnet, 1911

2106. Assassination has never changed the history of the world.
— Benjamin Disraeli, speech,
May 1, 1865

2107. If obedience is the result of the instinct of the masses, revolt is the result of their thought.
— Napoleon Bonaparte,
Maxims, 1804–15

2108. Without a revolutionary theory there can be no revolutionary movement.
— Lenin, "What Is To Be Done?" 1902

2109. All the world over, I will back the masses against the classes.
— William E. Gladstone, speech,
June 28, 1886

2110. Who stops the revolution half way? The bourgeoisie.
— Victor Hugo,
Les Misérables, 1862

2111. The time to stop a revolution is at the beginning, not the end.
— Adlai Stevenson, speech,
September 9, 1952

2112. I have been ever of opinion that revolutions are not to be evaded.
— Benjamin Disraeli,
Coningsby, 1844

2113. Without revolution no new history can begin.
— Moses Hess,
The Philosophy of the Act, 1843

2114. It is the quality of revolutions not to go to old lines or old laws; but to break up both, and make new ones.
— Abraham Lincoln, speech,
January 12, 1848

2115. We used to think that revolutions are the cause of change. Actually it is the other way around: change prepares the ground for revolution.

— Eric Hoffer,
The Temper of Our Time, 1967

2116. The brutalities of progress are called revolutions. When they are over we realize this: that the human race has been roughly handled, but that it has advanced.

— Victor Hugo,
Les Misérables, 1862

2117. Never contend with a man who has nothing to lose.

— Baltasar Gracián,
The Art of Worldly Wisdom, 1647

2118. In revolutionary times the rich are always the people who are most afraid.

— Gerald White Johnson,
American Freedom and the Press,
1958

2119. By a revolution in the state, the fawning sycophant of yesterday is converted into the austere critic of the present hour.

— Edmund Burke, *Reflections on
the Revolution in France*, 1790

2120. Radicalism itself ceases to be radical when absorbed mainly in preserving its control over a society or an economy.

— Eric Hoffer,
The Passionate State of Mind,
1954

2121. The most radical revolutionary will become a conservative the day after the revolution.

— Hannah Arendt, in
New Yorker, September 12, 1970

2122. The worst of revolutions is a restoration.

— Charles J. Fox, speech,
December 10, 1785

2123. All modern revolutions have ended in a reinforcement of the State.

— Albert Camus, *The Rebel*, 1951

2124. The urge to save humanity is almost always only a false-face for the urge to rule it.

— H. L. Mencken,
Minority Report, 1956

2125. More and more, revolution has found itself delivered into the hands of its bureaucrats and doctrinaires on the one hand, and to the enfeebled and bewildered masses on the other.

— Albert Camus, *The Rebel*, 1951

2126. "Revolution" today is taken for granted, and in consequence becomes rather dull.

— Wyndham Lewis,
The Art of Being Ruled, 1926

2127. Revolution, in order to be creative, cannot do without either a moral or metaphysical rule to balance the insanity of history.

— Albert Camus, *The Rebel*, 1951

2128. All destruction, by violent revolution or however it be, is but new creation on a wider scale.

— Thomas Carlyle,
Heroes and Hero Worship, 1840

2129. Be not deceived. Revolutions do not be backward.

— Abraham Lincoln, speech,
May 19, 1856

2130. I know, and all the world knows, that revolutions never go backward.

— William Henry Seward,
speech, October, 1858

2131. Revolutions never go backwards.

— Wendell Phillips, speech,
February 17, 1861

2132. I am opposed to every war but one ... and that is the worldwide war of social revolution.

— Eugene V. Debs, speech,
June 16, 1918

2133. *Ça ira.* (Things will work out.)

— Anonymous, ca. 1790,
French Revolution

2134. You cannot make a revolution with silk gloves.

— Joseph Stalin, attributed

2135. All great truths begin as blasphemies.
— George Bernard Shaw,
Annajanska, 1919

2136. It takes a revolution to make a solution.
— Bob Marley, in
To the Point International,
September 12, 1977

2137. The wind of revolutions is not tractable.
— Victor Hugo,
Les Misérables, 1862

2138. Ten days that shook the world.
— John Reed, book title
(about the Bolshevik Revolution
in 1919)

2139. It was the best of times, it was the worst of times.
— Charles Dickens,
A Tale of Two Cities, 1859

Revolution Is ...

See also Revolution

2140. A revolution is not the same as inviting people to dinner, or writing an essay, or painting a picture ... A revolution is an insurrection, an act of violence by which one class overthrows another.
— Mao Zedong,
Selected Works of Mao Zedong,
1965

2141. A revolution is not an easy thing to pull off.
— Edmund G. Brown, Jr.,
in *New York Times,*
December 28, 1991

2142. Revolutions are as a rule not made arbitrarily.
— Leon Trotsky,
Where is Britain Going? 1926

2143. Revolution is what societies do instead of committing suicide, when the alternatives are exhausted and all the connections that bind men's lives to familiar patterns are cut.
— Andrew Kopkind,
in *New York Times Magazine,*
November 10, 1968

2144. Revolutions are the locomotives of history.
— Nikita Khrushchev, in
Pravda, May 8, 1957

2145. Revolution is the festival of the oppressed.
— Germaine Greer,
The Female Eunuch, 1970

2146. Revolutions are not made; they come. A revolution is as natural a growth as an oak. It comes out of the past. Its foundations are laid far back.
— Wendell Phillips, speech,
January 8, 1852

2147. A riot is a spontaneous outburst. A war is subject to advance planning.
— Richard M. Nixon, speech,
December 8, 1967

2148. Revolution is a transfer of property from class to class.
— Leon Samson,
The New Humanism, 1930

2149. Revolution is not the uprising against the existing order, but the setting-up of a new order contradictory to the traditional one.
— José Ortega y Gasset,
The Revolt of the Masses, 1930

2150. Revolutions are brought about by men, by men who think as men of action and act as men of thought.
— Kwame Nkrumah,
Consciencism, 1964

2151. Revolutions are always verbose.
— Leon Trotsky, *The History of the Russian Revolution*, 1933

2152. A great revolution is never the fault of the people, but of the government.
— Johann Wolfgang von Goethe, in J. Eckermann, *Conversations with Goethe*, January 4, 1824

2153. Revolutions are not made for export.
— Nikita Khrushchev, speech, January 27, 1959

2154. The Revolution is like Saturn — it eats its own children.
— Georg Büchner, *Danton's Death*, 1835

2155. Every successful revolt is termed a revolution, and every unsuccessful one a rebellion.
— Joseph Priestly, letter, 1791

2156. Revolutions are celebrated when they are no longer dangerous.
— Pierre Boulez, in *Guardian*, January 13, 1989

2157. Everywhere revolutions are painful yet fruitful gestations of a people: they shed blood but create light, they eliminate men but elaborate ideas.
— Manuel González Prada, *Horas de lucha*, 1908

2158. Insurrection is an art, and like all arts has its own laws.
— Leon Trotsky, *The History of the Russian Revolution*, 1933

Revolutionaries

See also Fanatics; Revolution

2159. Like other revolutionaries I can thank God for the reactionaries. They clarify the issue.
— R. G. Collingwood, *An Autobiography*, 1939

2160. The duty of every revolutionary is to make a revolution.
— Fidel Castro, in H. Matthews, *Castro*, 1969

2161. A true revolutionary despises the philanthropies whereby misery is abated and revolution delayed.
— John Updike, in *New Yorker*, February 26, 1966

2162. A mark of many successful revolutionaries is their distaste for construction projects once the smoke has cleared.
— Alistair Cooke, *Six Men*, 1977

2163. It is easier to run a revolution than a government.
— Ferdinand Marcos, in *Time*, June 6, 1977

2164. To be a revolutionary is to love your life enough to change it, to choose struggle instead of exile, to risk everything with only the glimmering hope of a world to win.
— Andrew Kopkind, in *New York Times Magazine*, November 10, 1968

2165. Thinkers prepare the revolution; bandits carry it out.
— Mariano Azuela, *The Flies*, 1918

2166. All revolutions invariably encourage bad characters and potential criminals. Traitors throw off the mask; they cannot contain themselves amidst the general confusion that seems to promise easy victims.
— Ferdinand Delacroix, *Journal*, 1860

2167. Revolutionary movements attract those who are not good enough for established institutions as well as those who are too good for them.
— George Bernard Shaw, *Androcles and the Lion*, 1913

2168. Revolution only needs good dreamers who remember their dreams.
— Tennessee Williams,
Camino Real, 1953

2169. Whether a revolution succeeds or miscarries, men of great hearts will always be the victims.
— Heinrich Heine, *Salon*, 1834

2170. A revolution requires of its leaders a record of unbroken infallibility; if they do not possess it, they are expected to invent it.
— Murray Kempton,
Part of Our Time, 1955

2171. If there were more extremists in evolutionary periods, there would be no revolutionary periods.
— Benjamin R. Tucker,
Instead of a Book, 1893

2172. To be radical is, in the best and only decent sense of the word, patriotic.
— Michael Harrington,
Fragments of the Century, 1973

2173. *Radical* simply means "grasping things at the root."
— Angela Davis, speech,
June 25, 1987

2174. It is love of candor that makes men radical thinkers.
— Eric Bentley,
Thirty Years of Treason, 1971

2175. A radical is one who speaks the truth.
— Charles Lindburgh, in *Labor*,
June 15, 1957

2176. The radical of one century is the conservative of the next.
— Mark Twain, *Notebook*, 1935

2177. The radical invents the views. When he has worn them out the conservative adopts them.
— Mark Twain, *Notebook*, 1935

2178. We are revolutionaries, we Americans — although we abhor revolutions which are not made by our rules.
— James O. Robertson, *American Myth, American Reality*, 1980

2179. Oh, I'm a good old rebel, that's what I am.
— Innes Randolph,
A Good Old Rebel, ca. 1870

2180. Normal life cannot sustain revolutionary attitudes for long.
— Milovan Djilas, in
Guardian, April 9, 1990

2181. The nature of the true revolutionist excludes all romanticism, all tenderness, all ecstasy, all love.
— Sergei Nechayev, in Gunther,
Inside Russia Today, 1958

2182. Every revolutionary ends by becoming either an oppressor or a heretic.
— Albert Camus, *The Rebel*, 1951

2183. A revolutionary party is a contradiction in terms.
— R. H. S. Crossman, in
New Statesman, 1939

2184. The successful revolutionary is a statesman, the unsuccessful one a criminal.
— Erich Fromm,
Escape from Freedom, 1941

2185. The scrupulous and the just, the noble, humane, and devoted natures; the unselfish and the intelligent may begin a movement — but it passes away from them. They are not the leaders of a revolution. They are its victims.
— Joseph Conrad,
Under Western Eyes, 1911

2186. In revolutions there are only two sorts of men, those who cause them and those who profit by them.
— Napoleon Bonaparte,
Maxims, 1804–15

2187. Only those who have nothing to lose ever revolt.
— Alexis de Tocqueville,
Democracy in America, 1835

2188. Inferiors revolt in order that they may be equal, and equals that they may be superior.
— Aristotle, *Politics*, 4th c. B.C.

Rulers

See also Fanatics; Greatness; Leadership

2189. History has taught me that rulers are much the same in all ages, and under all forms of government; that they are as bad as they dare to be.
— Samuel Taylor Coleridge,
letter, April, 1798

2190. The first who was king was a fortunate soldier.
— Voltaire, *Mérope*, 1743

2191. War should be the only study of a prince. He should consider peace only as a breathing-time, which gives him leisure to contrive, and furnishes ability to execute.
— Niccolò Machiavelli,
The Prince, 1513

2192. A man may build himself a throne of bayonets, but he cannot sit on it.
— William Ralph Inge,
Philosophy of Plotinus, 1923

2193. To rule is not so much a question of the heavy hand as the firm seat.
— José Ortega y Gasset,
The Revolt of the Masses, 1930

2194. They that govern the most make the least noise.
— John Selden, *Table Talk*, 1686

2195. The subject's love is the king's best guard.
— Thomas Fuller,
Gnomologia, 1732

2196. No man ruleth safely but he that is willingly ruled.
— Thomas à Kempis,
Imitation of Christ, ca. 1420

2197. Uneasy lies the head that wears a crown.
— William Shakespeare,
Henry IV, Part II, 1597

2198. It is not easy for a person to do any great harm when his tenure of office is short, whereas long possession begets tyranny.
— Aristotle, *Politics*, 4th c. B.C.

2199. Kings are like stars — they rise and set, they have / The worship of the world, but no repose.
— Percy Bysshe Shelley,
Hellas, 1821

2200. A king is a thing men have made for their own sakes, for quietness' sake. Just as in a family one man is appointed to buy the meat.
— John Selden, *Table Talk*, 1686

2201. The king's name is a tower of strength.
— William Shakespeare,
Richard III, 1591

2202. There is something behind the throne greater than the king himself.
— William Pitt, speech,
March 2, 1770

2203. It is not with the words and explanations of theory that nations are governed.
— Napoleon Bonaparte, letter,
January 9, 1810

2204. Civilization is the process of setting man free from men.
— Ayn Rand,
The Fountainhead, 1943

2205. They should rule who are able to rule best.
— Aristotle, *Politics*, 4th c. B.C.

2206. To give the throne to another man would be easy; to find a man who shall benefit the kingdom is difficult.
— Mencius, *Works*, 4th c. B.C.

2207. No cross, no crown.
— William Penn, title of
pamphlet, 1669

2208. The good of subjects is the end of kings.
— Daniel Defoe,
The True-Born Englishman, 1701

2209. What is a King?—a man condemned to bear / The public burden of the nation's care.
— Matthew Prior, *Solomon*, 1718

2210. The prince is the first servant of the state.
— Frederick the Great,
Memoirs of the House of Branden-burg, 1758

2211. *Noblesse oblige.* (Rank has its obligations.)
— Gaston Pierre Marc,
Maxims and Reflections, 1808

2212. To be / Omnipotent but friendless is to reign.
— Percy Bysshe Shelley,
Prometheus Unbound, 1818–19

2213. The foremost art of kings is the power to endure hatred.
— Seneca, *Hercules Furens*, ca. 50

2214. Whom hatred frights, / Let him not dream on sovereignty.
— Ben Jonson, *Sejanus*, 1603

2215. Every noble crown is, and on earth will forever be, a crown of thorns.
— Thomas Carlyle,
Past and Present, 1843

2216. To govern is always to choose among disadvantages.
— Charles DeGaulle, in
New York Times,
November 14, 1965

2217. It is never possible to rule innocently.
— Louis de Saint-Just, speech,
November 13, 1792

2218. No one can rule guiltlessly, and least of all those whom history compels to hurry.
— Edgar Snow,
Journey to the Beginning,
1958

2219. To rule over oneself is the first condition for one who would rule over others.
— José Ortega y Gasset,
Invertebrate Spain, 1922

2220. Many a crown shines spotless now / That yet was deeply sullied in the winning.
— Johann Friedrich von Schiller,
The Death of a Wallenstein, 1798

2221. New nobility is but the act of power, but ancient nobility is the act of time.
— Francis Bacon, *Essays*, 1625

2222. Every ruler is harsh whose rule is new.
— Aeschylus, *Prometheus Bound*,
ca. 490 B.C.

2223. It should be noted that when he seizes a state the new ruler ought to determine all the injuries that he will need to inflict. He should inflict them once and for all, and not have to renew them every day.
— Niccolò Machiavelli,
The Prince, 1513

2224. It is not by whining that one carries out the job of king.
— Napoleon Bonaparte, letter,
August 13, 1809

2225. Mix kindness with authority; and rule more by discretion than rigor.
— William Penn,
Some Fruits of Solitude, 1693

2226. A prince who gets a reputation for good nature in the first year of his reign, is laughed at in the second.
— Napoleon Bonaparte, letter,
April 4, 1807

2227. Only strong personalities can endure history; the weak ones are extinguished by it.
— Friedrich Wilhelm Nietzsche,
Thoughts Out of Season, 1874

2228. Ill can he rule the great that cannot reach the small.
— Edmund Spenser,
The Faerie Queene, 1596

2229. Vulgarity in a king flatters the majority of the nation.
— George Bernard Shaw,
Man and Superman, 1903

2230. *L'état c'est moi.* (I am the state.)
— Louis XIV, remark,
April 13, 1655

2231. The rulers of the state are the only ones who should have the privilege of lying, either at home or abroad; they may be allowed to lie for the good of the state.
— Plato, *The Republic*,
ca. 370 B.C.

2232. Put not your trust in princes.
— Bible, *Psalms* 146:3

2233. All kings is mostly rapscallions.
— Mark Twain,
Huckleberry Finn, 1884

2234. Once you touch the trappings of monarchy, like opening an Egyptian tomb, the inside is liable to crumble.
— Anthony Sampson,
Anatomy of Britain Today, 1965

2235. Sawdust Caesar.
— George Seldes, title of book
(referring to Mussolini), 1932

2236. All human things are subject to decay, / And when fate summons, monarchs must obey.
— John Dryden,
Mac Flecknow, 1682

2237. There is not a single crowned head in Europe whose talents or merits would entitle him to be elected a vestryman by the people of any parish in America.
— Thomas Jefferson, letter,
May 2, 1788

2238. A throne is only a bench covered with velvet.
— Napoleon Bonaparte,
Maxims, 1804–15

2239. A monarch is the most expensive of all forms of government, the regal state requiring a costly parade, and he who depends on his own power to rule, must strengthen that power by bribing the active and enterprising whom he cannot intimidate.
— James Fenimore Cooper,
The American Democrat, 1838

2240. Royalty is a government in which the attention of the nation is concentrated on one person doing interesting actions.
— Walter Bagehot,
The English Constitution, 1867

2241. Kings are not born: they are made by artificial hallucination.
— George Bernard Shaw,
Man and Superman, 1903

2242. Divine right of kings means the divine right of anyone who can get uppermost.
— Herbert Spencer,
Social Statics, 1851

2243. Give me my robe, put on my crown; I have / Immortal longings in me.
— William Shakespeare,
Antony and Cleopatra, 1606–07

2244. The way in which the man of genius rules is by persuading an efficient minority to coerce an indifferent and self-indulgent majority.
— James F. Stephen,
Liberty, Equality and Fraternity,
1873

2245. The metaphor of the king as the shepherd of his people goes back to ancient Egypt. Perhaps the use of this particular convention is due to the fact that, being stupid, affectionate, gregarious, and easily stampeded, the societies formed by sheep are most like human ones.
— Northrop Frye,
Anatomy of Criticism, 1957

2246. If the blind lead the blind, both shall fall into the ditch.
— Bible, *Matthew* 15:14

2247. In the kingdom of the blind the one-eyed man is king.
— Desiderius Erasmus,
Adagia, 1500

2248. Let us now praise famous men, and our fathers that begat us.
— Bible, *Ecclesiasticus* 44:1

2249. For God's sake, let us sit upon the ground / And tell sad stories of the death of kings.
— William Shakespeare, *Richard II*, 1595

2250. The king never dies.
— William Blackstone, *Commentaries*, 1765

2251. Woe to thee, O land, when thy king is a child, and thy princes eat in the morning.
— Bible, *Ecclesiastes* 10:16

2252. The king reigns, but does not govern.
— Jan Zamoyski, speech, 1605

2253. The king reigns, and the people govern themselves.
— Adolphe Thiers, in *Le National*, January 20, 1830

2254. The Right Divine of Kings to govern wrong.
— Alexander Pope, *Dunciad*, 1742

2255. The king can do no wrong.
— Proverb

2256. That the king can do no wrong is a necessary and fundamental principle of the English constitution.
— William Blackstone, *Commentaries*, 1765

Security

See also Alliances; Appeasement; Fear

2257. A nation has security when it does not have to sacrifice its legitimate interests to avoid war and is able, if challenged, to maintain them by war.
— Walter Lippmann, *U.S. Foreign Policy*, 1943

2258. No nation ever had an army large enough to guarantee it against attack in time of peace or insure it victory in time of war.
— Calvin Coolidge, speech, October 6, 1925

2259. He that has gone so far as to cut the claws of the lion, will not feel himself quite secure until he has also drawn his teeth.
— Charles Caleb Colton, *Lacon*, 1820–22

2260. Most people want security in this world, not liberty.
— H. L. Mencken, *Minority Report*, 1956

2261. There is no security on this earth; there is only opportunity.
— Douglas MacArthur, in C. Whitney, *MacArthur: His Rendezvous with History*, 1955

2262. Only in growth, reform, and change, paradoxically enough, is true security to be found.
— Anne Morrow Lindbergh, *The Wave of the Future*, 1940

2263. The world must be made safe for democracy.
— Woodrow Wilson, speech, April 2, 1917

2264. To keep oneself safe does not mean to bury oneself.
— Seneca, *Epistolae Morales*, 1st c.

2265. To you who call yourselves men of peace, I say: You are not safe unless you have men of action on your side.
— Thucydides, *History of the Peloponnesian War*, 431–413 B.C.

2266. It is the moral strength of democracy which alone can give any meaning to the efforts at military security.
— Marshall McLuhan,
Understanding Media, 1964

2267. No one can build his security upon the nobleness of another person.
— Willa Cather,
Alexander's Bridge, 1912

2268. The protected man doesn't need luck; therefore it seldom visits him.
— Alan Harrington,
Life in the Crystal Palace, 1959

2269. He that's secure is not safe.
— Benjamin Franklin,
Poor Richard's Almanack,
August, 1748

2270. Walls have tongues, and hedges ears.
— Jonathan Swift, "A Pastoral Dialogue between Richmond Lodge and Marble Hall," 1727

2271. Careless talk costs lives.
— slogan, First World War

2272. Loose lips sink ships.
— slogan, Second World War

2273. *Taisez-vous! Méfiez-vous! Les oreilles ennemies vous écoutent.* Keep your mouth shut! Be on your guard! Enemy ears are listening to you.)
— French slogan, 1915

2274. The Xerox machine is one of the biggest threats to national security ever devised.
— Thomas Moorer, in *Time*,
June 17, 1985

2275. If when the chips are down the world's most powerful nation ... acts like a pitiful, helpless giant, the forces of totalitarianism and anarchy will threaten free nations and free institutions throughout the world.
— Richard M. Nixon, speech,
April 30, 1970

Slavery

See also Freedom; Revolution

2276. There is a peace more destructive of the manhood of living man than war is destructive of his material body. Chains are worse than bayonets.
— Douglas Jerrold,
The Wit and Wisdom of Douglas Jerrold, 1859

2277. There are many things more horrible than bloodshed; and slavery is one of them.
— Padraic Pearse,
The Coming Revolution, 1913

2278. In the final choice a soldier's pack is not so heavy a burden as a prisoner's chains.
— Dwight D. Eisenhower,
inaugural address,
January 20, 1953

2279. It is better to die on your feet than to live on your knees.
— Dolores Ibarruri, speech,
September 3, 1936

2280. While it is true that an inherently free and scrupulous person may be destroyed, such an individual can never be enslaved or used as a blind tool.
— Albert Einstein, *Impact*, 1950

2281. Men would rather be starving and free than fed in bonds.
— Pearl S. Buck,
What America Means to Me, 1943

2282. Lean liberty is better than fat slavery.
— Thomas Fuller, *Gnomologia*, 1732

2283. Freedom has a thousand charms to show, / That slaves, howe'er contented, never know.
— William Cowper,
Table Talk, 1782

2284. Better to reign in hell, than serve in heaven.
— John Milton,
Paradise Lost, 1667

2285. Man alone can enslave man.
— Simone Weil,
Oppression and Liberty, 1958

2286. If you put a chain around the neck of a slave, the other end fastens itself around your own.
— Ralph Waldo Emerson,
Essays, First Series, 1841

2287. No man can put a chain about the ankle of his fellow man without at last finding the other end fastened about his own neck.
— Frederick Douglass, speech,
October 22, 1883

2288. Familiarize yourself with the chains of bondage and you prepare your own limbs to wear them.
— Abraham Lincoln, speech,
September 11, 1858

2289. Hatred, slavery's inevitable aftermath.
— José Martí,
Woman Suffrage, 1887

2290. There is no slavery but ignorance.
— Robert G. Ingersoll,
The Liberty of Man, Woman and Child, 1877

2291. He who is by nature not his own but another's man, is by nature a slave.
— Aristotle, *Politics*, 4th c. B.C.

2292. The first slaves were made so by force, the state of slavery was perpetuated by cowardice.
— Jean-Jacques Rousseau,
The Social Contract, 1762

2293. There are few men whom slavery holds fast, but there are many who hold fast to slavery.
— Seneca, *Epistolae Morales*, 1st c.

2294. Slaves lose everything in their chains, even the desire of escaping from them.
— Jean-Jacques Rousseau,
The Social Contract, 1762

2295. It's often better to be in chains than to be free.
— Franz Kafka, *The Trial*, 1925

2296. Man is born free, and everywhere he is in chains.
— Jean-Jacques Rousseau,
The Social Contract, 1762

2297. Not all are free who scorn their chains.
— Gotthold Ephraim Lessing,
Nathan der Weise, 1779

2298. Man is created free, and is free, / Though he be born in chains.
— Johann Friedrich von Schiller,
The Word of the Faithful, 1797

2299. Slavery they can have anywhere. It is a weed that grows in every soil.
— Edmund Burke, speech,
March 22, 1775

2300. They are slaves who fear to speak / For the fallen and the weak.
— James Russell Lowell,
Stanzas on Freedom, 1843

2301. For every man who lives without freedom, the rest of us must face the guilt.
— Lillian Hellman,
Watch on the Rhine, 1941

2302. If men and women are in chains, anywhere in the world, then freedom is endangered everywhere.
— John F. Kennedy, speech,
October 2, 1960

2303. Either be wholly slaves or wholly free.
— John Dryden,
The Hind and the Panther, 1687

2304. Where slavery is, there liberty cannot be; and where liberty is, there slavery cannot be.
— Charles Sumner, speech,
November 5, 1864

2305. The man who asks of freedom anything other than itself is born to be a slave.

— Alexis de Tocqueville, *The Old Regime and the French Revolution*, 1856

2306. I believe that no people ever yet groaned under the heavy yoke of slavery but when they deserved it.

— Samuel Adams, in *Independent Advertiser*, 1748

2307. The individual who refuses to defend his rights when called by his government, deserves to be a slave, and must be punished as an enemy of his country and friend to her foe.

— Andrew Jackson, proclamation, September 21, 1814

2308. The chains which men bear they have imposed upon themselves; strike them off, and they will weep for their lost security.

— John Passmore, *The Perfectibility of Man*, 1970

2309. Americans are so enamored of equality that they would rather be equal in slavery than unequal in freedom.

— Alexis de Tocqueville, *Democracy in America*, 1835

Slogans and Mottoes

See also Battle Cries

2310. Be happy while y'er leevin, / For y'er a lang time deid.

— Scottish motto

2311. Defense, not defiance.

— motto of the Volunteers Movement, 1859

2312. Dig for victory.

— Reginald Dorman-Smith, radio broadcast, October 3, 1939

2313. Don't tread on me.

— motto of the first design of the American flag

2314. *E pluribus unum.* (One out of many.)

— Virgil, *Moretum*, 1st c. B.C., original motto of the United States, replaced by Congress in 1956 with "In God We Trust."

2315. *Ein Reich, ein Volk, ein Führer.* (One realm, one people, one leader.)

— Nazi slogan, 1930s

2316. I have not yet begun to fight.

— John Paul Jones, response to demand for surrender, September 23, 1779, and the motto of the U.S. Navy

2317. I Want You.

— motto of the U.S. Army

2318. In God We Trust.

— official motto of the United States, 1956, replacing *E pluribus unum.*

2319. Keep 'em flying.

— Harold N. Gilbert, slogan of the U.S. Air Force

2320. Kilroy was here.

— slogan popularized in the U.S. army, Second World War

2321. *Liberté! Égalité! Fraternité!* (Freedom! Equality! Brotherhood!)

— motto of the French Revolution, originally a motion passed on June 30, 1793 by the *Club des Cordeliers.*

2322. *Nemo me impune lacessit.* (No one provokes me with impunity.)

— Scottish regimental motto.

2323. Rebellion to tyrants is obedience to God.

— motto on Thomas Jefferson's seal.

2324. *Semper Fidelis.* (Always Faithful.)

— motto of the U.S. Marine Corps.

2325. *Semper Paratus.* (Always Ready.)
— motto of the U.S. Coast Guard

2326. *Sic semper tyrannis!* (Thus always to tyrants!)
— motto of the state of Virginia (also declared by John Wilkes Booth upon shooting Abraham Lincoln, April 14, 1865)

2327. SNAFU (acronym, Situation Normal, All Fouled Up)
— slogan popularized in the U.S. Army, Second World War

2328. *Ubi libertas ibi patria.* (Where liberty is, there is my country.)
— James Otis, motto

2329. The Yanks are coming.
— slogan, First World War

Soldiers

See also Duty; Glory; Honor; Patriotism

2330. When soldiers have been baptized in the fire of a battlefield, they have all one rank in my eyes.
— Napoleon Bonaparte, in R. W. Emerson, *Representative Men*, 1850

2331. The world continues to offer glittering prizes to those who have stout hearts and sharp swords.
— F. E. Smith, speech, November 7, 1923

2332. To be a successful soldier you must know history.
— George S. Patton, letter, June 6, 1944

2333. Soldiers are dreamers; when the guns begin / They think of fire lit homes, clean beds, and wives.
— Siegfried Sassoon, *Dreamers*, 1918

2334. The soldier, above all other people, prays for peace, for he must suffer and bear the deepest wounds and scars of war.
— Douglas MacArthur, speech, May 12, 1962

2335. There are few men more superstitious than soldiers. They are, after all, the men who live closest to death.
— Mary Stewart, *The Last Enchantment*, 1979

2336. Boys are the cash of war.
— John Ciardi, *This Strangest Everything*, 1966

2337. Soldiers were made on purpose to be killed.
— Napoleon Bonaparte, to Gaspard Gourgaud, 1815

2338. Soldier, rest! Thy warfare o'er, / Sleep the sleep that knows not breaking, / Dream of battled fields no more, / Days of danger, nights of waking.
— Walter Scott, *The Lady of the Lake*, 1810

2339. A soldier is a Yahoo hired to kill in cold blood as many of his own species, who have never offended him, as possibly he can.
— Jonathan Swift, *Gulliver's Travels*, 1726

2340. When the rich wage war it is the poor who die.
— Jean-Paul Sartre, *The Devil and the Good Lord*, 1951

2341. No soldier starts a war — they only give their lives to it. Wars are started by you and me, by bankers and politicians, excitable women, newspaper editors, clergymen who are ex-pacifists, and Congressmen with vertebrae of putty. The youngsters yelling in the streets, poor kids, are the ones who pay the price.
— Francis P. Duffy, sermon, January, 1931

2342. Ireland gives England her soldiers, her generals too.
— George Meredith, *Diana of the Crossways*, 1885

2343. They were expendable.
— William L. White,
title of book, 1942

2344. Horribly stuffed with epithets of war.
— William Shakespeare,
Othello, 1602–04

2345. I never expect a soldier to think.
— George Bernard Shaw,
The Devil's Disciple, 1901

2346. Children play soldier. That makes sense. But why do soldiers play children?
— Karl Kraus,
Sprüche und Widersprüche, 1909

2347. Do you know what a soldier is, young man? He's the chap who makes it possible for civilized folk to despise war.
— Allen Massie, in Fernie,
A Question of Loyalties, 1989

2348. And but for these vile guns, /
He would himself have been a soldier.
— William Shakespeare,
Henry IV, Part I, 1597

Strategy and Tactics

See also Battles; Force; Strength

2349. The art of war is simple enough. Find out where your enemy is. Get at him as soon as you can. Strike at him as hard as you can and as often as you can, and keep moving on.
— Ulysses S. Grant,
attributed remark

2350. Despise the enemy strategically, but take him seriously tactically.
— Mao Zedong, in *Time*,
March 22, 1963

2351. If your enemy turns to flee, give him a silver bridge.
— Proverb

2352. He that is not with me is against me.
— Bible, *Matthew* 12:30

2353. A secret foe gives a sudden blow.
— Proverb

2354. Wherever the enemy goes let our troops go also.
— Ulysses S. Grant, dispatch,
August 1, 1864

2355. When the enemy advances, we retreat. When he camps, we harass. When he tires, we attack. When he retreats, we pursue.
— Mao Zedong, in E. Wright,
History of the World, 1969

2356. A government needs one hundred soldiers for every guerrilla it faces.
— Fulgeñcio Batista y Zaldivar,
in *El Caribe*, January 1, 1959

2357. That is the whole secret of successful fighting. Get your enemy at a disadvantage; and never, on any account, fight him on equal terms.
— George Bernard Shaw,
Arms and the Man, 1898

2358. I say when you get into a war, you should win as quick as you can, because your losses become a function of the duration of the war. I believe when you get in a war, get everything you need and win it.
— Dwight D. Eisenhower, in
New York Times, March 16, 1968

2359. Never before have we had so little time in which to do so much.
— Franklin D. Roosevelt,
fireside chat, February 23, 1942

2360. Delays breed dangers.
— John Lyly,
Euphues: The Anatomy of Wit,
1579

2361. Delays have dangerous ends.
— William Shakespeare,
Henry VI, Part I, 1592

2362. All delays are dangerous in war.
— John Dryden,
Tyrannic Love, 1669

2363. The god of war hates him who hesitates.
— Euripedes, attributed

2364. It is all right to hesitate if you then go ahead.
— Bertolt Brecht,
The Good Woman of Setzuan,
1938–40

2365. In war nothing is impossible, provided you use audacity.
— George S. Patton,
War As I Knew It, 1947

2366. You must not fight too often with one enemy, or you will teach him all your art of war.
— Napoleon Bonaparte,
in R. E. Emerson,
Representative Men, 1850

2367. In crisis the most daring course is often safest.
— Henry Kissinger,
Years of Upheaval, 1982

2368. Take calculated risks. That is quite different from being rash.
— George S. Patton, letter,
June 6, 1944

2369. All the business of war, and indeed all the business of life, is to endeavor to find out what you don't know from what you do; that's what I call "guessing at what is on the other side of the hill."
— Arthur Wellesley,

Duke of Wellington, letter,
September 3, 1852

2370. Blunders are an inescapable feature of war, because choice in military affairs lies generally between the bad and the worse.
— Allan Massie, in Fernie,
A Question of Loyalties, 1989

2371. I fear all we have done is to awaken a sleeping giant and fill him with a terrible resolve.
— Isoruku Yamamoto, attributed
remark about the United States,
after the attack on Pearl Harbor,
December 7, 1941

2372. A horse! A horse! My kingdom for a horse.
— William Shakespeare,
Richard III, 1591

2373. An army marches on its stomach.
— Napoleon Bonaparte,
attributed

2374. In the end it is how you fight, as much as why you fight, that makes your cause good or bad.
— Freeman Dyson,
Disturbing the Universe, 1979

2375. All warfare is based on deception.
— Sun Tzu, *The Art of War*,
ca. 500 B.C.

2376. All policy's allowed in war and love.
— Susannah Centlivre,
Love at a Venture, 1706

2377. All's fair in love and war.
— Francis E. Smedley,
Frank Fairlegh, 1850

Strength

See also Aggression; Conflict; Expansion;
Force; Morale; Public Opinion

2378. The gods are on the side of the stronger.
— Cornelius Tacitus,
Histories, ca. 100

2379. As you know, God is usually on the side of the big squadrons against the small.
— Roger de Bussy-Rabutin,
letter, October 18, 1677

2380. God is on the side not of the heavy battalions, but of the best shots.
— Voltaire,
"The Piccini Notebooks,"
ca. 1750

2381. The winds and waves are always on the side of the ablest navigators.
— Edward Gibbon,
The Decline and Fall of the Roman Empire, 1776–88

2382. God is on everyone's side … in the last analysis, he is on the side of those with plenty of money and large armies.
— Jean Anouilh, *L'Alouette*, 1953

2383. To insist on strength … is not war-mongering. It is peace-mongering.
— Barry Goldwater, in
New York Times, August 11, 1964

2384. We have unmistakable proof that throughout all past time, there has been a ceaseless devouring of the weak by the strong.
— Herbert Spencer,
First Principles, 1861

2385. We live under a system by which the many are exploited by the few, and war is the ultimate sanction of that exploitation.
— Harold Laski,
Plan or Perish, 1945

2386. He who tugs Uncle Sam's beard too hard risks reprisal from the mightiest nation on the face of this earth.
— George McGovern, in
Observer, November 25, 1979

2387. Of the four wars in my lifetime, none came about because the U.S. was too strong.
— Ronald Reagan, in *Observer*,
June 29, 1980

2388. We shall win because we are the stronger.
— Paul Reynaud, speech,
September 10, 1939

2389. Freedom belongs to the strong.
— Richard Wright,
Long Black Song, 1936

2390. Once the bear's hug has got you, it is apt to be for keeps.
— Harold Macmillan,
regarding Communist expansion,
in *New York Herald Tribune*,
October 15, 1961

2391. In this age when there can be no losers in peace and victors in war — we must recognize the obligation to match national strength with national restraint.
— Lyndon B. Johnson, speech,
November 27, 1963

2392. Soft countries give birth to soft men.
— Herodotus, *The History*,
ca. 450 B.C.

2393. Human kindness has never weakened the stamina or softened the fiber of a free people. A nation does not have to be cruel to be tough.
— Franklin D. Roosevelt,
radio address, October 13, 1940

2394. Let us have faith that right makes might, and in that faith let us to the end do our duty as we understand it.
— Abraham Lincoln, speech,
February 27, 1860

2395. It is right that what is just should be obeyed; it is necessary that what is strongest should be obeyed.

—Blaise Pascal, *Pensées*, 1670

2396. Might makes right.

—Seneca, *Hercules Furens*, ca. 50

2397. Strength lies not in defense but in attack.

—Adolf Hitler, *Mein Kampf*, 1924

2398. The most important thing is to be strong. With strength, one can conquer others, and to conquer others gives one virtue.

—Mao Zedong, in *Time*, September 20, 1976

2399. The race is not to the swift, nor the battle to the strong.

—Bible, *Ecclesiastes* 9:11

2400. The race is to the swift, / The battle to the strong.

—John Davidson, "War Song," 1899

2401. The battle, sir, is not to the strong alone; it is to the vigilant, the active, the brave.

—Patrick Henry, speech, March 23, 1775

2402. The strongest of all warriors are these two—Time and Patience.

—Leo Tolstoy, *War and Peace*, 1865–69

2403. In a really just cause the weak conquers the strong.

—Sophocles, *Oedipus at Colonus*, 406 B.C.

2404. How many divisions has the Pope?

—Joseph Stalin, in *New York Times*, October 8, 1958

Tradition *see* History

Treason

See also Pacifism; Patriotism; Rebellion; Revolution

2405. Treason doth never prosper, what's the reason? / For if it prosper, none dare call it treason.

—John Harington, *Epigrams*, 1618

2406. If this be treason, make the most of it.

—Patrick Henry, speech, May 29, 1765

2407. All men should have a drop of treason in their veins, if nations are not to go soft like to many sleepy pears.

—Rebecca West, *The Meaning of Treason*, 1949

2408. The minority is always right.

—Henrik Ibsen, *An Enemy of the People*, 1882

2409. Treason in our time is a proof of genius. Why, I want to know, are not traitors decorated?

—Antoine de Saint-Exupéry, *Flight to Arras*, 1942

2410. The treason pleases, but the traitors are odious.

—Miguel de Cervantes, *Don Quixote*, 1605–15

2411. If I had to choose between betraying my country and betraying my friend, I hope I should have the guts to betray my country.

—E. M. Forster, *Two Cheers for Democracy*, 1951

2412. They talk of a man betraying his country, his friends, his sweetheart. There must be a moral bond first. All a man can betray is his conscience.

— Joseph Conrad,
Under Western Eyes, 1911

Treaties

See also Alliances; Diplomacy; Foreign Policy;
International Relations

2413. Treaties are observed as long as they are in harmony with interests.
— Napoleon Bonaparte,
Maxims, 1804–15

2414. Treaties are like roses and young girls. They last while they last.
— Charles DeGaulle, in
Time, July 12, 1963

2415. This is not a peace treaty, it is an armistice for twenty years.
— Ferdinand Foch, statement
at the signing of the Treaty of
Versailles, 1919

2416. The only treaties that ought to count are those which would effect a settlement between ulterior motives.
— Paul Valéry, *Reflections on the
World Today*, 1931

2417. Peace must have other guarantees than constitutions and covenants. Laws and treaties may help, but peace and war are attitudes of mind.
— Calvin Coolidge, speech,
September 6, 1924

2418. All treaties between great states cease to be binding when they come in conflict with the struggle for existence.
— Otto von Bismarck, attributed

2419. The fidelity of the United States to security treaties is not just an empty matter. It is a pillar of peace in the world.
— Dean Rusk, in *New York Times*,
April 30, 1985

2420. There can be no greater error than to expect or calculate upon real favors from nation to nation.
— George Washington,
farewell address,
September 17, 1796

2421. There is nothing more likely to start disagreement among people or countries than an agreement.
— E. B. White,
One Man's Meat, 1944

2422. When envoys are sent with compliments in their mouths, it is a sign that the enemy wishes for a truce.
— Sun Tzu, *The Art of War*,
ca. 500 B.C.

2423. More history's made by secret handshakes than by battles, bills, and proclamations.
— John Barth,
The Sot-Weed Factor, 1960

2424. You cannot shake hands with a clenched fist.
— Indira Gandhi,
in *Christian Science Monitor*,
May 17, 1982

2425. Bullets cannot be recalled. They cannot be uninvented. But they can be taken out of the gun.
— Martin Amis,
Einstein's Monsters, 1987

2426. The greatest honor history can bestow is the title of peacemaker.
— Richard M. Nixon,
inaugural address,
January 20, 1969

Tyranny

See also Fanatics; Freedom; Power; Rulers; Slavery

2427. No power ought to be above the laws.
— Cicero, *De Domo Sua*, 57 B.C.

2428. Wherever law ends, tyranny begins.
— John Locke, *Second Treatise of Government*, 1690

2429. As soon as the prince sets himself up above the law, he loses the king in the tyrant; he does to all intents and purpose unking himself.
— Jonathan Mayhew, *A Discourse concerning Unlimited Submission and Non-Resistance to the Higher Powers*, 1750

2430. Tyranny, like hell, is not easily conquered.
— Thomas Paine, in *The American Crisis*, 1776–83

2431. We grow tyrannical fighting tyranny.
— E. B. White, letter, April 27, 1952

2432. Old forms of government finally grow so oppressive that they must be thrown off even at the risk of reigns of terror.
— Herbert Spencer, *Education*, 1861

2433. We are not to expect to be translated from despotism to liberty in a feather bed.
— Thomas Jefferson, letter, April 2, 1790

2434. The willing sacrifice of the innocents is the most powerful retort to insolent tyranny that has yet been conceived by God or man.
— Mohandas K. Gandhi, in *Young India*, February 12, 1925

2435. The face of tyranny is always mild at first.
— Jean Racine, *Britannicus*, 1669

2436. Whoever has power in his hands wants to be despotic; the craze for domination is an incurable disease.
— Voltaire, letter, October 16, 1765

2437. O, it is excellent / To have a giant's strength, but it is tyrannous / To use it like a giant.
— William Shakespeare, *Measure for Measure*, 1604

2438. People complain of the despotism of princes; they ought to complain of the despotism of man.
— Joseph de Maistre, *Study on Sovereignty*, 1884

2439. Tyranny is always better organized than freedom.
— Charles Péguy, *Basic Verities*, 1943

2440. No country can be really well prepared for modern war unless it is governed by a tyrant, at the head of a highly trained and perfectly obedient bureaucracy.
— Aldous Huxley, *Ends and Means,* 1937

2441. The more complex the despotism, the more smoothly all things move on the surface.
— Elizabeth Cady Stanton, *History of Woman Suffrage*, 1881

2442. I suspect that in our loathing of totalitarianism, there is infused a good deal of admiration for its efficiency.
— T. S. Eliot, "The Idea of a Christian Society," 1939

2443. The totalitarian state is not power unchained, it is truth unchained.
— Bernard-Henry Lévy, *La Barbarie à visage humain*, 1977

2444. The only successful revolution of this century is totalitarianism.
— Bernard-Henry Lévy, in *Time*, September 12, 1977

2445. Revolutions have never lightened the burden of tyranny; they have only shifted it to another shoulder.
— George Bernard Shaw,
Man and Superman, 1903

2446. Every successful revolution puts on in time the robe of the tyrant it has deposed.
— Barbara Tuchman, attributed

2447. Government is an association of men who do violence against the rest of us.
— Leo Tolstoy, *The Kingdom of God Is Within You*, 1893

2448. I am the people — the mob — the crowd — the mass. / Do you know that all the great work of the world is done through me?
— Carl Sandburg,
I Am the People, the Mob, 1916

2449. The tyranny of a multitude is a multiplied tyranny.
— Edmund Burke, letter,
February 26, 1790

2450. Our supreme governors, the mob.
— Horace Walpole, letter,
September 7, 1943

2451. Great bodies of people are never responsible for what they do.
— Virginia Woolf,
A Room of One's Own, 1929

2452. When a nation has allowed itself to fall under a tyrannical regime, it cannot be absolved from the faults due to the guilt of that regime.
— Winston S. Churchill, message,
July 28, 1944

2453. Tyranny and despotism can be exercised by many, more rigorously, more vigorously, and more severely, than by one.
— Andrew Johnson, speech,
April 8, 1866

2454. We are more wicked together than separately. If you are forced to be in a crowd, then most of all you should withdraw into your self.
— Seneca, *Epistolae Morales*, 1st c.

2455. The mob has many heads but no brains.
— Thomas Fuller,
Gnomologia, 1732

2456. Mobs in their emotions are much like children, / subject to the same tantrums and fits of fury.
— Euripedes, *Orestes*, 408 B.C.

2457. The nose of a mob is its imagination. By this, at anytime, it can be quietly led.
— Edgar Allan Poe,
Marginalia, 1844–49

2358. When the multitude detests a man, inquiry is necessary; when the multitude likes a man, inquiry is equally necessary.
— Confucius, *Analects*,
ca. 480 B.C.

2459. Freedom of thought is the only guarantee against an infection of people by mass myths, which, in the hands of treacherous hypocrites and demagogues, can be transformed into bloody dictatorships.
— Andrei Sakharov,
Progress, Coexistence and Intellectual Freedom, 1968

2460. It has been discovered that the best way to insure implicit obedience is to commence tyranny in the nursery.
— Benjamin Disraeli, speech,
June 15, 1874

2461. Tyranny is a habit; it may develop, and it does develop at last, into a disease.
— Fyodor Dostoevski,
The House of the Dead, 1862

2462. The true courage of civilized nations is readiness for sacrifice in the service of the state, so that the individual counts as only one amongst many. The important thing here is not personal mettle but aligning oneself with the universal.
— Georg Wilhelm Friedrich Hegel,
The Philosophy of Right, 1821

2463. Except as its clown and jester, society does not encourage individuality, and the State abhors it.
— Bernard Berenson,
Aesthetics and History, 1948

2464. Whatever crushes individuality is despotism, by whatever name it may be called.
— John Stuart Mill,
On Liberty, 1859

2465. I have sworn upon the altar of God, eternal hostility against every form of tyranny over the mind of man.
— Thomas Jefferson, letter,
September 23, 1800

2466. Tyrants have not yet discovered any chains that can fetter the mind.
— Charles Caleb Colton,
Lacon, 1820–22

2467. Enlighten the people generally, and tyranny and oppressions of body and mind will vanish like evil spirits at the dawn of day.
— Thomas Jefferson, letter,
April 24, 1816

2468. Make men large and strong, and tyranny will bankrupt itself in making shackles for them.

— Henry Ward Beecher, *Proverbs from Plymouth Pulpit*, 1887

2469. Oppression makes the wise man mad.
— Robert Browning, *Luria*, 1846

2470. The most potent weapon in the hands of the oppressor is the mind of the oppressed.
— Steve Biko, speech, 1971

2471. The history of an oppressed people is hidden in the lies and the agreed-upon myths of its conquerors.
— Meridel Le Sueur,
Crusaders, 1955

2472. The more a regime claims to be the embodiment of liberty, the more tyrannical it is likely to be.
— Ian Gilmour, *Inside Right*, 1977

2473. Persecution is the first law of society because it is always easier to suppress criticism than to meet it.
— Howard Mumford Jones,
Primer of Intellectual Freedom,
1949

2474. You have not converted a man because you have silenced him.
— John Morley, *On Compromise*,
1874

Tyrants

See also Power; Revolution; Tyranny

2475. A tyrant ... is always stirring up some war or other, in order that the people may require a leader.
— Plato, *The Republic*,
ca. 370 B.C.

2476. Any excuse will serve a tyrant.
— Aesop, *Fables*, "The Wolf and the Lamb," ca. 550 B.C.

2477. Tyrants seldom want pretexts.
— Edmund Burke,
Letter to a Member of the National Assembly, 1791

2478. And with necessity, / The Tyrant's plea, excused his dev'lish deeds.
— John Milton,
Paradise Lost, 1667

2479. Nature has left this tincture in the blood, / That all men would be tyrants if they could.
— Daniel Defoe,
The History of the Kentish Petition, 1712–13

2480. Do not put such unlimited power into the hands of the husbands.

Remember, all men would be tyrants if they could.
— Abigail Adams, letter,
March 31, 1776

2481. You need neither art nor science to be a tyrant.
— Jean de La Bruyère,
Characters, 1688

2482. It is ill putting a sword in a madman's hand.
— Proverb

2483. Tyrants never perish from tyranny, but always from folly.
— Walter Savage Landor,
Conversations, 1824–53

2484. For how can tyrants safely govern home, / Unless abroad they purchase great alliance?
— William Shakespeare,
Henry VI, Part III, 1592

2485. In every tyrant's heart there springs in the end / This poison, that he cannot trust a friend.
— Aeschylus, *Prometheus Bound*,
ca. 490 B.C.

2486. To be feared is to fear; no one has been able to strike terror into others and at the same time enjoy peace of mind himself.
— Seneca, *Epistolae Morales*, 1st c.

2487. Dictators ride to and fro upon tigers which they dare not dismount. And the tigers are getting hungry.
— Winston S. Churchill,
While England Slept, 1936

2488. The right of a nation to kill a tyrant in case of necessity can no more be doubted than to hang a robber, or kill a flea.
— John Adams, *Constitution of
Massachusetts: Declaration of
Rights*, 1780

2489. The tree of liberty grows only when watered by the blood of tyrants.
— Bertrand Barère de Vieuzac,
speech, 1792

2490. Despots themselves do not deny that freedom is excellent; only they desire it for themselves alone, and they maintain that everyone else is altogether unworthy of it.
— Alexis de Tocqueville,
*The Old Regime and the French
Revolution*, 1856

2491. God himself has no right to be a tyrant.
— William Godwin,
Sketches of History, 1784

2492. Whoever puts his hand on me to govern me is a usurper and a tyrant; I declare him my enemy.
— Pierre Joseph Proudhon,
Confessions of a Revolutionary,
1849

2493. Kings will be tyrants from policy, when subjects are rebels from principle.
— Edmund Burke, *Reflections on
the Revolution in France*, 1790

2494. The limits of tyrants are prescribed by the endurance of those whom they suppress.
— Frederick Douglass, letter,
March 30, 1849

2495. "The consent of the governed" is more than a safeguard against ignorant tyrants: it is an insurance against benevolent despots as well.
— Walter Lippmann,
A Preface to Politics, 1913

2496. The benevolent despot who sees himself as a shepherd of the people still demands from others the submissiveness of sheep.
— Eric Hoffer,
The Ordeal of Change, 1964

2497. The tyrant grinds down his slaves and they don't turn against him; they crush those beneath them.
— Emily Brontë,
Wuthering Heights, 1847

2498. No one can terrorize a whole nation, unless we are all his accomplices.
— Edward R. Murrow,
radio broadcast, March 7, 1954

2499. The worst of tyrants, an usurping crowd.
— Homer, *The Iliad*, ca. 700 B.C.

2500. Tyrants are but the spawn of Ignorance, / Begotten by the slaves they trample on.
— James Russell Lowell, "Prometheus," 1843

2501. Whom the gods wish to destroy, they first make mad.
— Euripedes, *Fragment*, 5th c. B.C.

2502. Great ambition unchecked by principle or the love of glory, is an unruly tyrant.
— Alexander Hamilton, letter, January 16, 1801

2503. To be a great autocrat you must be a great barbarian.
— Joseph Conrad, *The Mirror of the Sea*, 1906

2504. They who study mankind with a whip in their hands will always go wrong.
— Frederick Douglass, speech, August 1, 1860

2505. Cruelty is a tyrant that is always attended with Fear.
— Thomas Fuller, *Gnomologia*, 1732

2506. Cruelty is the law pervading all nature and society; and we can't get out of it if we would.
— Thomas Hardy, *Jude the Obscure*, 1895

2507. Opinions which justify cruelty are inspired by cruel impulses.
— Bertrand Russell, *Unpopular Essays*, 1950

2508. Lay the proud usurpers low! / Tyrants fall in every foe! / Liberty's in every blow! / Let us do or die!
— Robert Burns, *Scots Wha Hae*, 1794

2509. When you stop a dictator there are always risks. But there are greater risks in not stopping a dictator.
— Margaret Thatcher, on *BBC TV*, April 5, 1982

Valor *see* Courage

Veterans

See also Soldiers

2510. How different the new order would be if we could consult the veteran instead of the politician.
— Henry Miller, *The Wisdom of the Heart*, 1941

2511. Men acquainted with the battlefield will not be found among the numbers that glibly talk of another war.
— Dwight D. Eisenhower, speech, June 2, 1946

2512. The only war is the war you fought in. Every veteran knows that.
— Allan Keller, in *New York World-Telegram and Sun*, August 24, 1965

2513. Now tell us about the war, / And what they fought each other for.
— Robert Southey, *The Battle of Blenheim*, 1798

2514. War talk by men who have been in a war is always interesting; whereas moon talk by a poet who has not been in the moon is likely to be dull.
— Mark Twain, *Life on the Mississippi*, 1883

2515. The war stories, instead of repelling young men, bewitch them; the suffering is alluring and promises redemption. War teases them: the wounds they are ready for are painted on and can be washed off like graffiti; they believe the wounds will give them importance.
— Gloria Emerson,
Some American Men, 1985

2516. The history of a soldier's wounds beguiles the pain of it.
— Laurence Sterne,
Tristram Shandy, 1760

2517. You know — we've had to imagine the war here, and we have imagined that it was being fought by aging men like ourselves. We had forgotten that wars were fought by babies. When I saw those freshly shaved faces, it was a shock. "My God, my God -" I said to myself, "it's the Children's Crusade."
— Kurt Vonnegut, Jr.,
Slaughterhouse-Five, 1969

2518. All wars are boyish, and are fought by boys.
— Herman Melville, *Battlepieces and Aspects of the War*, 1866

2519. What war has always been is a puberty ceremony. It's a very rough one, but you went away a boy and came back a man, maybe with an eye missing or whatever but godammit you were a man and people had to call you a man thereafter.
— Kurt Vonnegut, Jr., in
City Limits, March 11, 1983

2520. War may make a fool of man, but it by no means degrades him; on the contrary, it tends to exalt him, and its net effects are much like those of motherhood on women.
— H. L. Mencken,
Minority Report, 1956

2521. And when he goes to heaven / To Saint Peter he will tell: / Another Marine reporting, sir; / I've served my time in hell!
— Anonymous, epitaph for
PFC Cameron, who died at
Guadalcanal, 1942

2522. I have seen war ... I hate war.
— Franklin D. Roosevelt,
speech, August 14, 1936

2523. Look at an infantryman's eyes and you can tell how much war he has seen.
— Bill Mauldin, *Up Front*, 1944

2524. Grim-visaged war hath smoothed his wrinkled front.
— William Shakespeare,
Richard III, 1591

2525. Nations may make peace. It is harder for fighting men.
— William Manchester, in
New York Times Magazine,
June 14, 1987

2526. A man who is good enough to shed his blood for the country is good enough to be given a square deal afterwards.
— Theodore Roosevelt, speech,
June 4, 1903

2527. The nation which forgets its defenders will be itself forgotten.
— Calvin Coolidge, speech,
July 27, 1920

Victory

See also Conquest; Defeat; Glory; Strength

2528. Victory is a thing of the will.
— Ferdinand Foch,
message, 1914

2529. It is fatal to enter any war without the will to win it.
— Douglas MacArthur,
speech, July 7, 1952

2530. Victory is the beautiful, bright-colored flower.
— Winston S. Churchill,
The River War, 1899

2531. What red-blooded American could oppose so shining a concept as victory? It would be like standing up for sin against virtue.
— Matthew B. Ridgway,
The Korean War, 1967

2532. You cannot fight hard unless you think you are fighting to win.
— Theodore Roosevelt,
letter, July, 1912

2533. In war there is no substitute for victory.
— Douglas MacArthur,
speech, April 19, 1951

2534. If you think you can win, you can win. Faith is necessary to victory.
— William Hazlitt,
Literary Remains, 1836

2535. 'Tis man's to fight, but Heaven's to give success.
— Homer, *The Iliad*, ca. 700 B.C.

2536. No one can guarantee success in war, but only deserve it.
— Winston S. Churchill,
Their Finest Hour, 1949

2537. There is hardly such a thing as a war in which it makes no difference who wins. Nearly always one side stands more or less for progress, the other side more or less for reaction.
— George Orwell, "Looking Back on the Spanish War," 1943

2538. There are not fifty ways of fighting, there is only one: to be the conqueror.
— André Malvaux, *L'Espoir*, 1937

2539. Winning isn't everything. It is the only thing.
— Vince Lombardi, in *Newsweek*,
November 19, 1979

2540. We are not interested in the possibilities of defeat.
— Victoria, letter concerning the
Boer War, December, 1899

2541. The power to wage war is the power to wage war successfully.
— Charles Evans Hughes,
*The Supreme Court of
the United States*, 1928

2542. When there is no peril in the fight, there is no glory in the triumph.
— Pierre Corneille, *Le Cid*, 1636

2543. Poor is the triumph o'er the timid hare!
— James Thomson,
The Seasons, 1746

2544. Force complete, absolute, overpowering was applied until the enemy's will to resist and capacity to exist as a nation were broken. This was victory.
— Dean Acheson,
Power and Diplomacy, 1958

2545. If we win, nobody will care. If we lose, there will be nobody to care.
— Winston S. Churchill,
speech, June 25, 1941

2546. The victor belongs to the spoils.
— F. Scott Fitzgerald,
The Beautiful and Damned, 1922

2547. Triumph cannot help being cruel.
— José Ortega y Gasset,
Notes on the Novel, 1925

2548. Generous victors are rare.
— Amos Elon, in
New Yorker, April 23, 1990

2549. When you have gained a victory, do not push it too far; 'tis sufficient to let the company and your adversary see 'tis in your power but that you are too generous to make use of it.
— Eustace Budgell, in
The Spectator, 1711–12

2550. Sweet mercy is nobility's true badge.
— William Shakespeare,
Titus Andronicus, 1590

2551. In war there is no second prize for the runner-up.
— Omar Bradley, in
Military Review, February, 1950

2552. Commonly, people believe that defeat is characterized by a general bustle and a feverish rush. Bustle and rush are the signs of victory, not of defeat. Victory is a thing of action.
— Antoine de Saint-Exupéry,
Flight to Arras, 1942

2553. Don't persist in a losing cause unless you truly know you can turn it into a winning one.
— Robert Heller,
The Super Managers, 1984

2554. The tragedy of life is not that man loses but that he almost wins.
— Heywood Broun, *Pieces of Hate, and Other Enthusiasms*, 1922

2555. In war, whichever side may call itself the victor, there are no winners, but all are losers.
— Neville Chamberlain,
speech, July 3, 1938

2556. War will of itself discover and lay open the hidden and rankling wounds of the victorious party.
— Cornelius Tacitus,
Histories, ca. 100

2557. It is expedient for the victor to wish for peace restored; for the vanquished it is necessary.
— Seneca, *Hercules Furens*, ca. 50

2558. Victory at all costs, victory in spite of all terror, victory however long and hard the road may be; for without victory there is no survival.
— Winston S. Churchill,
speech, May 13, 1940

2559. Victory attained by violence is tantamount to a defeat, for it is momentary.
— Mohandas K. Gandhi,
leaflet, May 3, 1919

2560. Those who know how to win are much more numerous than those who know how to make proper use of their victories.
— Polybius, *History*, ca. 125 B.C.

2561. It is not the cause for which men took up arms that makes a victory more just or less, it is the order that is established when arms have been laid down.
— Simone Weil, "The Great Beast: Conclusion," 1939–40

2562. Another such victory and we are ruined.
— Pyrrhus, in Plutarch, *Lives*,
ca. 1st-2nd c.

2563. It is true that we have won all our wars, but we have paid for them. We don't want victories anymore.
— Golda Meir, in *Life*,
October 3, 1969

2564. Who, apart / From ourselves, can see any difference between / Our victories and our defeats?
— Christopher Fry,
Thor, with Angels, 1948

2565. For what are the triumphs of war, planned by ambition, executed by violence, and consummated by devastation? The means are the sacrifice of many, the end, the bloated aggrandizement of the few.
— Charles Caleb Colton,
Lacon, 1820–22

2566. "And everybody promised the duke, / Who this great fight did win." / "But what good came of it at last?" / Quoth little Peterkin. / "Why, that I cannot tell," said he; / "But 'twas a famous victory."
— Robert Southey,
The Battle of Blenheim, 1798

2567. The important thing in life is not the victory but the contest; the essential thing is not to have won but to have fought well.
— Pierre de Coubertin,
speech, July 24, 1908

2568. You win the victory when you yield to friends.
— Sophocles, *Ajax*, ca. 447 B.C.

2569. Minds are conquered not by arms, but by love and magnanimity.
— Baruch Spinoza, *Ethics*, 1677

2570. Be ashamed to die until you have won some victory for humanity.
— Horace Mann, speech, 1859

2571. To give victory to the right, not bloody bullets, but peaceful ballots only, are necessary.
— Abraham Lincoln, speech, May 18, 1858

2572. He that returns a good for evil obtains the victory.
— Thomas Fuller, *Gnomologia*, 1732

2573. In a serious struggle there is no worse cruelty than to be magnanimous at an inopportune time.
— Leon Trotsky, *The History of the Russian Revolution*, 1933

2574. In war, resolution; in defeat, defiance; in victory, magnanimity; in peace, goodwill.
— Winston S. Churchill, in E. Marsh, *A Number of People*, 1939

2575. The problems of victory are more agreeable than those of defeat, but they are no less difficult.
— Winston S. Churchill, speech, November 11, 1942

2576. Whether in chains or in laurels, Liberty knows nothing but victories.
— Wendell Phillips, speech, November 1, 1859

2577. As always, victory finds a hundred fathers but defeat is an orphan.
— Galeazzo Ciano, *Ciano Diaries, 1939–43*, September 9, 1942

2578. A victorious general has no faults in the eye of the public, while a defeated general is always wrong no matter how wise his conduct may have been.
— Voltaire, *Le Siècle de Louis XIV*, 1751

2579. That's the way it is in war. You win or lose, live or die — and the difference is just an eyelash.
— Douglas MacArthur, *Reminiscences*, 1964

2580. Beware of rashness, but with energy and sleepless vigilance go forward and give us victories.
— Abraham Lincoln, letter to General J. Hooker, January 26, 1863

2581. History ... keeps her eyes fixed on the victories, and leaves the vanquished in the shadows.
— Stefan Zweig, *The Right to Heresy*, 1936

2582. Of war men ask the outcome, not the cause.
— Seneca, *Hercules Furens*, ca. 50

2583. In starting and waging a war, it is not Right that matters, but Victory.
— Adolf Hitler, speech, August 22, 1939

2584. They laugh that win.
— William Shakespeare, *Othello*, 1602–04

2585. There is no pain in the wound received in the moment of victory.
— Publilius Syrus, *Moral Sayings*, 1st c. B.C.

2586. On the day of victory no one is tired.
— Proverb

2587. Victory is gay only back home. Up front it is joyless.
— Marlene Dietrich, *Marlene Dietrich's ABC*, 1962

2588. No triumph of peace is so great as the supreme triumph of war.
— Theodore Roosevelt, speech, 1895

Vietnam

See also Futility of War

2589. I predict you will sink step by step into a bottomless quagmire, however much you spend in men and money.
— Charles DeGaulle, statement to John F. Kennedy on involvement in Vietnam, 1961

2590. Ignorance was not a factor in the American endeavor in Vietnam pursued through five successive presidencies, although it was to become an excuse.
— Barbara Tuchman, *The March of Folly*, 1984

2591. Vietnam was lost in the living rooms of America — not on the battlefields of Vietnam.
— Marshall McLuhan, in *Montreal Gazette*, May 16, 1975

2592. North Vietnam cannot defeat or humiliate the United States. Only Americans can do that.
— Richard M. Nixon, speech, November 3, 1969

2593. Above all, Vietnam was a war that asked everything of a few and nothing of most in America.
— Myra MacPhearson, *Long Time Passing: Vietnam and the Haunted Generation*, 1984

2594. Tonight — to you, the great silent majority of my fellow Americans — I ask for your support.
— Richard M. Nixon, speech on his policies in Vietnam, November 3, 1969

2595. The men and women who served in Vietnam were heroes. Not just because of their deeds of valor, but because they served at a time when words like duty, honor and country lost their meaning for many.
— Dan Quayle, speech, July 13, 1990

2596. The war the soldiers tried to stop.
— John Kerry, comment on Vietnam, in *Evening Star*, April 26, 1971

2597. I don't object to its being called "McNamara's war." I think it is a very important war and I am pleased to be identified with it and do whatever I can to win it.
— Robert McNamara, on the Vietnam War, in *New York Times*, April 25, 1964

2598. Vietnam was the first war ever fought without any censorship. Without censorship, things can get terribly confused in the public mind.
— William C. Westmoreland, in *Time*, April 5, 1982

2599. ...The first clear failure in our history.
— Bruce Palmer, on the fall of South Vietnam, in *New York Times*, April 15, 1985

2600. Our purpose in Vietnam is to prevent the success of aggression. It is not conquest, it is not empire, it is not foreign bases, it is not domination. It is, simply put, just to prevent the forceful conquest of South Vietnam by North Vietnam.
— Lyndon B. Johnson, in *Time*, March 4, 1966

2601. Vietnam was our longest, costliest, and, as it went on, our least popular war; it was also the least understood. And the more attempts were made to explain, the more puzzling it became.
— Merle Miller, *Lyndon: An Oral Biography*, 1980

2602. No event in American history is more misunderstood than the Vietnam War. It was misreported then, and it is misremembered now.
— Richard M. Nixon, in *New York Times*, March 28, 1985

2603. Our numbers have increased in Vietnam because the aggression of others has increased in Vietnam. There is not, and there will not be, a mindless escalation.
— Lyndon B. Johnson, in
Time, March 4, 1966

2604. It became necessary to destroy the town in order to save it.
— Anonymous, statement by a
U.S. officer in Vietnam,
February 8, 1968

2605. The Vietcong are going to collapse within weeks.
— Walt Rostow, in *Look*,
December 12, 1967

2606. Rarely have so many people been so wrong about so much.
— Richard M. Nixon,
No More Vietnams, 1985

2607. As this long and difficult war ends, I would like to address a few special words to ... the American people: Your steadfastness in supporting our insistence on peace with honor has made peace with honor possible.
— Richard M. Nixon, speaking
on the end of the Vietnam War,
January 23, 1973

2608. The war in Vietnam threatened to tear our society apart, and the political disagreements that separated each side continue to some extent. It's been said that these memorials reflect a hunger for healing.
— Ronald Reagan, speech about
the Vietnam War Memorial,
November 11, 1984

2609. It's a gravestone.
— Nelson DeMille, about the
Vietnam War Memorial,
Words of Honor, 1985

War and Peace

See also Pacifism; Peace

2610. War, the begetter of all things, the creature of all things, the river with a thousand sources, the sea without a shore: begetter of all things except peace, so ardently longed for, so rarely attained.
— Fernand Braudel,
The Mediterranean, 1949

2611. Not war but peace is the father of all things.
— Willy Brandt,
Über den Tag hinaus, 1974

2612. He that will not have peace, God gives him war.
— Proverb

2613. Better an egg in peace than an ox in war.
— Proverb

2614. Better a lean peace than a fat victory.
— Thomas Fuller,
Gnomologia, 1732

2615. It is far easier to make war than to make peace.
— Georges Clemenceau,
speech, July 14, 1919

2616. There never was a good war or a bad peace.
— Benjamin Franklin, letter,
September 11, 1783

2617. To be prepared for war is one of the most effectual means of preserving peace.
— George Washington, speech,
January 8, 1790

2618. Let us therefore follow after the things which make for peace.
— Bible, *Romans* 14:19

2619. Peace hath higher tests of manhood / Than battle ever knew.
— John Greenleaf Whittier,
"The Hero," 1853

2620. The will for peace on the part of the peace-loving nations must express itself to the end that nations that may be tempted to violate their agreements and the rights of others will desist from such a course. There must be positive endeavors to preserve peace.
— Franklin D. Roosevelt, speech, October 5, 1937

2621. If we do not abolish war on this earth, then surely one day war will abolish us from the earth.
— Harry S Truman, speech, 1966

2622. If we are to promote peace on earth, we must have a great deal more than the power of the sword. We must call into action the spiritual and moral forces of mankind.
— Calvin Coolidge, speech, June 3, 1925

2623. Peace hath her victories no less renowned than war.
— John Milton, *Sonnet 16*, 1652

2624. Let us ever remember that our interest is in concord not in conflict, and that our real eminence as a nation lies in the victories of peace, not those of war.
— William McKinley, speech, 1890

2625. The inglorious arts of peace.
— Andrew Marvell, *Upon Cromwell's Return from Ireland*, 1650

2626. In the arts of peace Man is a bungler.
— George Bernard Shaw, *Man and Superman*, 1903

2627. I do not want to read about the war. I was going to forget the war. I had made a separate peace.
— Ernest Hemingway, *A Farewell to Arms*, 1929

2628. Hath his bellyful of fighting.
— William Shakespeare, *Cymbeline*, 1609–10

2629. The mere absence of war is not peace.

— John F. Kennedy, State of the Union address, January 14, 1963

2630. Where they make a desert, they call it peace.
— Cornelius Tacitus, *Agricola*, ca. 98

2631. Don't tell me peace has broken out, when I've just bought fresh supplies.
— Bertolt Brecht, *Mother Courage*, 1939

2632. The no-man's-years between the wars.
— Herbert Reed, *Annals of Innocence and Experience*, 1940

2633. Let war yield to peace, laurels to paeans.
— Cicero, *De Officiis*, 44 B.C.

2634. The eagle has ceased to scream, but the parrots will now begin to chatter. The war of the giants is over and the war of the pigmies will now start to squabble.
— Winston S. Churchill, remark on V-E day, May 7, 1945

2635. The Great War and the Petty Peace.
— H. G. Wells, *The Outline of History*, 1920

2636. War makes thieves and peace hangs them.
— Proverb

2637. War its thousands slays, Peace its ten thousands.
— Bailey Ports, *Death*, 1759

2638. Men grow tired of sleep, love, singing and dancing sooner than war.
— Homer, *The Iliad*, ca. 700 B.C.

2639. The deliberate aim at Peace very easily passes into its bastard substitute, Anesthesia.
— Alfred North Whitehead, *Adventures of Ideas*, 1935

2640. The cankers of a calm world and a long peace.
— William Shakespeare, *Henry IV, Part I*, 1597

2641. Peace! Impudent and shameless Warwick, peace; / Proud setter up and puller down of kings.
— William Shakespeare,
Henry VI, Part III, 1592

2642. Now we suffer the woes of long peace. Luxury, more savage / Than war, has smothered us, avenging the world we ravage.
— Juvenal, *Satires*, ca. 100

2643. If few can stand a long war without the deterioration of soul, none can stand a long peace.
— Oswald Spengler,
The Hour of Decision, 1934

2644. The German soul is opposed to the pacifist ideal of civilization, for is not peace an element of civil corruption?
— Thomas Mann, *Reflections of a Non-Political Man*, 1917

2645. Mankind will never win lasting peace so long as men use their full resources only in tasks of war.
— John Foster Dulles,
War or Peace, 1950

2646. Mankind has grown strong in eternal struggles and it will only perish through eternal peace.
— Adolf Hitler,
Mein Kampf, 1924

2647. It is easier to lead men to combat and to stir up their passions than to temper them and urge them to the patient labors of peace.
— André Gide, *Journals*,
September 13, 1938

2648. Who would prefer peace to the glory of hunger and thirst, of wading through mud, and dying in the service of one's country?
— Jean Giraudoux,
Amphitryon 38, 1929

2649. It is better we disintegrate in peace and not in pieces.
— Benjamin N. Azikiwe, in
Newsweek, August 8, 1966

2650. There could be real peace only if everyone were satisfied. That means there is not often a real peace. There are only actual states of peace which, like wars, are mere expedients.
— Paul Valéry, *Reflections on the World Today*, 1931

2651. Nobuddy ever fergits where he buried a hatchet.
— Frank McKinney Hubbard,
Abe Martin's Broadcast, 1930

2652. We do not admire a man of timid peace.
— Theodore Roosevelt, speech,
April 10, 1899

2653. Peace, like war, can succeed only where there is a will to enforce it, and where there is available power to enforce it.
— Franklin D. Roosevelt, speech,
October 21, 1944

2654. Whatever enables us to go to war, secures our peace.
— Thomas Jefferson, letter,
July 11, 1790

2655. The legitimate object of war is a more perfect peace.
— William T. Sherman, speech,
July 20, 1865

2656. We are going to have peace even if we have to fight for it.
— Dwight D. Eisenhower, speech,
June 10, 1945

2657. Ef you want peace, the thing you've got to do / Is jes' to show you're up to fightin', tu.
— James Russell Lowell,
The Bigelow Papers, Series II, 1866

2658. The more bombers, the less room for doves of peace.
— Nikita Khrushchev, speech,
March 14, 1958

2659. What we need is Star Peace and not Star Wars.
— Mikhail Gorbachev, speech,
November 28, 1986

War Is ...

See also Peace Is ... ; War and Peace

2660. War is the national industry of Prussia.
— Comte de Mirabeau, attributed

2661. War is a blessing compared with national degradation.
— Andrew Jackson, letter, May 2, 1845

2662. War is a kind of superstition; the pageantry of arms and badges corrupts the imagination of man.
— Percy Bysshe Shelley, *A Philosophical View of Reform*, 1819

2663. War is an invention of the human mind. The human mind can invent peace.
— Norman Cousins, *Who Speaks for Man?* 1953

2664. War is not an instinct but an invention.
— José Ortega y Gasset, *The Revolt of the Masses*, 1930

2665. War is both the product of an earlier corruption and a producer of new corruptions.
— Lewis Mumford, *The Conduct of Life*, 1951

2666. War, *n.* A by-product of the arts of peace.
— Ambrose Bierce, *The Devil's Dictionary*, 1906

2667. War is not neat. War is not tidy. War is a mess, and you have to be sure the stakes justify what you are doing.
— William J. Crowe, Jr., in *Los Angeles Times*, November 29, 1990

2668. War is not at all such a difficult art as people think ... In reality it would seem that he is vanquished who is afraid of his adversary and that the whole secret of war is this.
— Napoleon Bonaparte, to Czar Alexander, 1807

2669. War challenges virtually every other institution of society — the justice and equity of its economy, the adequacy of its political systems, the energy of its productive plant, the bases, wisdom and purposes of its foreign policy.
— Walter Millis, *The Faith of an American*, 1941

2670. War! It is too serious a matter to leave to the military.
— Georges Clemenceau, in G. Saurez, *Clemenceau*, 1886

2671. War is itself a political act with primarily political objects and under the American form of government political officials must necessarily direct its general course.
— Dudley W. Knox, *A History of the United States Navy*, 1936

2672. *War* is the highest form of struggle for resolving contradictions when they have developed to a certain state, between classes, nations, states, or political groups, and it has existed ever since the emergence of private property and of classes.
— Mao Zedong, *Quotations from Chairman Mao*, 1956

2673. War is capitalism with the gloves off and many who go to war know it but they go to war because they don't want to be a hero.
— Tom Stoppard, *Travesties*, 1975

2674. War is nothing but a duel on an extensive scale.
— Karl von Clausewitz, *On War*, 1833

2675. The American approach to war is that it's like football, only with guns.
— David Evans, in *Chicago Tribune*, June 9, 1991

2676. In fact, it's getting harder to differentiate between war and football. Which is reality and which is metaphor?
— Daniel Golden, in
Boston Globe, January 20, 1991

2677. War is the trade of kings.
— John Dryden,
King Arthur, 1691

2678. The chase, the sport of kings; / Image of war, without its guilt.
— William Somerville,
The Chase, 1735

2679. War is a game that is played with a smile. If you can't smile, grin. If you can't grin, keep out of the way till you can.
— Winston S. Churchill, in W. Manchester, The Last Lion, 1983

2680. War's a game which were their subjects wise / Kings would not play at.
— William Cowper,
The Task, 1785

2681. War is a game in which princes seldom win, the people never.
— Charles Caleb Colton,
Lacon, 1820–22

2682. War is just like bush-clearing— the moment you stop, the jungle comes back even thicker, but for a little while you can plant and grow a crop in the ground you have won at such a terrible cost.
— Kenneth Kaunda,
Kaunda on Violence, 1980

2683. War is not the natural state of the human family in its higher development, but merely a feature of barbarism lasting on through the transition of the race, from the savage to the scholar.
— Elizabeth Cady Stanton,
History of Woman Suffrage, 1881

2684. War is, after all, the universal perversion.
— John Rae,
The Custard Boys, 1960

2685. As peace is of all goodness, so war is an emblem, a hieroglyphic, of all misery.
— John Donne, Sermons, 1622

2686. War, it would appear, is a normal attribute to human life.
— Jean de Bloch,
The Future of War, 1903

2687. With men, the state of nature is not a state of peace, but war.
— Immanuel Kant,
Perpetual Peace, 1795

2688. War represents a vice that mankind would like to get rid of but which it cannot do without. Man is like an alcoholic who knows that drink will destroy him but who always has a reason for drinking.
— Thomas Merton,
Love and Living, 1980

2689. Either war is obsolete or men are.
— R. Buckminister Fuller, in
New Yorker, January 8, 1966

2690. You cannot qualify war in harsher terms than I will. War is cruelty, and you cannot refine it.
— William T. Sherman, letter,
July 12, 1864

2691. War is not an adventure. It is a disease. It is like typhus.
— Antoine de Saint-Exupéry,
Pilote de guerre, 1942

2692. War is a contagion.
— Franklin D. Roosevelt, speech,
October 5, 1937

2693. But what is war? ... The aim of war is murder.
— Leo Tolstoy,
War and Peace, 1865–69

2694. War is death's feast.
— Proverb

2695. Blood is the god of war's rich livery.
— Christopher Marlowe,
Tamburlaine the Great, 1587

2696. War is the slaughter of human beings, temporarily regarded as enemies, on as large a scale as possible.
— Jeanette Rankin, speech, 1929

2697. War is the supreme drama of a completely mechanized society.
— Lewis Mumford,
Technics and Civilization, 1934

2698. War is pillage versus resistance and if illusions of magnitude could be transmuted into ideals of magnanimity, peace might be realized.
— Marianne Moore, in
Dial, April, 1929

2699. They were going to look at war, the red animal — war, the blood-swollen god.
— Stephen Crane,
The Red Badge of Courage, 1895

2700. The essence of war is violence, and ... moderation in war is imbecility.
— Thomas Babington,
*Essays Contributed to the
Edinburgh Review*, 1843

2701. Old, unhappy, far-off things, / And battles long ago.
— William Wordsworth,
The Solitary Reaper, 1807

2702. War is the child of Pride.
— Jonathan Swift,
The Battle of the Books, 1697

2703. There is many a boy here today who looks on war as all glory, but, boys, it is all hell. You can bear this warning voice to generations yet to come. I look upon war with horror.
— William T. Sherman, speech,
August 11, 1880

2704. War is hell and all that, but it has a good deal to recommend it. It wipes out all the small nuisances of peacetime.
— Ian Hay,
The First Hundred Thousand,
1916

2705. We are having one hell of a war.
— George S. Patton, letter,
December 15, 1944

Weapons

See also the Atomic Age; the Cold War; Morale;
Power; Propaganda; Strategy and Tactics; Strength

2706. Don't forget your great guns, which are the most respectable arguments of the rights of kings.
— Frederick the Great, letter,
April 21, 1759

2707. Guns will make us powerful; butter will only make us fat.
— Josef Göbbels,
radio broadcast, 1936

2708. Bombs do not choose. They will hit everything.
— Nikita Khrushchev, in
New York Herald Tribune,
August 12, 1961

2709. From the earliest dawnings of policy to this day, the invention of man has been sharpening and improving the mystery of murder, from the first rude essays of clubs and stones, to the present perfection of gunnery.
— Edmund Burke, *A Vindication
of Natural Society*, 1756

2710. Weapons are like money; no one knows the meaning of *enough*.
— Martin Amis,
Einstein's Monsters, 1987

2711. At the rate science proceeds, rockets and missiles will one day seem like buffalo — slow, endangered grazers in the black pasture of outer space.
— Bernard Cooper, in
Gettysburg Review, Summer, 1989

2712. Our swords shall play the orators for us.
— Christopher Marlowe,
Tamburlaine the Great, 1587

2713. A sword never kills anybody; it's a tool in the killer's hand.
— Seneca, *Letters to Lucilius*, 1st c.

2714. Wars may be fought with weapons, but they are won by men. It is the spirit of the men who follow and of the man who leads that gains the victory.
— George S. Patton, in *Cavalry Journal*, September, 1933

2715. Weapons are an important factor in war, but not the decisive one; it is man and not materials that counts.
— Mao Zedong, "Problems of War and Strategy," November 6, 1938

2716. The power which establishes a state is violence; the power which maintains it is violence; the power which eventually overthrows it is violence.
— Kenneth Kaunda, *Kaunda on Violence*, 1980

2717. Terrorism has become the systematic weapon of a war that knows no borders or seldom has a face.
— Jacques Chirac, speech, September 24, 1986

2718. Barbarism is the absence of standards to which appeal can be made.
— José Ortega y Gasset, *The Revolt of the Masses*, 1930

2719. Russians can give you arms but only the United States can give you a solution.
— Anwar al-Sadat, in *Newsweek*, January 13, 1975

2720. Arms alone are not enough to keep peace. It must be kept by men.
— John F. Kennedy, State of the Union address, January 11, 1962

2721. Since, in the main, it is not armaments that cause wars but wars (or the fears thereof) that cause armaments, it follows that every nation will at every moment strive to keep its armaments in an efficient state as required by its fear; otherwise styled security.
— Salvador de Madariaga, *Morning Without Noon*, 1974

2722. There is still one absolute weapon ... That weapon is man himself.
— Matthew B. Ridgway, speech, November 10, 1953

2723. Science has brought forth this danger, but the real problem is in the minds and hearts of men.
— Albert Einstein, regarding nuclear weapons, in *New York Times Magazine*, June 23, 1946

2724. It is ideas, not vested interests, which are dangerous for good or evil.
— John Maynard Keynes, *The General Theory of Employment, Interest and Money*, 1936

2725. Ideas are indeed the most dangerous weapons in the world.
— William O. Douglas, *An Almanac of Liberty*, 1954

2726. To live without killing is a thought which could electrify the world, if men were only capable of staying awake long enough to let the idea soak in.
— Henry Miller, *Sunday after the War*, 1944

2727. I am proud of the fact that I never invented weapons to kill.
— Thomas Edison, in *New York Times*, June 8, 1915

Winning *see* Victory

INDEX OF PERSONS

INDEX OF KEY
WORDS IN CONTEXT

abandon: the ocean 1284
   willingly a. 1796
abate: changes that will a.
   729
abated: misery is a. 2161
abatement in the hostility
   613
abhor: revolutions which are
   not made by our rules 2178
   sufficiently a. it 1890
abhors: state a. it 2463
abilities: uncommon a. 1343
ability: height of a. 1471
   to execute 2191
   to get men to do 1352
   to get to the verge of
     war 1907
   to improve 1347
   to suspend the func-
     tioning of the
     imagination 418
   to will either good or
     evil 964
able: if challenged 2257
   in the least a. 1471
   men 1679
   to answer the essential
     question 1076
   to command 1377
   to destroy 1487
   to prevent a third
     world war 1914
   to procure 1716
   to sing his praise 1366
ablest navigators 2381
abnegation: courage and a.
   1706
abnormal energy 1730
abolish war 1599, 2621
abolished: was can be a.
   1594

abolition: complete a. 1580
abomination can be committed 1326
above the law 2427, 2429
abroad: home or a. 2231
   innocents a. 785
   peaceful relations a.
     777
   sent to lie a. 555
   they purchase great
     alliance 2484
   when you're a. 553
absence: in the a. 1277
   of fear 358
   of mind 285
   of standards 2718
   of war 1697, 2629
absent: hates you a. 697
   the other is a. 1818
absolute: and sublime 964
   complete a. overpow-
     ering 2544
   freedom 1337
   power 1727, 1786, 1792
   power is a. 1411
   right of the state 1934
   weapon 2722
absolutely: absolute power
     corrupts a. 1786
   corrupts a. 1793
   essential to national
     defense 1392
   in our power 1791
   lust for power which
     corrupts a. 1787
   powerlessness frus-
     trates a. 1789
   rules a. 1818
absolutes: procession of false
   a. 1189
absolved from the faults 2452

absorbed mainly in preserving its control 2120
abstract: plenty of courage
   among us for the a. 322
absurd: war becomes a. 1602
abuse: group that gets it will
   a. it 1823
   liable to a. 1759
   more dangerous the a.
     1803
   of greatness 1030
   ought to be reformed
     2052
abuses: and encroachments
   1743
   correction of a. 2053
abyss: dark a. 947
accept: civilization as it is
   1842
   the doctrine 1848
   the values of war 1499
acceptable: a government
   more a. 2078
acceptance: speed of his a.
   83
accepted: definition 308
   surrender can be a. 545
accepts: excuse history never
   a. 1146
accident: promoting a. 1093
acclaim earned in the blood
   of his followers 1460
accompanied by prestige
   1451
accomplices: we are all his a.
   2498
accomplish: means to a. 838
accomplished: look at what
   he a. 1453
   never a. 1350
   nothing was a. 541

169

never get in the b. 1957
which contain no lies
1084
will be burned 1933
boots: have one's b. on 1876
border: army on the b. 1375
move across every b.
1672
this is the Libyan b.
2073
borders: knows no b. 2717
bore: becomes a b. at last
1062
born: and die 64
fortunate who are b.
233
free 2296
great 992
in chains 2298
in the minds 800
in them 1406
kings are not b. 2241
out of the understand-
ing 1355
slaves 662
to be a slave 2305
to know you 874
borrow it for a while 1422
borrowed from their mass
1406
Boston Neck 1899
both: are the slaves 887
part of himself in b.
1768
bottle: two scorpions in a
b. 254
bottom: at b. every state
regards another 1533
fellows at the b. 1465
man at b. 1160
of the deep 1230
bottomless quagmire 2589
bought: at the price of
national honor 1225
for nothing 816
fresh supplies 2631
bound: to forgive an enemy
614
to trust him 614
boundaries: state b. 651
boundary: every border and
every b. 1672
of the march of a
nation 650
bounds: liberty is never out
of b. 872
of the continent 658

to every government
1991
bourgeoisie: who stops the
revolution half way the
b. 2110
bows and arrows 1851
boy: fell dead 427
here today 2703
went away a b. 2519
boyish: wars are b. 2518
boys: are not going to be
sent into any foreign wars
1866
are the cash of war
2335
Asian b. 1868
fought by b. 2518
rally round the flag b.
808
send American b. 1868
trust in God my b.
1903
brace ourselves to our duties
1662
brain: easy on the b. 531
brains: madness left in their
b. 1679
mob has many heads
but no b. 2455
branch of the art of lying
1948
branches: most lucrative of
its b. 1603
brand of whiskey 1475
brave: act of valor 317
active the b. 2401
and hated 1623
be b. or else be killed
343
boisterous battle 149
everyone becomes b.
339
fortune favors the b.
365
from a safe distance
325
good and the b. 1622
home of the b. 320
I'm very b. generally
324
makes a b. man braver
331
man 308, 379, 397,
572, 705
man's choice 391
man's wounds 367
men 193, 370, 372

none but the b. 301
not truly b. 396
resistance 278
some have been
thought b. 378
war spares not the b.
405
weapon of the b. 300
braver but less daring 331
bravery: as a quality
brings b. to the surface
934
is knowledge of the
cowardice in the
enemy 408
is the capacity to per-
form properly 357
never goes out of fash-
ion 299
stands upon compar-
isons 333
bravest: are the b. 377
often fall by the hands
of cowards 341
sight in the world 1019
spirits 307
brawls: chaotic b. 1249
bread broken with comrades
1499
break: a man's spirit 1736
all records 1514
their fetters 2080
up both 2114
breakdown of policy 786
breaking: succeed in b. 2049
breathing of strength 287
breathing-time which gives
him leisure 2191
breed: best ye b. 661
endless war still b. 901
breeds reptiles of the mind
2028
bribing the active and enterprising 2239
bridge: a b. too far 126
give him a silver b.
2351
the gap 804
brief: triumph has been b. 26
bright honor 1230
bright-colored flower 2530
brilliance without wisdom
84
brilliant triumph 1063
bring: to the fight 1482
war to the heavens
1929

and despair 338
as distinguished from
    panic 418
baseness and c. 475
compromise does not
    mean c. 523
conscience and c. 399
ferocity and c. 403
in the enemy 408
is incorrigible 415
is made respectable
    416
modern c. 417
perhaps c. 388
perpetuated by c.
    2292
shameful c. 1683
that one is his c. 389
utter c. 359
cowardly: dogs bark loudest
    409
    heart 414
    not the brave but the
        c. 405
    submission to wrong
        52
    too c. to fight 404
    when they are dead is
        c. 1749
coward's: legs 419
    revenge 411
    sword 371
cowards: a plague on all
    c. 412
    die many times before
        their deaths 383
    die often 381
    established by c. 385
    goes to the heads of c.
        343
    hands of c. 341
    in scarlet 402
    nothing that makes
        more c. 2021
    of c. no history is writ-
        ten 386
    use their might 406
    will not preserve it
        385
    word that c. use 400
cowheartedness: rashness
    and c. 328
cradles: tattooed in our c.
    1525
craft or cruelty 1802
craven: morally c. 380
craze for domination 2436

crazy: flew them and was c.
    896
    to fly 896
create: and civilize a state
    1392
    impulse to c. 1738
    light 2157
    one's future 1115
    power to c. 1737
    those who c. 1810
    those who love and c.
        1401
created free 2298
creates a belief 720
creating: a true ensemble
    1086
    new methods 1911
creation: on a wider scale
    2128
    stages of c. 193
creative: in order to be c.
    2127
creature: dangerous c. 1808
    history-making c. 1074
    of all things 2610
    who has no chance of
        being free 815
creatures of more common
    stuff 6
credible: must be c. 1945
    deterrent 1947
credulities of mankind 1372
credulity encourages 1964
creed: of slaves 206
    perverted c. 247
    single dogmatic c. 1847
creeds and institutions 1106
crime: against humanity 1317
    because it is unjust
        1317
    in the statesman 1378
    rest is c. 202
    successful c. 931
    that of the individual
        c. 1600
crimes: and misfortunes 1185
    are committed in thy
        name 846
    excuse for his c. 389
    follies and misfortunes
        1186
criminal: unsuccessful one a
    c. 2184
criminals: bad characters and
    potential c. 2166
    I don't mean the c.
        1744

crimson splendor 303
crippling thwarting thing
    460
crises: have their advantages
    1272
    that spin out of con-
        trol 176
crisis: a c. invited 515
    in c. the most daring
        course is often
        safest 2367
    in perspective 1113
    will in this c. 1624
critic of the present hour
    2119
critical: lovers of America
    1620
    moments 1504
    pretending that the
        trivial is c. 576
criticizes his country 1646
critics: in times of peace the
    c. 684
crooked designs 1647
crop in the ground 2682
cropper: come a c. 1018
cross: no c. no crown 2207
    the Charles River 1899
crosses: between the c. row
    on row 431
crowd: forced to be in a c.
    2454
    nor a nation 709
    of spectators 2048
    the mass 2448
    usurping c. 2499
    will always save Barab-
        bas 606
crown: head that wears a c.
    2197
    no cross no c. 2207
    noble c. 2215
    of thorns 2215
    put on my c. 2243
    shines spotless now
        2220
crowned head 2237
crucified: who is to be c.
    606
cruel: and unrelenting
    enemy 278
    however c. 601
    impulses 2508
    to be tough 2393
    triumph cannot help
        being c. 2547
cruelty: craft or c. 1802

ways of f. 2538
worth f. for 1319
fights: interval between f. 1694
   swords it f. with 347
   whoever f. monsters 1245
figures: three sets of f. 1956
fill him with a terrible resolve 2371
final: choice 2278
   humility 1496
   sacrifice 1479
   test of a leader 1358
   war for human liberty 1859
find: it strongest 1521
   the solution 1578
   themselves possessed 1331
   very difficult 1565
finding: new words 1911
   the other end fastened 2287
finest: goal 1919
   hour 1662
finger: never have lifted a f. 72
finish: cannot so f. 1901
finished: thoroughly f. 128
fire: don't f. unless fired upon 105
   don't one of you f. 92
   faster 108
   horizon blazing with f. 2072
   lit homes 2333
   of a battlefield 2330
   smoke and f. 1425
   their shots 2048
   when you are ready 110
   worse than raging f. 398
fired upon 105
firing: line is invisible 212
   no f. till you see the whites of their eyes 91
firm seat 2193
firmly seated in authority 1719
first: and most imperative necessity 288
   blow is half the battle 148
   duty of man 742

last and always 781
law for the historian 1078
   principle of a civilized state 1760
   rank 155
   requirement of a statesman 774
   time 1129, 1247
   to discover your mistakes 631
fishes: so are the f. 142
fission: living with nuclear f. 82
fist: at the conference table 1359
   clenched f. 2424
   I feel an army in my f. 1484
   of patriotism 1631
fit: of absence of mind 285
   to be trusted 1807
   to live 2085
   to sit in judgment 1335
fits of fury 2456
fixed: eyes f. on the victories 2581
flag: rally round the f. 808
flagrant: most f. of all the passions 1732
Flanders: in F. fields the poppies blow 431
flare up 259
flat: thing would fall f. 563
flatters the majority 2229
flattery: implies f. 1749
flea: kill a f. 2488
fleckless: heroes should be f. 1071
flee: enemy turns to f. 2351
   let the sound of it f. 135
   the wicked f. 967
   those who f. 1210
fleece of gold 193
flesh: soul over the f. 1063
flew: them and was crazy 896
   where a standard never f. 162
flock of sheep 1433
flop: worse f. 1592
flourish: monstrously f. 956
   then do patriots f. 1648
flourishes: dramatic f. 801
flow from ourselves 951

flower: bright-colored f. 2530
fluid prejudice 1138
fly: fight nor f. 728
   had to f. 896
   more missions 896
   when they see death 393
   would not hurt a f. 1596
flying: keep 'em f. 2319
foaming with much blood 1832
foe: call no man f. 599
   friend and f. 1580
   friend to her f. 2307
   oppose any f. 827
   overcome but half his f. 765
   secret f. 2353
   tyrants fall in every f. 2508
   very quickly by a f. 632
foes: are mortal 611
   chivalrous f. 1258
   from whom we pray to be delivered 171
   greatest f. 1494
   judge of a man by his f. 635
   woes unite f. 24
fog: gleams through the f. 1080
folk: civilized f. 2347
follies: appetites and f. 171
   crimes, f., and misfortunes 1186
   of all f. 670
follow: men who f. 2714
   other men's habits 2016
   the current of opinion 1984
   those who have been despised 2025
followers: are without number 416
   blood of his f. 1460
   of a great man 1366
following your methods 1911
follows that every nation 2721
folly: always from f. 2483
   war contains so much f. 1581
fond: grow too f. of it 1394
   of truth 2014

battalions 2380
hand 2193
yoke of slavery 2306
hedges ears 2270
heed: take h. of enemies 617
the teachings of his-
tory 1224
heels: follow truth too near
the h. 1079
height: of ability 1471
of feeling 1666
of moral cultivation
1679
of psychological luxury
1487
heightens the dignity of all
men 1747
held in reverence 1985
hell: belief in h. 476
better to reign in h.
2284
boys it is all h. 2703
contagion of h. 1244
get the h. out of here
107
if Hitler invaded h. 36
of a war 2705
on the feet 531
opens 1242
peace will be h. 1414
scare the living h. out
of me 1453
served my time in h.
2521
tell him to go to h. 106
tell you to go to h. 549
tossed to h. 1464
tyranny like h. 2430
war is h. 2704
with you 1935
hell-raising: all around h.
1637
help: appeal for h. 1294
in persuading people
1402
neither glory nor any
h. 1210
nowhere in the world
to go for h. 1043
you to prevent war
1911
helpless giant 2275
helps: them to deceive themselves 1968
us to make a decision
2004
hereditary leisure class 1396

heretic: oppressor or a h.
2182
hero: acted like a h. 1068
becomes a bore at last
1062
cannot be a h. 1051
conquering h. 276
country that needs a h.
1053
don't want to be a h.
2673
for fifteen minutes
1065
is a man 1049
show me a h. 1073
the h. acts 1045
with coward's legs
419
heroes: are created by popular demand 1058
are very human 1061
as quickly as of h. 343
fame of h. 1060
have no time to think
1054
history selects its h.
1057
in obscurity 1067
murderers as well as h.
1779
served in Vietnam were
h. 2595
sons of h. 1054
to have no h. 1055
heroic: deeds 1059
dimension 1051
enterprise 1587
man does not pose
1064
wishes to be thought
h. 1064
world 1052
heroism: deeds of h. 1067
does not require spiri-
tual maturity 1072
feels and never reasons
1070
fight with h. 1069
is endurance 1056
is the brilliant triumph
1063
is the dazzling and glo-
rious 1063
opportunities for h.
1056
piety without h. 1063
poetry of h. 1047

hero-worship is strongest
1386
hesitate if you then go ahead
2364
hesitates: him who h. 2363
Hesperides: apples of the H.
193
hidden: and rankling wounds
2556
in the lies 2471
most estimable when
h. 336
hieroglyphic of all misery
2685
high: estate 1726
intellectual quality
1435
point 1173
higher: development 2683
tests of manhood 2619
highest: form of vanity
1459
lesson of statecraft 1719
reality 352
highly trained and perfectly
obedient bureaucracy
2440
high-spirited: proud and h.
1225
hill: or high point 1173
other side of the h.
2369
hills: fight in the h. 2074
him who loves his country
125
hired to kill in cold blood
2339
Hiroshima: bomb at H. 55
bomb fell over H. 70
turned back to look at
H. 69
historian: an unsuccessful
novelist 1091
comes along 1090
duty of the h. 1097
essentially wants more
documents 1088
first law for the h. 1078
is a prophet in reverse
1096
must not try to know
what is truth 1085
tell me the acts O h.
1089
trade of h. 1094
who fails in his duty
1100

soldiers were made on
p. 2337
spiritual p. 1547
was to be left alone 676
purposes: all intents and p.
2429
of its foreign policy
2669
purse: thumb on the p. 1767
pursue: free to p. 865
when he retreats we p.
2355
pursued through five successive presidencies 2590
pursuit: of peace 1689
of war 1587
push: it too far 2549
of bayonets 91
put a chain around the neck
2286
putting them together again
1824
putty: vertebrae of p. 2341
puzzling: more p. it became
2601
pygmies: retarded p. 1891
war of the p. 2634
pyramids: from the summit
of these p. 1492

quagmire: bottomless q.
2589
quaint and curious 1259
qualify war in harsher terms
2690
qualities: good q. in action
1214
quality: courage is a q. 353
high intellectual q.
1435
in the captain 1378
of human nature 344
of revolutions 2114
primary political q.
1363
vital q. 1483
which knows no fear
308
quarrel: a national q. 179
between two states 534
in a false q. 340
in a faraway country
1293
ruler has a q. 235
with one another 258

quarrels not their own 236
quarters nor provisions 125
queer: you look so q. 425
queries: answer all q. 1668
question: inevitably arises
1109
interesting q. 1441
of history 1076
of the heavy hand 2193
soldier's first q. 1498
there is no q. 1211
questioned: fitness is q. 1450
questions: study of q. 1179
quick: to flare up 259
touched to the q. 427
win as q. as you can
2358
quickest way of ending a war
492
quickly: go over very q. 1854
the glory 922
very q. by a foe 632
quiet: all q. along the Potomac 220 433
all q. on the Western
Front 113
conscience 1665
world 1638
quietly: building new structures 1700
can be q. led 2457
quietness' sake 2200
quit: Americans never q.
2066
quite secure 2259

race: between education and
catastrophe 1135
controls the r. 1937
human r. 186, 459,
1114, 1349, 1638,
2116
is not to the swift 2399
is to the swift 2400
nation and the r. 1050
transition of the r.
2683
we are a conquering r.
273
races of men on the earth
259
racket: stop the r. 292
radiation poisoning 82
radical: ceases to be r. 2120
invents the views 2177

is one who speaks the
truth 2175
of one century 2176
revolutionary will be-
come a conserva-
tive 2121
simply means grasping
things at the root
2173
thinkers 2174
to be r. 2172
radicalism itself ceases to be
radical 2120
radically opposed to liberty
2098
raft: passing r. 579
rain: as clouds carry r. 291
command the r. 1377
rainbow that rises in showers
of blood 906
rains: as soon as it r. 560
raise the anchor 1556
ran the risk 1314
range of angry men 179
ranges: summits of r. 1005
rank: a battle of the first r.
155
has its obligations 2211
in my eyes 2330
no merit without r.
1436
relative r. 1441
title and r. 1438
rankling wounds 2556
rape and plunder 1402
rapscallions: all kings is
mostly r. 2233
rare: generous victors are r.
2548
insanity is r. 1530
rarely attained 2610
rash: calls the brave man r.
397
different from being r.
2368
rashness: and cowhearted-
ness 328
beware of r. 2580
rate science proceeds 2711
rather: be equal in slavery
2309
give my life 708l
have peace 1669
see America save her
soul 544
starve than sell our
national honor 1226

world to w. 2164
  your peace or buy it 41
wind of revolutions 2137
winding stair 1014
winds and waves 2381
wine the strongest heads
  1800
wings: fear gives w. 730
  hear the beating of his
    w. 452
winners: history is written
  by the w. 1204
  there are no w. 2555
winning: at the moment
  1745
  isn't everything 2539
  sullied in the w. 2220
  sure of w. 395
  turn it into a w. one
    2553
wins: he almost w. 2554
  makes no difference
    who w. 2537
  or it loses 783
  the victory 1482
wipes out all the small nuisances 2704
wisdom: and purposes 2669
  beginning of w. 749
  brilliance without w.
    84
  of states 1109
  seldom the truest w.
    1766
  true w. 1831
  we had w. 1715
  will grow with our
    power 1717
wise: become as the unwise
  1752
  enough 1297, 1357,
    1806
  he is w. who tries
    everything before
    arms 521
  how w. his conduct may
    have been 2578
  learn many things 629
  man 633, 2469
  men pass for w. 1753
  no less w. 1112
  not always w. 1002
  to kill 1470
  too w. to govern the
    world 655
  were their subjects w.
    2680

wisely: behave w. 519
wish: as loudly as you w.
  1675
  believe that they w.
    1969
  for nothing but chaos
    1287
  for peace 2557
  know how to w. 2093
  men to be virtuous
    1644
  my first w. 1233
  to avoid foreign colli-
    sion 1284
  to destroy 1034
  to know a man 1750
wished-for state 1141
wishes: for a truce 2422
  to be thought heroic
    1064
withdraw into your self
  2454
withdrawal from it 2078
without: revolution 2113
  the means of its con-
    servation 2045
withstand the force 1994
witness: of the past 1083
  that testifies to the
    passing of time
    1171
witnesses: to do without w.
  360
  to our success 643
  to the desolation of war
    899
wits: knocked out of his w.
  227
wives: clean beds and w.
  2333
woe: to the defeated 111
  to thee 2251
woes: of long peace 2642
  unite foes 24
  world's most basic w.
    526
woman: fought over a w. 210
women: and children 227
  excitable w. 2341
  indecently dressed w.
    659
  laughing at them 1398
  men and w. 233, 1624,
    2302, 2595
  motherhood on w.
    2520
women's rights 894

won: a battle w. 496
  all our wars 2563
  at such a terrible cost
    2682
  by men 2714
  enjoying what they
    have w. 1054
  never w. a battle 151
  not to have w. but to
    have fought well
    2567
  on the playing fields of
    Eton 156
  some victory for
    humanity 2570
  they have been w. over
    613
  war has been w. 1548
wonder where war lived 175
wondering what you were
  doing morally 897
wooden swords 1442
word: become a bad w. 1141
  can be put in one w. 44
  cast into the midst of
    the people 2090
  civilization 460
  described by one w.
    778
  heathen w. for power
    1764
  in a w. we may gather
    1112
  is not French 1493
  last w. 1265
  possibilities of the w.
    1636
  sense of the w. 2172
  state is identical 177
  take my w. for it 1264
  that cowards use 400
  the w. war 177
  when I use the w. 460
  which always com-
    memorates 1632
words: and explanations 2203
  finding new w. 1911
  make these w. 1239
  of his mouth 537
  other men's w. 2016
  outcome of w. 1390
  people do not want w.
    1488
  repeating your w. 1911
  some with w. 17
  to the American peo-
    ple 2607